# SOUTH I

is a journey of exploration through the history, culture, wildlife, art, architecture, landscapes and communities of Tamil Nadu, Kerala, and Goa, with their diverse traditions of Hinduism, Christianity, and here and there Judaism, Islam and Jainism. From coastal Madras to the religious centres of Kanchipuram and Madurai, from the rock fort of Trichy to the tip of Cape Comorin, Philip Ward has wandered far and wide in the land of the Tamils.

Kerala too is diverse and tropically lovely, with seaports and inland waterways, palaces and bazaars, wildlife sanctuaries and Kathakali dance festivals.

Goa has become established as one of the world's most attractive beach-holiday resorts, but there is much to see in historic, abandoned Old Goa and its offshoot Panaji; in lakes and nature reserves; fascinating churches and inland temples, coastal forts and traditional Portuguese-style mansions.

*South India* describes the cool hill-station still called 'Snooty Ooty', the great art gallery of Tanjore, the former French enclave of Pondicherry, and the rock-cut shrines and sculpture of 7th to 8th-century Mamallapuram.

Intended for first-time visitors as well as experienced travellers who wish to understand the background to the vision, *South India* provides a sympathetic and thoughtful companion to some of India's most spectacular attractions.

PHILIP WARD, FRGS, ALA, FRSA, has spent much of the last 35 years in Africa and Asia, including 8 years in Libya and nearly 2 in Indonesia. His latest books include *Japanese Capitals*, *Travels in Oman*, *Ha'il: Oasis City of Saudi Arabia*, and *Bulgaria* which won the International Travel Writers Competition (First Prize), 1990. He is the author of *The Oxford Companion to Spanish Literature* and the acclaimed novel of the Mexican Conquest, *Forgotten Games*. His first book about India was *Rajasthan, Agra, Delhi*, and he returns to India for his next book *Western India: Karnataka, Maharashtra, Bombay*.

# SOUTH INDIA
## Tamil Nadu · Kerala · Goa

## A Travel Guide

## Philip Ward

**Oleander**

The Oleander Press
17 Stansgate Avenue
Cambridge CB2 2QZ

The Oleander Press
80 Eighth Avenue (Suite 303)
New York, N.Y. 10011
U.S.A.

**British Library Cataloguing in Publication Data**

Ward, Philip, 1938-
    South India. Tamil Nadu, Kerala, Goa:
    a travel guide. –
    (Oleander travel books; 18)
    1.  India (Republic). Tamil Nadu – Visitors' guides
    2.  India (Republic). Kerala – Visitors' guides
    3.  India (Republic). Goa – Visitors' guides
    I.  Title
    915.40452

    ISBN 0-900891-31-9

Printed and bound in Great Britain

# Contents

# Acknowledgements

As usual, readers are asked kindly to allow for my conflating several journeys into one apparently seamless itinerary, avoiding explanations about returning to Europe and back to India. Those readers travelling for several months at a time will thus be able to use the book for reference; those travelling for shorter periods will dip into whichever narrative they need by using the contents list and index.

For part of my time in India I was Writer-in-Transit as a guest of Exodus Expeditions of London, whom I thank for their collaboration. Mostly I travelled solo on buses, trains, boats and on foot and no praise is too high for the efficient, patient and underrated punctuality and frequency of Indian transportation systems, not to mention their exceptionally good value for money.

In unwitting preparation for the Goan period I studied Portuguese language and culture at the University of Coimbra many years ago: to that team of dedicated scholars my grateful thanks. Veena Chopra taught me the Hindi I wanted for everyday use among those (and they are few in South India) who use it every day, and for this gift I shall always be grateful.

My wife, Audrey, and my daughters Carolyn and Angela, have made my life as tranquil as may be, in a lifetime where an individual cannot be sure in which continent he will find himself next month.

PHILIP WARD

# Introduction

My purpose while travelling the length and breadth of South India has been to select the solid information and personal impressions of places likely to interest a reader or traveller keen to experience at first or second hand the subcontinent's diversity of humanity, landscape, art, architecture, and historical development.

*South India* is a companion volume to my *Rajasthan, Agra, Delhi* and will, I hope, appeal to the same wide audience. 'South India' is a generic description denoting different ideas to different people. I have described under that heading the two southernmost states of India: Tamil Nadu to the east, and Kerala to the west, plus the ever-popular half-westernised territory of Goa.

Some understand Karnataka to form a part of South India, and some believe it to be a part of Western or Central India, for it is so vast that Gersoppa Falls and Bijapur seem half a world away from Bangalore or Mysore. So I include Karnataka in my next book with adjoining Maharashtra and its capital Bombay.

Tamil Nadu understandably receives the lion's share of attention in this book because of its vast size of 130,000 square kilometres (bigger than Austria and Denmark combined) and the immense significance of Tamil culture and the Hindu artistic and architectural tradition that has flowered here almost without interruption from northern invaders. If you did not appreciate Hindu temples and the associated bazaar cities before, prepare to enjoy them now.

Kerala may be a good deal smaller in area, but its traditions are well-defined, proudly maintained, and the coastal landscapes and inland waterways make of it a paradise for the traveller, even if Keralans themselves feel daunted by lack of employment opportunities.

Goa, tiny by Indian standards, has an equally clear artistic and historic personality, and deserves close study for its buildings and social life, its turbulent evolution and its tolerant individuality.

Festivals in Goa, Trichur, Madurai are among the most colourful on earth, giving the visitor a chance to immerse himself or herself in the delights of Holi or Pongal, Christmas or Shigmo.

I suggest arriving in Madras, and travelling roughly clockwise, ending up at Goa, from whose Dabolim Airport one can return to Europe direct or more usually via Bombay.

The best months to visit South India are during the height of the North American and European winter: between early December and late February. Domestic tourism to Goa peaks in May.

Most of these itineraries depend on road transport, usually inter-city buses, and auto-rickshaws locally. A rail journey would be slightly different. Those able to hire private cars and drivers are in a way to be envied, because they will waste less time. But they miss that vital element of any true Indian adventure: the Indians themselves as one mingles in their inquisitive company. And they retain that terrible temporal straitjacket that we in the West believe to be 'normal'.

How strange we are! Our sense of time is so anxious that we fill every minute on calendars, diaries, notebooks, so that no time is 'wasted'. Punctuality is a fever, telling the truth is an agonising series of conscientious moves, measures of tact and politeness are weighed in the mind like coins in the hand, and class is a minutely-observed sequence of interactions, as meticulous in observance as a chemical experiment where lives are at risk.

Being 'correct' about grammar, being 'exact' with facts, telling jokes showing the relationship of teller to told as much as their sense of humour. The German or Englishman is a stickler for information. What kind of a bird is that? What is the date of this pot? What is the number of that train, the name of that village, the meaning of that picture? The craze for knowing things hobbles one's imagination like a donkey at a rough, simple, stake. The Vedas, the Diamond Sutra, Guru Granth Sahib, the Jaina Sutras: none of these assumes an exact knowledge, yet they support and inspire the beliefs of most Indians, for whom time and place alike, as much as identity, will always remain in the realm of illusion, like suffering and even life itself. They do not think: they *suffer sensations*. They may take advantage of situations in the short term, but tend not to plan ahead too far, for that is to preempt the prerogative of divinity. If they did, their conclusions would reveal the fallibility of their short-term manoeuvres. Can they be right? Very probably. For if you add up all the notions, facts and words ever uttered, and ask yourself what *difference* they had made, 99.9% of all utterances or actions would be seen as useless, absurd, wrong, or simply *unnecessary*. You look around, and in a skirmish of temporary despair soon forgotten, you realise that too many people have always been unnecessary, a realisation which gives general death particular dignity.

Westerners often come to India to find a simple solution to their own complexities, whether in a commune or at a beach, using hallucinatory drugs, free expression, ascetic discipline, transcendental meditation, or one of a hatful of yogic practices, with a selection of vegetarian, vegan or mind-stretching obsessions. They go to theosophical classes at Adyar, Madras; Sri Aurobindo's ashram at Pondicherry; Hindu temples such as

Rameshwaram; hash parties at Anjuna in Goa; even the ancient Jewish synagogue in Cochin or Christian missionary societies in Kottayam (Kerala) or Pilar (Goa).

I cannot make any concrete suggestions, because every traveller is unique, and the traveller's experience in each place is unique. You might find nirvana in the mountain mists at Kodaikanal, deep satisfaction in the great temples of Kanchipuram, or a blinding revelation in the sea at Kaniya Kumari, where India comes to an abrupt southern end. You may, on the other hand, return home with a disconsolate feeling that what you were seeking you had left at home, and needed only to recover a lost equilibrium. Teeming millions, endless poverty, squalor and pollution: India has a way of putting into perspective the lesser problems of the rest of the world.

There is nothing intentionally or potentially definitive about *South India*. Its chief aim is to suggest that you stop what you are doing and find out how Tamil Nadu, Kerala, and Goa can change your life, and how comparatively rich it will be when you return with your memories, your books, films, postcards, spices, shawls, photographs. After the Indian experience, nobody is ever the same again.

# Illustrations

Photographs are by the Author and maps by the Government of India unless otherwise stated. Colour illustrations for the cover were kindly supplied by the Government of India Tourist Office (Hindu woman; Kerala bazaar; rock-cut temple at Mamallapuram, Tamil Nadu).

# 1: TAMIL NADU: TEMPLES AND BAZAARS

'Tamil Nadu' is the country of the Tamils, inhabiting predominantly a huge area of 130,000 square kilometres – an area as large as Austria and Denmark combined – in the south-east of the Indian subcontinent. Its modern capital of Madras, only three and a half centuries old, was established here by the East India Company and preserves some of the most celebrated of all British colonial buildings.

Tamil Nadu, vast as it is, comprises but a fraction of the land once known as the Madras Presidency, which in the 17th century formed roughly a third of India, the other presidencies being Bombay and Bengal.

The Coromandel Coast on the east of India may have not lent itself geographically to the prosperity assumed by the western Malabar Coast: it did not face Europe, Africa, and entrepôts such as Bahrain or Basra, but it traded profitably with Japan, China, and the Spice Islands of the Philippines, Indonesia and Malaysia long before the British contemplated their fort and factory there.

In Calcutta and Bombay you know that you are in vast conurbations; in Madras, like Delhi, the atmosphere is that of a series of villages, more or less merging into each other but not before establishing their own identity: the Fort, Guindy, Georgetown and Mylapore, Mount Road, Marina, Triplicane, Adyar and St Thomas' Mount.

It seems almost inconceivable, but Madras accommodates nearly four million people, and the tendency to move citywards from the countryside grows with every passing year.

The endless traffic in Madras reminded me of the Bachelor of Arts in R.K. Narayan's amusing novel of that title (1965), whose B.A., Chandran, arrived from his native town numb at the hotel opposite the People's Park, 'wishing that the people of Madras were more human; they were so mechanical and impersonal; the porter at the station had behaved as if he were blind, deaf and mute; now this hotel man would not even look at his guest; these fellows simply did not care what happened to you after they had received your money; the *jutka* man had departed promptly after he received the rupee, not uttering a single word...'. But then, all cities are like Madras in such impersonality: I even enjoy the feeling of separateness, being responsible for nobody, to

1

*Map of Tamil Nadu*

nobody. The *jutka*, a two-wheeled coffin like the rickety *cranchee* of Calcutta drawn by a sad nag, may derive its name from the Hindi *jhatka*, quick, though it would be a dilemma to point out a slower conveyance unless one were to harness Madras Snake Garden's Aldabra tortoise.

Forty km north of Madras lies Pulicat (Palaverkatu), the first Dutch settlement in India, dating from 1605. The English tried to trade nearby, but the Dutch understandably resisted this encroachment, so the English moved first north to Armagaon (Durgarayapatnam) in 1626 then in 1632 to Masulipatam and finally south in 1639 to Madras, after plans to make their headquarters at Pondicherry, Kunimedu and Covelong.

Nobody knows what 'Madras' means; the name occurs as Madrazpatam (1640) and as Chennapattanamu (Telugu) and Shennaippatanam (Tamil) or similar transliterations. It sounds very like 'madrasa', the Arabic word for a school or college, but this folk etymology appears to have no real validity. The English founders called it Fort St George after their original fortified compound, and did not risk living outside the fort, which was the first major enterprise of the English East India Company and begun in 1644, five years after Francis Day founded the settlement. Development in the second half of the 17th century was swift beyond the fort into the 'Black Town', and when the English colonials ventured beyond the walls in the 18th century they created splendid neo-classical villas in luxuriant gardens, and many of these survive to this day, as do the Indo-Saracenic glories of the 19th century, due in great measure to the energetic vision of Robert Fellowes Chisholm.

## Fort St George

Polygonal Fort St George grew gradually, and in 1694 the Fort House was pulled down to give way to a new Fort House, now the Secretariat, and Fort Square was created by razing some inner walls in 1711. Briefly taken by the French, it was briefly endangered by Haidar Ali's siege of 1769. In 1781 the British captured Pulicat from the Dutch and held it except for eight years from 1818. Though the civil and military government of Tamil Nadu is quartered at Fort St George, the visitor is free to wander around Fort Square and the various buildings, of which the most important are the Fort Museum and St Mary's Church, though Robert Clive's House (plaque) opposite St Mary's is worth seeking out, as is the small museum devoted to Clive in the Pay and Accounts Office.

The Fort Museum, open as such since 1948, faces the northern gate, and occupies the site of a private merchant's house, replaced by this edifice by 1790. A bank operated on the ground floor and the old Madras Exchange on the upper floor, with a lighthouse, dismantled in 1841, rising almost a hundred feet above the low shoreline, above the Exchange. Later it became an Officers' Mess, and now offers the visitor

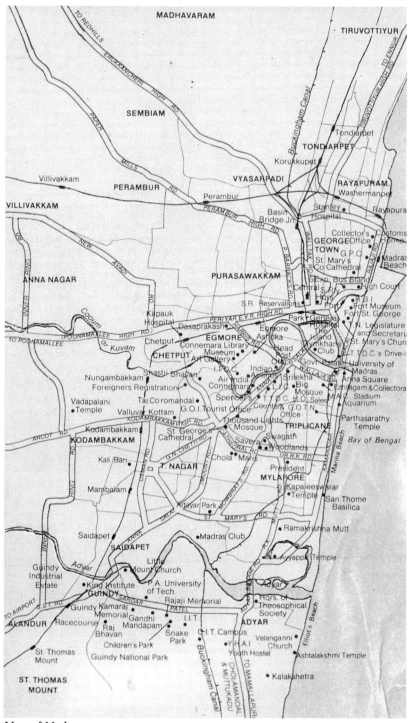

*Map of Madras*

*Madras. Fort St George. The Exchange, now Fort Museum*

the consolation of nostalgia: a corner of 'White Town' in a city spreading its tentacles more widely and thickly than ever the British imagined. Even now, Madras remains the fourth largest city in India.

Weapons and uniforms, flags and armour in the first gallery remind you that Madras was held only by force of arms. The staircase is flanked by an impressive statue of Lord Cornwallis, made by Thomas in 1800, formerly on Fort Square. Porcelain once owned by the Arcot Nawabs and stamps are shown near a coronation mug of Edward VIII. Portraits by the highly-reputed Ravi Varma (born in Travancore in 1848) go part of the way to repudiating the generalisation of the Jaganmohan Palace catalogue (1980): 'The 19th century was a period of progressive degradation in Indian art, particularly painting'. Church silver on display

5

comes from Pulicat (early 17th century), the Zion Church in Tranquebar (1717) and St Mary's (1780). Exhibits are devoted to coins, Indo-French culture, the achievements of the Wadiyar dynasty of Mysore, and prints of Madras. The upper floor, spacious and elegant, has unexpected pleasures: 'Queen Alexandra' and 'Edward VII' by Luke Fildes; 'George III' and 'Queen Charlotte Sophia' attributed optimistically to Allan Ramsay; 'Robert Clive' (1725-74) by Thomas Day and 'Streynsham Master' (1640-1724), the Governor of Madras who commissioned St Mary's, by Charles D'Agar. How evocative are these Daniell prints of the ruined interior of Madurai Palace and Trichy in 1792, of Madras 'Black Town' in 1793, and J.B. East's prints of the hazardous landings on Madras beach!

St Mary's Church, the earliest surviving Anglican Church east of Suez (1678-80), echoes to the sound of tombs and heroes, soldiers and diplomats, spies and civil servants: Hastings and Hobart, Keble and Russell, Pigot and Hood, Sir Thomas Munro and Sir Henry Ward. Flaxman was responsible for the monuments to Josiah Webbe (1804) who died at 37 'a martyr to an uncongenial climate' and to Revd. C.W. Gericke, frightened to death by monkeys at Vellore in 1803. St Mary's survived because of its privileged position within the fort, and because its outer wall is four feet thick; the roof is also of brick, and the only timber used in the construction is to be found in windows and doors. A banner reads 'Be still: God is near' but He cannot easily be coaxed into this stern white air, its lectern stiff like a starched white collar, surviving all those aristocratic Governors and fine ladies, such as Jane Amelia, wife of Sir Henry Russell, whom John Bacon Jr. has immortalised in a beautiful memorial: alack, dear Jane, she died within two months of her wedding day. The garden of St Mary's is tended as a place of contemplation, but the cemetery lies some way off, near the War Graves Cemetery at the General Hospital.

### Pantheon

In the 18th century the Pantheon resounded to dance orchestras and the tinkle of glasses at society balls, but nowadays Pantheon Road is a cultural centre, comprising the Victoria Memorial Hall and Technical Institute (designed by Henry Irwin, 1909) now a spacious Art Gallery, with only a small number of select exhibits; the Museum Theatre, expanded from its 18th-century origins; Irwin's Connemara Public Library (1896); and the Government Museum (1854), the most important museum (with Tanjore) south of Bombay.

To summarise the Art Gallery first, portraits of notables such as Annie Besant and Rabindranath Tagore in a small side room make a disconcerting prologue to the main hall, itself strangely eclectic. We expect the South Indian traditional 17th-century *Coronation of Yudis-*

*thira* and characteristic 19th-century paintings from Tanjore influenced by European art conventions, and even three exquisite bronzes from Vadakhuppanaiyur (Rama, flanked by Sita and Lakshman) which prefigure the many superb Chola bronzes you will discover in Tanjore Art Gallery; but to find first-rate Mughal paintings (17th-18th centuries) as far south as Madras is a great surprise: for the connoisseur there is a classic Mughal miniature of two fighting bulls and King Nushirwan with his court.

The Government Museum (closed only on public holidays) has no guidebook and no postcards, catastrophically, for nobody will be able to memorise all the museum's wonders. Highlights include 2nd-3rd century Buddhist limestone sculptures from Goli and Jaggayyapeta; Chalukya work from Badami; a recumbent Sri Ranganatha with two consorts from South Arcot; and snakestones as votive objects from infertile couples whose curse is attributed by some to their killing of a cobra in this or a previous existence.

An infertile couple sets up one of these magic cobra stones. In many parts of South India the cobra stone symbolises Subrahmanya, son of Lord Shiva, conceived by the Ganges from Shiva's seed and known in the North as Kartikeya or Senapati. The cobra stone is believed to be most effective if set up at Rameshwaram.

Sculpture from Bengal has come from Pala artists of 9th-century Bengal, Buddhists tolerant of Hinduism, and their Hindu successors, the Senas. If you have not been able to see Mohenjodaro in Pakistan, a few (insignificant) examples can be inspected here; and the same applies to the Greco-Buddhist art of Gandhara, which can be found too in the British Museum. The British Museum has some examples from the great dismantled stupa at Amaravati, once the largest in eastern Deccan, but the largest collection is found here in Madras and, with figures from Nagarjunakonda (Andhra Pradesh), is of cardinal significance for an understanding of Buddhist iconography. The earliest Amaravati work comes from the first stupa (200 B.C.), extended in the 2nd and 3rd centuries A.D.: a model has been reconstructed to show its appearance before it fell into disrepair about the 12th century. The subject of the frieze scenes, apart from floral elements, is the sequence of the life and incarnations of the Buddha, or Jataka tales, including a Parinirvana and Mayadevi's dream reminiscent in their subtlety and compositional beauty of the Renaissance Gateway to Paradise panels by Ghiberti on the Florentine Baptistery (1425-52). Limestone wears away in time, but Gautama subduing the elephant, and devotees raising the bowl, preserve their antique majesty in miniature. Most memorable of all is the depiction of the stupa in relief, with devas and devis flying above in the manner of angels in Western art.

Off the Amaravati hall, a Buddhist room reconstructs the Nagarjunakonda site (still amply worth seeing today, with a museum on site) and shows discoveries from Sankaram, near Anakapalli (Andhra Pradesh); a Jain room has the usual figures of Mahavira and other tirthankaras, with a great Parshvanatha from Danavulapadu ('village of demons') in Cuddapah district, north-west of Madras.

Stones commemorating the death of widows (sati) or wives (sumangali) touch our sympathies. Arm bangles on a wife's stone shows that her husband is still alive, and the sun and moon show that her memory will last as long as the planets themselves: an interesting example from Penukonda (Anantapur district) has a 16th-century inscription in Kannada. Tantalising examples of sculptured women from Bhubaneshwar nudge one to visit Orissa. In the next room a headless Suragama blowing a conch reminded me of boys selling trumpet conches on South Beach.

The bronze gallery has small examples of Hindu sculpture from the Pallava school of the 9th century, but the later Chola images stand out in any company, especially if we think of 11th and 12th century art in England or Germany, hesitant and naive. The Tiruvengadu Shiva Nataraja springs from a tradition both confident and sophisticated, strong yet delicate, like the seated Shiva from Kilapuddanur. Some might prefer the more languid Late Chola Parvati from Kodaikkadu, or the Vijayanagar-period Krishna dancing on a snake from Nilappadi. Whatever your preference, the Madras Museum will deepen your appreciation of South Indian religious art, and repay close study.

### Sri Parthasarathy

From the Museum it is a short rickshaw ride to Lord Vishnu's temple once outside Madras proper, in the suburb of Triplicane, but now fully integrated into the city. It is called Sri Parthasarathy, and was originally a 7th or 8th-century Pallava foundation, but in its present form is of Vijayanagar date (1564), renovated in 1975. *Partha* is another name for Arjuna, hero of the *Bhagavadgita*, and *sarathy* denotes a charioteer, so the temple is devoted to Lord Krishna – whose plenary expansion is Lord Vishnu – as charioteer of Arjuna. Photography anywhere in the temple is prohibited, and non-Hindus are forbidden access to the shrines of Lord Krishna and his beloved Rukmini, who was betrothed to Sisupala, King of Chedi, but on her way to the wedding 'Krishna saw her, took her by the hand, and carried her away in his chariot', proving that a charioteer may have other than military aims in mind. The gopurams on east and west are both open, and each enclosure has its own fascination, crowded with Vaishnavite pilgrims from morning till night. *K.P. Ranu Electricals, Madras* advertised in the compound, but devotees crowded into the shrines to make offerings before the principal deities. Popular religion and popular films have become virtually interchangeable in Tamil Nadu since the megastar M.G. Ramachandran became Chief Minister, and the gods and heroes he portrayed in 42 years of films are confused in sixty million Tamil minds with the life and thoughts of their guru or 'Vaathiar'. Gemini Film Studios, where so many interchangeable Tamil films have been churned out, stand on Gemini Circle close to Sri Parthasarthy.

## Sri Kapalishwaram

Along Ice House Road you will see the Skin and Leprosy Clinic, and the hostel of Lady Willingdon College of Education, Queen Mary's College, All-India Radio, the Portuguese Cathedral of São Thomé (locally pronounced Sántom) and the Shaivite temple dedicated to Sri Kapalishwaram, Lord of the Skulls, who is Rudra, the roarer, the terrible aspect of Lord Shiva. It is said – and one is conscious of never questioning such sayings – that in this temple Parvati, Lord Shiva's consort, appeared here in the form of a peacock or 'maila', since when the peacock has been sacred in Hinduism and this district was called Mailampuram (now Mylapore), the town of the peacock.

As the oldest and most august Shaivite temple in Madras, the Kapalishwaram is the focus of numerous festivals and its sacred tree and sacred pool are visited daily by thousands of worshippers. *Gita* cassettes for divine grace were on sale, and the usual colourful human turbulence flowed around and about, irresistible as the sea. At least two millennia old, the original buildings were demolished by proselytising Portuguese in 1566, and the present structures have been renovated several times since its reconstruction in the 16th century by the rulers of Vijayanagar. The great gopuram tapers over 36 metres high, and a great many (is it 63?) Shaivite saints are figured in bronze around the outer courtyard, then carried in a procession on the 8th day of the ten-day festival (March-April) known as Aruvathumuvai.

## Churches

A few hundred metres away stands the Cathedral Basilica of St Thomas the Apostle, who is thought to have landed at Cranganore in 52 and been martyred at St Thomas' Mount in 72. His putative tomb is sunk in front of the altar. With so many Hindu miracles jostling for credibility, what can the Catholics do but compete? So this basilica of 1896 cherishes in its crypt a small bone from the apostle's hand and the lance-head once used to attack him... Nestorian Christians originating from Persia first built a chapel over the saintly remains. The Portuguese founded a church nearby shortly after their arrival in 1521, and this became a cathedral in 1606, demolished in 1893. The present neo-Gothic structure has been the seat of 'episcopus Meliaporensis' and since 1952 the 'archiepiscopus': the present incumbent in Monsignor G. Casimir (1987- ). A plaque claims that the first mass was said in the

9

original church by Rev. Antonio Gil in 1521. Pope John Paul II visited in 1986. The interior in conventional neo-Gothic basilican style has a tablet 'In Honour of Our Lady of the Rosary of Valle di Pompei' and an altar to Our Lady of Mylapore, where St Francis Xavier resided for 4 months in 1545 with the then Vicar, Fr. Gaspar Coelho.

Much more interesting architecturally is the barrel-vaulted Church of Our Lady of Light, in honour of the Virgin who was alleged by Portuguese mariners at sea to have succoured them and brought them to safe harbour during a storm. I didn't know how to reach the Luz Church (dated on the west front 1516) so I asked the first passer-by. Vivian Francis not only offered to show me the Luz Church, but eagerly offered me tiffin of idli sambar in a nearby restaurant and asked my birth date so he could send me a card. 'I was brought by God to help you', explained this practising Catholic, with a charming smile. The Luz, graceful in its white façade and elevated by steps above the surrounding streets, survives in its tree-lined cul-de-sac quiet and comtemplative amid the surrounding traffic. Fr. Thomas Charadh, the parish priest, offers mass for the benefit of his parish's 320 catholic families in Tamil throughout the week, and once in English on Sunday evenings. His home next door is in a dignified building also occupied by a retired archbishop and a retired monsignor. Nuns run a hospital at the rear. The ornate baroque gilded altar dedicated to the Blessed Virgin Mary might be anywhere in Beira Alta, were it not for the shock of an Armenian tomb next to a Portuguese tomb of 1817. The de Vries funerary monument adds further diversity. De Vries is the commonest name in the Amsterdam telephone book. All local priests are buried in the cemetery to the right of the church courtyard. It was 6.10 in the evening, and darkling as an old lady in a black shawl knelt before the altar and made the sign of the cross: we might have been in Evora or Viseu.

Next morning I pursued the Portuguese pilgrimage to Chinnamali, the Little Mount, where a cave is reputed to have sheltered the Apostle Thomas, martyred by Hindus who took exception to his mission on the west coast and the east coast. He preached, it is said, to crowds who gathered below this cave, which now has an altar with a small Greek cross said to date from the time of the Apostle. A church, commissioned in 1612 by a pious Goanese, Antonio Gonsalves de Taide, has risen above the cave, and in front of a holy spring.

Three km from Little Mount is St Thomas' Mount, ninety metres high, dominating the colonial flat-roofed bungalows of the Old Cantonment. St Thomas' Church is another Portuguese edifice of the early 16th century, though an archway is dated 1726. You are told various legends as if the truth made no difference: the painting of the Madonna was painted by St Luke and brought here by St Thomas; St Thomas was kneeling on this altar stone at the moment of his martyrdom; the cross,

10

with a Pahlavi inscription interpreted as 'The pure in heart are beloved of Him who carried the Cross', bleeds in sympathy with the Crucifixion. St Thomas' Mount lies near the road to Meenambakkam International Airport, where most foreign travellers arrive in Madras.

## Harbour

Anyone arriving by sea has the surprise of Alexandria, for lowlying Madras seems to emerge equally suddenly, when you are virtually within the harbour, fully-fledged like a butterfly needing no chrysalis. The sheltered harbour in front of Georgetown (the old 'Black Town') makes little impact compared with the long narrow expanse of Marina Beach, seldom crowded except at weekends and on public holidays, and the even quieter Elliot's Beach farther south. The harbour was begun in 1875 to alleviate the anxieties of the ship-to-shore *masula* craft, fragile and liable to overturning. The northern end, Anna Square, commemorates Dr Conjeevaram Natarajan Annadurai, the great Tamil leader who died in 1969, after less than two years as Chief Minister. The so-called Great Moderate of the South, he founded the Dravida Munnetra Kazhagam party, promising the masses a new sovereign Dravida Nadu, or confederation of four southern states until he moved into a period of 'India First' statesmanship in 1962, but persuaded New Delhi to allow Tamil Nadu state to teach in only Tamil and English. He deplored the effects of the caste system, strove to combat poverty and religious factionalism, and must be honoured as a great Indian statesman, whose funeral called forth lamentations reminiscent of Gandhi's and Nehru's. 'Anna engalay vittu poivittaingalay' came the cry from every side: 'Elder Brother, you have left us and departed'. If you assess a city's mood and sympathies by its memorials (Nelson and Albert in London; Lenin in Moscow; Stalin in Tirana), then Madras can be judged by Anna Square's memorial pillar and eternal flame, as well as the memorials to Mahatma Gandhi; to the first Governor-General Rajagopalachari affectionately known as Rajaji; and to K. Kamaraj, a southern hero of India's freedom movement. These three memorials can be found near Raj Bhavan, originally the Government House of 1817 built for Sir Thomas Munro, a pleasant colonial-style bungalow in the southern suburb of Guindy. Guindy National Park forms the chief part of a green belt running from Madras Racecourse to the lush, magnificent wilderness of the Adyar estuary's sandbanks and mangroves, kept pristine by the determination of the Theosophical Society. Ornithologists trill and whoop with pleasure on seeing godwit and avocet, flamingo and hoopoe, woodpecker and wagtail above a sanctuary for fox and jungle cat, lynx and sea turtle.

## Adyar

Col. Henry S. Olcott and Mme. Helena Petrovna Blavatsky founded the Theosophical Society in New York in 1875, but even then the crass materialism of Manhattan proved recalcitrant to a spiritual movement advocating Universal Brotherhood. Rejecting Bombay, they finally selected Madras as the home of the society in 1882, and established its world headquarters there four years later, responding to the peace and beauty of the estuary at the mouth of the southern river in Madras, the Adyar, for the northern river, the Cooum, had already been built up to north and south, the latter beyond Triplicane to Mylapore.

Of all the bodies of religious belief that India and Indianness have spawned, none is more bizarre than the Theosophists. Colonel Olcott seems to have been a genuine seeker after universal brotherhood, but Mme. Blavatsky claimed that she was in touch with adepts known as the Brotherhood of Luxor, a branch of 'the Great White Brotherhood' operating from the Himalaya. Her *Isis Unveiled* and subsequent *Secret Doctrine* became key works for devotees, though there is nothing interesting in them that cannot be found in gnostic and paragnostic speculations. To put Theosophy into perspective, read John Symonds' *Madame Blavatsky, medium and magician* (1959). Theosophists take for granted a great deal: clairvoyance and reincarnation, the astral plane and occult chemistry, but if one jibs at their philosophical and scientific fallacies, there is no doubting the warm goodness of the central impulses leading to tolerance and harmony. Annie Besant, a theosophical luminary, has written of her faith: 'Amid class hatreds and warring sects it raises this sublime banner of human love, a continual reminder that essentially all humanity is one, and that the goal to which we travel is the same for all. Without this recognition of Brotherhood all science is useless and all religion is hypocrisy'.

Such determined comradeship is reflected at Adyar, where visitors are welcome on weekdays (8-11 and 2-5). The Garden of Remembrance offers a quiet and serene refuge; each religion has its own shrine and garden: for Sikhs and Zoroastrians, a chapel for Christians, a temple for Hindus and Buddhists, and a model of the Pearl Mosque at Agra for Muslims. You are a Theosophist *as well* as a religious believer, not instead. Colonel Olcott's private library has become a major scholarly resource in the course of more than a century. The main house for the Society originally belonged to a civil servant called John Huddlestone, who negotiated with Tipu Sultan in 1784, but the Great Hall was added by the Theosophists, and makes reference by symbol, quotation or figuration to Zoroaster, Buddha, Jesus, Krishna, al-Qur'an al-Karim, Moses, Lao-tze, Confucius, Guru Nanak of the Sikhs, Mahavira of the Jains, Mithras, Orpheus and Osiris, overseen by statues of Blavatsky and Olcott. Do not miss the extraordinary banyan tree, its enormous branches shading more than forty thousand square feet.

Nearby is the Adyar Club (1891), which merged with the older Madras Club (1832) in 1963, when the stiff British male-dominated club gave way to Indian membership, then to 'amenities for ladies and social activities such as dancing'. Though not as old as the Bengal Club, the Madras Club was known as 'the best Club in India', by which the stalwarts may have silently signified the exclusion (even after World War I) of Indians, non-British Europeans and even Americans. The original Madras Club building no longer survives, but the new Madras Club stands proudly in George Moubray's Adyar home dating to the last quarter of the 18th century. Contemporary with Moubray's house is Quibble Island's James Brodie's castle (1776), so called because of twin turrets facing Adyar river. You may visit Brodie's Castle for public concerts, because it now houses the College of Carnatic Music.

Colonial architecture springs to the eye elsewhere in Adyar: look for Chettinad Palace (close to the Theosophical Society) to find Somerford, a house in the garden; and the Maharajah of Travancore's garden house called Ramalayam. Crossing Adyar Bridge Road and turning right into São Thomé High Road you emerge onto Marine Beach Road, officially Kamarajar Salai, designed by Grant Duff in the 1880s. Shallows of the Bay of Bengal ripple towards Lady Willingdon Training College (1917), then its circular hostel (1842), built as an ice house then for some time a widows' home, the domed University Examinations Hall, the red sandstone Presidency College, which was formerly a High School (1840) founded by the Cambridge graduate Eyre Burton Powell and now occupies two buildings, one relatively new and the earlier by Robert Fellowes Chisholm (1865-71). The parade of distinguished edifices continues with the Secretariat of Public Works (1870) and Chepauk Palace, divided nowadays between the Public Works and the Revenue. It was built in 1768 by Philip Stowey for Muhammad Ali Wallajah, Nawab of the Carnatic, but the British took it over for offices in 1855 when the last titular Nawab died. Chepauk is the home of Madras Cricket Club (that other M.C.C.), where cricketers such as Rusi Modi (203 v. an Australian Services XI in 1946), Conrad Powell Johnstone and Ram Singh made their reputation. Though India was admitted to the Imperial Cricket Conference as late as 1932, records at Chepauk go back to 1848, and only the Calcutta club has a longer record in the annals of Indian cricket.

Senate House (1873) is another splendid essay in the so-called Indo-Saracenic style owed to the ebullient Chisholm, whose fascination with the Gothic is here allowed to obtrude.

The Marina Aquarium has little to commend it (the Taraporevala Aquarium in Bombay is more representative of Indian marine fauna) and if it's wild life you're after then Romulus Whittaker's Crocodile

Farm on the road south to Mahabalipuram is more interesting. Best of all is the Snake Garden in Guindy National Park just south of the Rajaji Memorial, west of Adyar. Of the 3,000 species of snakes, 23% are found in India, the commonest poisonous varieties being the cobra, krait, Russell's Viper, and the saw-scaled viper. On average ten thousand Indians die every year from snakebite, though all of the seventeen species of freshwater snake are harmless. A 14-year-old cobra had just died at Guindy, but iguana babies had been born. A regal python thirty-three feet long is capable of swallowing a small deer; other menacing shapes included a vine snake, a rat snake, a striped keelback, and cobras. Here are water monitors from the mangrove swamps, colossal Aldabra tortoises, and fifteen recently-hatched marsh crocodiles. Lecture-demonstrations are held every hour on the hour, during which the timid are encouraged to handle harmless reptiles. I was chatting to a specialist from the National Institute of Communicable Diseases in Delhi about the deaths by reptiles. 'The real problems are still in water-borne parasites, like the Guinea-worm, which has been eradicated from Tamil Nadu recently, and is now confined to parts of Madhya Pradesh and Rajasthan.'

## Marina

Marina Beach has a lighthouse which can be visited from 2 to 4, but just strolling on the sand has its own fascination, with snack stalls offering fish and samosas, candy floss and cold drinks. Where an English beach will be aflutter with the mew of grey and white seagulls, Madras beach snarls with querulous black crows, blustering and flapping, sullen as punk rock stars at a funeral. At one stall you can fire pellets at balloons with a rifle; at another plastic trinkets such as yellow and red trumpets invite the petulant urchin to plead for a rupee from his indulgent mother, who has as they say 'a soft corner' for him. 'That is a third-class trumpet', she complained, 'what for you are wanting it? No-no, don't be a botheration.' A harassed Tamil in a striped pullover was cranking up a little hand-manipulated merry-go-round with wooden horses. Effluent wafted its scent over the fish canteens, and its foamy fluff at the tidemark. Several stalls with shell ornaments, depressing in their similarity and vulgarity, stood near each other, each reducing the others' potential sale. Why prompt price comparisons? In wells sunk below beach level men were washing, slapping their chest and haunches, and throwing each other slivers of soap. A barefoot ice-cream seller with a kerchief on his head rested beside his bright orange cart, near a queue which had formed for a horse-ride along the sands. Nobody risked bathing: it is in fact not an Indian custom at all. In 1844 Grant Duff called his promenade the Marina 'from old Sicilian recollections' and it is still as attractive as any Sicilian beach at Siracusa or Trapani.

*Madras. Marina. Horse-rides and ice-cream*

Across the road the Indo-Saracenic style of Major Charles called 'Mad' Mant burgeons in the University campus, in the gardens of the Nawab of the Carnatic's palace. That almost hysterically eclectic style wills in stone a spurious unity that could never be achieved in economic, political or architectural terms without vulgar hybridisation: a quixotic vision even when Mant arrived in 1859. Now the style possesses the respectability of a century's patina, but the palaces of Baroda, Kolhapur and Dharbanga have an unsatisfactory mixture of the European Gothic, the Islamic, and the native Indian, and though many enjoy their grandiose exuberance, I cannot believe that anyone moved by Chartres, Isfahan or Jodhpur will welcome such deliberate stylistic dilution. Mant died in his forties, and R.F. Chisholm completed the Lakshmi Vilas at Baroda in 1890, having already endowed Madras with its Indo-Saracenic heritage and headed (since 1855) the Madras School of Industrial Arts, now the Fine Arts School, taking as his model the South Kensington museums, especially the Victoria and Albert. The Italo-Saracenic Presidency College (1865-71) sorts oddly, to my eyes, with the Indo-Saracenic-Byzantine feel of Senate House, but there is an endearing larger-than-life boldness about the whole enterprise, with a British arrogance bordering on the majestic.

Just think: it is possible to roam Madras and close one's eyes entirely, if one were so bigoted, to any Tamil intrusion. Ripon Buildings, named for a former Governor-General, shimmers in cricket-flannel white; it was built in 1900 to a design by Harris and houses Madras Municipal Corporation. George Hardinge's massive Gothic Central Railway Station, the southern terminus of the mainline system, dates from 1868-72, while Chisholm's neighbouring Egmore Station makes its eloquent Indo-Saracenic point, another opulent work in the era of Henry Irwin. If you find these works daunting, then pluck up your courage to the sticking-point for the riotous red walls and ornamented Mughal domes of the High Court (1888-92) begun by J.W. Brassington and finished by Irwin and J.H. Stephens. The central tower is topped by a lighthouse, and can usually be visited by those willing to make the strenuous effort to reach the top, from which Madras is seen like a counterpane. Opposite stands the Bank of Mysore, formerly the Madras Christian College.

## More Churches

Christian churches had played no small part in the life of Madras, as we have seen in Fort St George, and the Portuguese-influenced Catholic churches. St George's Anglican Cathedral (1814-16) dominates the south side of Mount Road where Nungambakkam High Road meets St George's Cathedral Road. Conceived on the model of London's St Giles-in-the-Fields, its Ionic exterior and interior consort oddly with stained-glass windows and a 140-foot spire, but the white stucco facing glints like marble and within a fine Flaxman memorial to Archdeacon John Mousley (1823) repays contemplation. St Andrew's Kirk (1818-21) is by the same architects, Major T.F. de Havilland and Colonel James Caldwell, and reflects their passion for Ionic, with a spire and a steeple 165 feet high, but this time their pattern was St Martin-in-the-Fields, on Trafalgar Square. Massive white Corinthian columns rise like great trees in the graceful circular interior under a starry dome. St Andrew's is open for prayer daily from 8 to 7, with Church of South India services on Sundays at 9 and 6. Its garden has an avenue lined with palms and behind it is a recreation centre and a Day Care Centre for the handicapped.

Venture to the 18th-century Armenian Church of St Mary and you will find the sprawling hubbub of Georgetown, once the 'native quarter' behind the pukka sahibs' Fort. It is laid out in the grid pattern which will later characterise 'modern' Chandigarh: a proper town self-contained in commerce - Armenians settled here in large numbers - and in religion, with the Roman Catholic St Mary of the Angels, the Church of Holy Emmanuel, mosques, Jain shrines and Hindu temples, most strikingly the twins Chennakeshvarar and Chennamalikeshvarar, rebuilt in 1762 near the Flower Bazaar police station.

I always prefer the rumbunctious bazaars in Indian towns to their well-guarded luxury hotels, and if you can't manage to reach Madurai, Madras's Georgetown Bazaar makes a good substitute, especially the Kotawal Chavadi market in southern Georgetown, with more varieties of fruit and vegetables than you will see in the most sophisticated supermarket. By night, too, Georgetown bristles with colour and commotion, its narrow streets colourful with saris and movie posters. Women whose raven hair is plaited with flowers swing gracefully across the narrow roads.

## Arts and Crafts

By night there is never any shortage of dance, drama or music in Madras. Madras Music Academy at 115 Mowbray's Road provides an annual festival, and other venues include Rajah Annamalai Hall on the Esplanade and Sitraragam. A *sabha* is a musical subscription society offering a weekly concert, but some tickets may be on sale at the door, so you can try the Sri Krishna Gana Sabha on Griffith Road, the Narada Gana Sabha at 254 Mowbray's Road, or the Rasika Ranjani Sabha at 1 Sundareshvarar Street, Mylapore.

Kalakshetra is a hundred-acre campus founded by Rukmini Devi Arundale in 1936, where Indian classic arts are taught in a beautiful environment reminiscent of Adyar, close by. Classical Indian music and dance, weaving and textile design are taught. A similar school for traditional arts and crafts is the Kumararaja Muthiah School, with Tanjore-style paintings, metal sculpture and handwoven textiles.

Beyond Kalakshetra, on the coast road south, Cholamandal is an artists' village with a permanent selling exhibition. It was begun in 1966 by Professor Paniker, former head of the College of Arts, and the crafts here include batik, terra cotta, metalwork, and sculpture, as well as painting and drawing. The Lalit Kala Akademi has its southern branch in Madras: a national art centre where Indian arts are studied, exhibited and sometimes also sold. Private art galleries include the Kala Yatra, Le Gallery, and Sakshi.

In Nungambakkam, near the junction of Kodambakkam High Road and Village Road, stands the white Valluvar Kottam (1976), or memorial to the poet-saint Thiru Valluvar, whose book the *Holy Kural*, written about 100 B.C., corresponds quite closely to the Greek ethical teachings and to the Sanskrit *Rgveda*. 'Kural' is that short rhymed couplet form in which Valluvar wrote. Of the 133 chapters of ten couplets each, the first four are introductory, the next 34 are devoted to ethics or *Aram*; the next 70 to wealth or *Porul*; and the last 25 to love or *inbam*. These correspond closely to the Sanskrit *Dharma*, *Artha*, and *Kama*, and like most poets Valluvar is at his most eloquent when celebrating secret, guilty love as in the *Song of Solomon* or *Romeo and Juliet*. In *Aram*, the sage can tell us:

> Self-control will lead to heaven,
> lack of control to hell

while confessing in his *Inbam*:

> Can the world of the God with lotus eyes
> be sweeter than the arms of my beloved?

and

> Joyously we two embrace
> letting no air between.

But married love is a corollary to these earlier furtive encounters and Valluvar is eloquent here too: separation and reunion remind one of the Rama and Sita episodes of the *Ramayana*, here universalised by Valluvar.

It is a great pity that a 'lifesize' statue of Valluvar is erected in the shrine, for we have no authentic idea of what he looked like; equally disappointing is the sub-Chola, sub-Pallava architecture of the ensemble and concrete shrine in the form of the temple chariot at Tiruvarur. The barn-like hall seating four thousand is open on three sides to benefit from any sudden breeze.

If you want bookshops in Madras, the best is the atmospheric old Higginbotham's at 814 Mount Road (1844), with a second-hand department upstairs discreetly distant from the big sellers in English and Tamil: the *Limca Book of Records* (an Indian-style *Guinness Book*) and T. Janakiraman's *The Sins of Appu's Mother*, Frederick Forsyth and Catherine Cookson. It is sad to quote N. Subrahmanian on modern Tamil letters: 'Whatever talent there is has adjusted itself to the puerile level of an imaginary mediocrity, of a semi-literate "weekend journal-reading" public.' Other bookshops on Mount Road include Pai & Co (no. 152) and Kennedy Book House at 155. Hotel bookshops are run by Danai (Taj Coromandel, Sindoori and Adyar Gate) and Giggles (Connemara).

### Shopping

Shopping is one of the major national pastimes of India, and Madras is a cynosure for silk enthusiasts, who delight in Kanchipuram's handwoven silks, often glittering with gold threads and decorated with temples or abstract designs. Kanchipuram cottons with designs similar to those on silks can be found at the Tamil Nadu Handloom Weavers' Co-operative and the Co-optex shops and silk shops near Panagal Park. The Victoria Technical Institute at 765 Mount Road is trustworthy for hand-embroidered linen, lace and wall-hangings (but it closes on Saturday afternoons), and also on Mount Road you could try Panneerdas at no.

40, Indian Arts Museum at 151, Kashmir Art Palace at 156, Mini Khadi Kraft at 172 and Poompuhar at 818. The choice of jewellers is just as broad: each major hotel is represented, and you could try Bapalal at 24/1 Cathedral Road or Vummidi Bangaru at 603 Mount Road. 'Madras diamonds' are zircons, and local gold- and silver-smithing continue to impress. Look too for the local 'temple jewellery' (specialists include Murthi's in Mylapore) which is used by Bharata Natyam dancers: it is gold-plated silver jewellery set with sometimes artificial stones that gives a stunningly opulent effect with the right sari and the right skin-colouring. Definitely not for the English Rose! And don't forget the enormous selection in leather: handbags, suitcases, jackets, shoes and sandals, at prices far lower than you would pay in Paris or New York. Beside Kashmir Handicrafts Emporium two Canadian ladies with identical maple-leaf holdalls looked at each other meaningfully then scowled at the gutter wreckage close to their careful feet, with the clear implication: 'Give us two Brillo pads and we can clean up the whole of Madras by sundown'.

Similarly low-priced are the meals: no matter where you choose to dine, prices will be spectacularly below those for similar repasts in Munich or Houston. Of course, vegetarians are catered for at most restaurants such as the Woodlands Drive-In on Cathedral Road and Hotel Kanchi and Hotel Palmgrove, but Madras has become particularly well-known for non-vegetarian cuisine originating from Chettinad, south of Trichy. Ponnusamy's in Royapettah (between the Cathedral and the Marina) leads the way in this 'military' cuisine, which gives its name to Velu's Military Hotel, where Chettinad meals are on offer, as at the newer Raintree restaurant at the Connemara, Binny's Road, off Mount Road. Fast foods from the U.S.A. now compete with the steamed rice cake (*idli*) and fried savoury doughnut (*vada*) familiar everywhere in South India, and the Udipi 'meals' which consist of a tray of different vegetables and curries encircling a central mound of rice. Widely-based South Indian restaurants include the Mysore at Taj Coromandel and the Meenam at Harrison's Hotel, 154-5 Village Road. Chinese eating-houses proliferate as tastes become more sophisticated: the Golden Dragon at the Taj Coromandel, the Sagari in the Chola Sheraton, the Chungking and the Dynasty at Harrison's. The best buffet must surely still be the renowned Regency in the Park Sheraton, and among the spreading Continental-type restaurants, one must nominate the Gatsby.

Outside enclaves of former colonial control such as Pondicherry, Tamil Nadu had long and gamely tried to fulfil Gandhiji's aim of outlawing alcohol, which he believed would cause the downfall of the rural peasantry. But the prohibition laws passed in several states, including Tamil Nadu, have proved impossible to enforce; Tamil Nadu alone has over 400,000 cases pending connected with alleged prohibition offences, and bootlegging has proved a boon only to the bribed and the untaxed. Many peasants have died from drinking contaminated liquor made by themselves or at illicit bars, so the Dravida Munnetra Kazhagam government of Tamil Nadu passed in 1990 regulations permitting its own 'country liquor' to be brewed in its own distilleries under quality control and sold to villagers at reasonable prices.

This new policy, it is hoped, will sweep away at one blow the bribery, corruption, dangerous hooch, and revenue loss to the state which had resulted from prohibition. Whether it will have the desired effect is another matter.

### Kanchipuram

'Wear helmet avoid death' admonished a road sign, as if Madras City Corporation had suddenly realised the key to immortality.

I passed the Egmore Wesley Church (services at 8.30 and 6) just after dawn to catch the early bus, and paused at R.K. Medicals, a long, narrow shop on the corner of Poonamalle High Road announcing 'Blood Transfusion Services' and with the hundreds of vehicles already thundering by I wondered how many transfusions would be needed that day for road accidents. R.K. himself shuffled Nestlé's Milkmaid and

*Madras. Parry's Corner. Fruit vendors*

Cuticura; I glimpsed a garlanded teak Ganesha amid the Strepsils and Riogel against flatulence. Cows rootled in the wayside garbage, and nervous dogs backed away first from one trouble, then another. A little round red letterbox marked 'Madras 600084 No clearance on Sundays or Holidays' cluttered the pavement.

Parry's Corner, that focus of Madrasi traffic, is named for Parry & Company, the firm in the building facing the Law Courts where the Esplanade meets First Line Beach. This is where you catch the public bus departing every half hour for Kanchi, though if you are really pushed for time and can spend only one hectic day in the environs, the India Tourism Development Corporation offers at a giveaway price a daily tour from 7.30 to 6 p.m. also visiting Tirukkalukunram and Mahabalipuram.

The 76 bus was nearly full, and ragged orange-vendors shouted their wares along the aisle before we jolted off, the genial conductor in khaki selling us tickets with much jingling of change. A Tamil next to me had fallen asleep with his head on my shoulder, despite the driver's incessant hooting and the incredible din from all sides. I do not travel in India for a quiet life, but I need at least three weeks to recover from the emotional and physical battering, every sense assaulted. Our bus narrowly missed a sauntering cow on the right and a lorry heaped chockfull with laden banana branches, as we ploughed gamely through the road west and crossed the Cooum River towards slightly more open country then padi fields: it takes a hundred minutes to cover the 74 km to Kanchi.

Rickshaw drivers stood expectantly as we emptied the bus: Selvaraj hailed me, and I breezed nonchalantly through the hail of 'me guide sir!' 'you want nice silk?' after negotiating a fair price for the day's riding from temple to temple. Usually one haggles a fare to a destination, with or without waiting, but in certain towns a rate for the day or half-day to include all waiting seems much fairer to both parties. Selvaraj started, as I expected, at Kailasanatha Temple, in the northwest area of Shiva Kanchi, almost out in the fields. The town of 125,000 is divided into Shiva Town with most of the important Hindu shrines, the smaller Vishnu Town, and the Jain area of Tiruparuttikunram.

### Kailasanatha

Kailasanatha means Lord of Kailasa, Shiva's mountain abode, and this sandstone temple is a precious reminder of the 7th-9th centuries, when the Pallava dynasty ruled from this capital, with Mamallapuram, also known as Mahabalipuram, as their local port. Rajasimha (c.700-28) is best remembered as a Pallava ruler for this temple, alive with chipmunks but bereft of priests or worshippers, for it now belongs to the Archaeological Survey. The first stone monuments in South India are the related temples at Mamallapuram, begun by Mahendravarman I

*Kanchipuram. Rickshaw-wallah*

(*c*.600-30), which seems very odd, given the fact that the Pallavas (believed to be Telugu in origin) ruled the Kanchi region from the third century A.D. and they were of course preceded by many other equal or lesser dynasties. There was no lack of stone, so what happened? In his essay in *Studies in Indian Temple Architecture* (ed. by P. Chandra, Delhi, 1975), K.R. Srivanasan propounds the idea that megalithic stone-built burials connected stone with death so rulers might feel that temples in which the living were to worship might treat the material as tabu. Of course, there must have been structures in flimsier materials: wood, brick, and perhaps others, but since there was no large-scale demolition of religious sites by opposing fanatics like that experienced in North India, we cannot be convinced that a once-thriving tradition was razed. They seem to have even resisted the temptation to carve out religious caves until Pallava times, yet Ajanta caves are both much more developed and much earlier. The question remains unresolved.

Kailasanatha consists of two principal elements: the long, symmetrical, and highly elaborate enclosure wall, and the great vimana, or towered sanctuary incorporating seven small cell-shrines, each with an image of Lord Shiva and at the back a panel showing Shiva, his consort Parvati and their son known variously as Subrahmanya, Kumara or Skanda. Though there are, surprisingly, no Chola-age accretions to this

*Kanchipuram. Kailasanatha Temple. Alcoves against the wall*

Pallava shrine, Rajasimha's son did add a lingam shrine to Shiva named in honour of Mahendravarman, a Pallava ruler of the 7th century, decorated on the outer walls with Shiva in the form of a wandering beggar, Shiva with Parvati, and the dancing Shiva.

The inner wall of the great courtyard is lined with intimate alcoves, carved on the exterior, and painted (later) within. Originally, all the sculptures were painted, and traces of these vegetable colours (dominantly yellow and red), and white from crushed shells, remain to tantalise one with the vision of what they once might have been. If you enjoy the 'Descent of the Ganges' at Mamallapuram, Kanchi's seaport, you will prize the same scene here behind the sanctuary envisaged while Lord Shiva is still trying to prevent the waters from drowning the earth: the earlier phase of the same legend.

A seated Nandi, Lord Shiva's bull, views Kailasanatha with an air of millennial resignation, from well outside the temple precinct, secure in the knowledge that lines of miniature bulls and alis (half-lion-half-elephant) protect each alcove in the main court.

### Iravataneshvara

I resisted the temptation to head straight for the later Ekambareshvara in order to see this Pallava shrine, like Kailasanatha of the early 8th century. Its square sanctuary has carvings of Lord Shiva as master of the world, through dance and through knowledge, below water monsters (makaras). Slightly later are the Mukteshvara and Matangeshvara temples to the south, both to the right of the main Madras road, and both square with pyramid-shaped towers.

## Ekambareshvara

Shiva's principal active temple in Kanchi is named for the Lord of the Mango, an ancient tree which you can circle in worship for it too is a manifestation of Lord Shiva. You circle clockwise of course, the unnamable 'other direction' being ill-omened in India. Monotheists persist in misunderstanding the rôle of nature worship in Hinduism; like Buddhism it recognises different stages in spiritual evolution, from the insensible to the enlightened, and suggests that, as in any other kind of education, one teaches and explains only at a level appropriate to the student. So while a child may see an image of Shiva, or touch an ancient mango tree, the partially aware adult can see – if fleetingly – a numinous of intangible reality behind the world of the senses. A Hindu may elude the idol-barrier as simply and purely as a Christian, if he prefers to do so, but Hinduism is clearly more tolerant than the younger faiths of Judaism or Islam, for example, in its ability to accept multifarious forms of worship.

Your first impression, from the pavilion in the long street where leather-sellers try to sell you a pair of open sandals, is of a mighty gopuram announcing in eight gradually diminishing storeys the might of Krishnadeva Raya of the Tuluva dynasty of Vijayanagar, who ruled from 1509 to 1529 and created this 190-foot gateway in the first year of his reign. Originally a Pallava foundation, the Mango Temple was enlarged by the Cholas and then by Vijayanagar as a showpiece, and pilgrims even now fill the temple from morning till night, though it covers nine hectacres. You will be hunted by temple officials to pay for using your camera even if you don't, and there is no shortage of touts self-appointed as 'guides' but as always there is nothing they can show you that you cannot easily find for yourself: follow the flow, sit cross-legged in a corner and watch the Indians in their infinite variety of race, class, caste, colour, age and attitude. Pigeons peck and squuck restlessly, for in Hindu tradition they were unquiet humans that the exasperated Shiva transmogrified in frustration that they would not keep *still*; now they seek for all eternity the release that only Lord Shiva may grant them.

As I completed my circle of the sacred mango tree, the priest by the entrance smudged ash on my forehead which was silently intended to represent wood ash from the mango, and to produce rupees for the outstretched palm. Tree worship among the Tamils may go as far back

*Kanchipuram. Ekambareshvara Temple. Courtyard*

as stone-worship: the erection of megaliths known equally widely in prehistoric Europe. Water-spirits were worshipped at rivers, lakes and sea-shores, The banyan is from early times thought to incorporate the spirit of Shiva, the Kadamba tree the spirit of Murugan, the South Indian name of Kartikeya, Shiva's son, and other trees possessed of spirits were thought to include the pipal, the jujube or Zizyphus and the vanni or Prosopis. At first, worshippers would surround the protected tree with a rail, and then a wall, followed by a shrine. Certain totem trees would come to be associated with a given dynasty: the *panai* with the Cheras, the *ati* with the Cholas, and the *nim* with the Pandyas.

This huge active temple has a mandapam called the Hall of a Thousand Pillars, though I counted scarcely more than half that optimistic figure. One can wander at will as far as the entrance to the sanctum, marvelling at the excellent pillar-carving. I watched ritual bathing in a stepped tank on the northern side, and was welcomed by an English-speaking priest into a shrine with a Shiva Nataraja as centre-piece. Visitors involved with the dance professions must feel gratified that their disciplined way of life is so deeply honoured by Hindu symbolism: the Lord of the Universe as Sacred Dancer. And – unlike our impoverished Puritanism – Hindu temples continue to honour Lord Shiva with temple dancing, temple music, and in many cases the sculptural representation of sensual love which the Indian spirit so accurately relates to spiritual love.

We are accustomed to palace-forts in Rajasthan and elsewhere, but temple-forts are common in South India; Ekambareshvara saw such service in the 18th century. The French drove out the Muslims, to be succeeded in 1759 by the British, who were followed in 1780 by the forces of Haidar Ali.

The main shrine's idol is an earth lingam worshipped by Shiva's consort Parvati here known as the 'wanton-eyed' or Kamakshi. Similar images can be seen in the surrounding portico. I dropped down on to my haunches in shadow to observe the strange, rich variety of life around me: a family was unwrapping cloths to reveal their meal, sloe-eyed children forming an expectant semicircle round their scarlet-saried mother. A limping sadhu with a white-flecked grey beard chanted to himself before disappearing round a corner.

### Kamakshi Temple
In a side-street to the south-east I found this greatly remodelled temple dedicated to the wanton aspect of Parvati. The new pyramidal towers surmount a Vijayanagar gate, and most of the buildings we see now date from around the 17th century, though a Shiva temple just beyond its north-eastern corner is clearly Chola. Kamakshi's mandapam, or columned hall, is decorated with a frieze showing divinities, and each col-

*Kanchipuram. Kamakshi Temple, with elephant*

umn, pilaster and bracket is intricately carved. The main shrine to Parvati has a gilded tower, but there is a range of smaller shrines around it, each with its own appeal. Kamakshi's site goes back to Pallava times, when it was traditionally the funeral-temple of the Hindu philosopher Shankara (788-820), poet of *stotras* or hymns of praise, and commentator on the Vedanta Sutras of Badarayana (*c*.500 B.C.) still available in paperback from Dover, New York, or Constable, London. Shankara was a great theological disputant and traveller, who roved India to debate with Buddhists and other 'heretics', defending the ultimate truth and consistency of the sacred Vedic literature. His admittedly double standard of truth resembled the bold, sweeping reasoning of Thomas Aquinas' *Summa*. On one level, he argued, the world as produced by Brahma evolved in a manner already explained by the Sankhya School.

27

On a much higher level, the whole universe of phenomena has no objective existence: it is illusion, the realm of *maya*. The only reality behind appearances is the World Soul, or Brahman, of the Upanishads, which can be attained only through meditation. This so closely resembles the Buddhist view of Nirvana that many Hindu opponents accused him of crypto-Buddhism, though he propounded Advaita (literally non-dualism, that is monism). Shankara's influence has spread from South India to all parts of the country, and from the ninth century to every succeeding epoch, including our own. In Kanchipuram his sect is headed by His Holiness Jayendra Saraswati, who spent nine years in study and meditation before taking up his duties as pontiff when nominated by his predecessor. *Vedanta for the Western World* (1948) edited by Christopher Isherwood is just one sign of Vedanta's popularity. Aldous Huxley called it 'the perennial philosophy' and the Ramakrishna Vedanta Centre in London founded in 1948 represents a powerful spiritual line running through Shankara to Sri Ramakrishna (1836-86) and his pupil Swami Vivekananda. Ian Davie of Ampleforth College, York, has produced a book providing a coherent Jesuology on the basis of Vedanta, suggesting a Hindu dimension within Christian thought. But Westerners have little or no chance of penetrating the mysteries of Advaita Vedanta because their heredity and environment give them no preparation to cope with a religious society deriving every action from a mystical origin. High-caste Hindus are effortlessly superior, disregard convention, and move between garrulity and silence, somnolence and hyperactivity with a consummate ease born of scorn for worldliness. A Westerner has virtually no chance of meeting true Hindu mystics, because their verbal language and spiritual language are alike totally diverse from ours. The entire Upanishad called *Mandukya* is devoted to one word, *om*, which is considered the verbal equivalent to the Brahman, or universal, eternal reality. A mystic chanting the word from the pit of his stomach releases sounds and powers which no amount of translation into Western languages could embody or even roughly indicate. The spring into faith, the leap into the dark: these inhere in *om*.

In Pondicherry we shall see the ashram of the yogi Sri Aurobindo, another Vedantist of the main stream. The Ramakrishna Centre teaches three 'fundamental truths': man's real nature is divine; the aim of human life is to unfold and manifest this divine nature; and, truth is universal, and not the exclusive possession of any one creed, race or epoch. Because these beliefs are deeply ingrained in Hindu thought processes, it is easy to understand how Russians and Germans, Americans and Italians, Arabs and Englishmen are implicitly tolerated, and why Indians in cities such as Madras find no paradox in seeing a mosque, temple and church on the same street.

28

## Vaikuntha Perumal

Turn right off the road to the rail station and you enter the Vaishnavite world of Kanchi. A Pallava structure of the later 8th century, it was endowed by Nandivarman II, and has a vimana, or towered sanctuary, higher even than the Shaivite Kailasanatha: could the superior height have been in direct competition? The most interesting feature for the art connoisseur is a panel-sequence on the colonnade walls recounting the history of the Pallava dynasty: a full account can be found in C. Minakshi's *The Historical Sculptures of the Vaikuntha Perumal Temple, Kanchi* (Delhi, 1941). Despite the erosions of time one can make out battle scenes, coronation scenes, and court ceremonies. The entrance hall is a Vijayanagar accretion, but the main sanctuary has three inner sanctums, in which as you ascend you find Vishnu standing, seated and reclining. A mandapam is situated on the western side.

## Varadaraja Swami Temple

'Varada' is a bestower of boons, Lord of the World, and 'swami' denotes a spiritual master. It is the leading Vishnu temple in Kanchi and dates in its present form from Chola times, but any guide will assure you that Brahma made a fire sacrifice to raise Vishnu here on a high altar, and this modern temple allegedly reflects the said altar. Srinivasan names the kalyana mandapam here as 'one of the finest examples'. Look closely at the corners of the overhanging cornices, or kapotas, where great stone chains and the corner-pieces from which they hang are each carved from a single stone. The purpose of the kapota (it literally means 'dove') is of course not decorative, but was to allow rains to run off, protecting beams, joist-ends, and worshippers below. The function of the kalyana mandapam was to provide the stage for the ceremonial reenactment of the wedding of god and goddess in the form of processional bronze icons once a year.

Barrett has compared the temple-building passion of the Cholas to the pervasion of village churches throughout England: by the year 1000 A.D. Chola imperial sway extended far from Tamil Nadu to Kerala and Karnataka, coastal Andhra Pradesh, and to islands from Sri Lanka and the Laccadives to Andaman and the Maldives.

The Varadaraja we see now, however, dates from later times when the grandeur of Tanjore's Brihadeshvara had given way to more modest enterprise. Look first at the western gopuram, certainly no earlier than the 12th century, and the Vijayanagar-period eight-storey eastern gopuram, probably of the 16th century. The Vijayanagar mandapam has ninety-six columns to which you might devote at least a day, for their intricate range of Vaishnavite scenes and legends, interspersed by these virtuoso sculptors with erotic figures and holy men. Damage was done by soldiers when the temple was used as a barracks. More familiar scenes from the Ramayana have been carved on the basement. A tank with a charming pavilion lies to the north. Entering the third precinct you come to pavilions with sculptures of royal donors on the column bases. The next mandapam has Chola-period columns and a small Chola shrine to a Vaishnavite saint, Anantalvar. The main sanctuary beyond an 11th-century gateway possesses bronzes of Vishnu with his consorts, but as always one is not allowed past the entrance to the inner shrine. Everywhere you will see worshippers with a white 'V' on their brow bisected by a vertical red line: the sign of a Vaishnavite. The Aiyengar Brahman caste retains a sector of the temple for continuous recitation of the Vedas.

### Vardhamana Jain Temple
Take a rickshaw from Vishnu Kanchi along the banks of the Vegavati, and cross the river to Tiruparuttikunram, the Jain area. Vardhamana, 'the prosperous one', was born of a princely family in 599 B.C. according to tradition, or 549 or 539 B.C., according to Western scholars. At the age of thirty, he abandoned the world to live like a beggar and observe the realities of sickness, disease, old age, and death. Like his contemporary, Gautama Buddha, he sought release from the material world, but unlike the advocate of the Middle Way, Vardhamana preached the need for great austerities as a means to liberation, the achievement (siddhi) of the perfect ones (siddhas). He is called a ford-maker (tirthankar) for his ability to show his followers a way from the world of illusion to the world beyond. The Jaina Sutras (Dover, New York; Constable, London) show Vardhamana, known in Jainism as Mahavira, 'the great hero', to have been an eloquent preacher, an ardent ascetic, and a great organiser, who composed the differences of the school of Parshva, his predecessor and teacher. He stressed non-violence and that sacred duty to protect all living things exemplified by the Jain practice of covering one's mouth to ensure that no flying creatures are accidentally swallowed. He stressed repentance, and the spiritual cognition of the cosmos which, by processes of faith and works, illumination and asceticism, will lead the soul from this present dark age in its present stark environment to the very summit where the perfected ones reside for all eternity.

I looked first at the 9th-century Pallava temple to the seventh tirthankar, Chandraprabha, then at the later Chola twin-shrine temples of Vardhamana, with 17th-century ceiling paintings on the mandapam to illustrate Hindu and Jain legends. As I left the quiet shrine, a woman in a yellow sari spat a red flow of betel saliva onto the ground like a viper's tongue suddenly bloodied and loosed from the mouth. My rickshaw driver, spreadeagled on the passenger seat like a Hollywood gun-battle victim, rose from his torpor, and cycled gamely off to the Hotel Tamil Nadu near the rail station. There in the quiet, dusky garden I sipped a cool Gold Spot orange drink, and waited for peacocks.


## Vellore

Highway 4 westward from Madras to Chittoor and Bangalore branches north from Arcot, and I took instead Highway 46 from Arcot in the direction of Krishnagiri, to Vellore. The original settlement was Vellappadi, nowadays a suburb, so called from its grove of vela or babul trees, *acacia arabica*, the suffix 'ur' denoting a settlement. Its babbling bazaar and colourful street life stunned me into a seated trance beside a bangle-stall, but eventually the heat and dust of midday drove me towards a cold drinks stall. Bullocks steadily plodded past, pulling their carts oblivious to all around them. The heat seems to radiate like turned-up bars of electric fires from the rocky hills topped by three peaks: Sajjarao, Gajjarao, and Murti, dominating the town from the east. The great granite Vellore Fort might have been laid out, as locals claim, in the last years of the 13th century by a man from Bhadrachalam called Bommi Reddy, granted permission to settle here by the Chola king of the time. The upper brick parapets pierced with embrasures are clearly not Indian in style, and are presumably the work of Italian engineers, either of the same period or slightly later. However, it is unlikely that the fort and associated temple date from before the mid-14th century, according to an inscription on the walls of a temple in the Gudiyattam taluq. It passed to King Narasingha Raya of Vijayanagar about 1500, and in the mid-17th century it was taken by the Sultans of Bijapur but after a short period of Muslim sovereignty it fell to Tukoji Rao's Marathas in 1677. Daud Khan, a Mughal general and Nawab of the Carnatic, expelled the Marathas in 1708 and his family held Vellore until 1763, when the fort and surrounding area was captured by the British allied with Nawab Muhammad Ali. Tipu Sultan's family members in Vellore fomented the unsuccessful Vellore Mutiny of 1806 in which 350 sepoys were killed. Nowadays Vellore Fort is used for offices, like Fort St George in Madras, but Vellore is the more picturesque, and for connoisseurs of military architecture must be one of the treasures of South India. Its water supply is assured both by the nearby Palar river (which has a duct leading to the temple), and, by an underground system deriving from the Suryagunta bathing tank. The massive structure is four-sided, but irregular, with moated ramparts strengthened by bastions and round towers. Below the ramparts a *fausse-braie* with machicolated turrets is separated from the solid masonry counterscarp by a broad ditch varying in width. The crenellated parapets have broad merlons suitable for defence by musketeers: I dodged out of the way in deference to a volley from an imagined Porthos. A modern church stands to the southeast of the Fort; in a Christian cemetery stands a mute memorial dated 1863-4 to those who fell in the 1806 mutiny; as a matter of interest, about four hundred members of Tipu Sultan's family are buried about 1½ km east of the fort, just south of the Kanchi Road and beyond the Christian Medical College Hospital. Some of the most significant tombs are those to his wife, Padshah Begum, and to Mirza Raza, who married one of Tipu's daughters. After the mutiny, understandably enough, the remaining family members of Tipu Sultan were removed to Calcutta.

The temple of Jalakanteshvara, or 'Shiva Residing in the Waters', situated within the fort walls, was desanctified for some time, as blood had been shed within it, and run by the Archaeological Survey, but in 1981 it was rededicated. Entry is by the southern gopuram of seven levels, along one passage of which you find a representation said to be of that Reddy who was responsible for both fort and temple. As usual, what is said may be taken with a pinch of salt and simultaneous silence, for the fort is clearly earlier than the temple of 1566, which is in that full Vijayanagar style we shall see in Karnataka at Srirangam and Hampi. The kalyana mandapam, just inside the temple enclosure, is a riot of sculptural masterpieces, each pillar with its own personality, and the roof ornaments dazzling in their virtuosity: three circles of parrots hang head down with a lotus flower in beak and claw, each carved from a monolith as if such extraordinary delicacy were the most natural art in the world.

At the northwest corner it is worth noting a well with a pivotal stone doorway below the customary water level: here a subterranean mandapam has a passage obviously connecting with the river Palar. The temple has a Shiva Nataraja shrine to the north and a lingam shrine to the west, opening off the same mandapam.

Vellore Government Museum was closed that day, so I took a Kanchi-bound bus at the adjacent bus stand and headed back eastward to the Hotel Tamil Nadu in Kanchi. Moonlight imprinted its official silver hallmark on all the edges of houses and of huts.

### Chingalpat and Tirukkalukunram

Next morning, faced with the choice between a train or bus to Chingalpat ('Lotus Town'), I opted for the latter, and walked through the cool, radiant dawn light to the bus station, where cows, freshly turned out of family courtyards, were beginning to mooch hopefully from one pile of garbage to another. An ancient man with a gunny bag in one hand and a stout walking-stick in the other gazed abstractedly around him, caught in the miasma of old age.

None of the buses jolting in or out bore any script but Tamil, so I asked for the bus to Chingalpat, and was motioned to a vehicle encrusted with grime and, having checked his destination with my neighbour, sagged down, to be assailed by sellers of lottery-tickets, bangles, bananas, and popcorn. For breakfast I bought a cold drink and a packet of Marie biscuits, while a whitebeard heaved himself on to the bus, wafted incense over the passengers, and unsolicited brushed the incense into our unsuspecting hair. I am sweetly scented on an Indian bus - at last! The bus eased its honking way among yoked bullocks, past the International Taekwondo Association of India, up Gandhi Road, and past the Modern English College and Coffee and Tiffin Hotel, on to the open road. Of course Tamil Nadu buses have seats for either two Tamils or three Tamils, but not one Tamil plus Fat Englishman, or two Tamils plus F.E. The dilemma is: do I hog the place of one Tamil and squeeze the remainder to pulp; or two Tamils and face the wrath of those standing who count that there is place for one more Tamil? We ended by doing what everyone else does: squeezing.

Chingalpat Fort is a Vijayanagar structure of the later 16th century, surrounded by water on three sides. Decayed and dilapidated, it has been bisected by the modern railway line, so that you pass through it without even knowing. The Chariot Palace or Ther Mahal is the only significant building left, though it has lost a storey. The temple chariot of the Varadaraja Temple at Kanchi was visible from the top by the ladies of the palace. If you think that the nearby former Hindu temple looks mysteriously Islamic, you are right: it was transformed into a mosque, with characteristic arches, when captured by the Muslims.

The bus to Mahabalipuram from Chingalpat stops at Tirukkalukunram ('Hill of the Holy Eagles'), and there one alights for the temple complex at the foot of the hill and – stamina willing – a steep climb to the top, less interesting intrinsically than for the legend that two pilgrims commuting daily between Benares and Rameshwaram drop in for lunch about noon, disguised as eagles. A cave has been sculpted in Pallava style near this upper temple, but the views towards the sea and inland – truly an eagle's eye view – are worth any amount of climbing, though doolis (covered baskets with long handles for porters) are available for the aged and infirm.

### Mamallapuram

Back in the village centre I boarded the next bus for Mahabalipuram, better known in Tamil as Mamallapuram from the Pallava ruler Narasimhavarman I (630-668). He was known as 'the Great Wrestler' or Mahamalla, later corrupted to Mamalla, under whom the city first flourished. The bus was crowded to the doors, and the usual teeming throng of extras pushed and shoved to get a slice of the action on board, but as my grandmother once sternly pointed out in a voice to transfix the wayward: 'Jumping in first doesn't make the bus start any earlier'. To the usual tolerant amusement of those already aloft I apologetically tried to insert a hand between two jampacked Tamils, but found myself clutching only empty air and fell away. The next bus would take just the same time to get there, and in the meantime I quaffed a sociable Limca with Asoke Kumar Dutta of the Tyre Corporation of India, who handed me his card with a slight bow and begged me to honour his house when I next visited Madras. How does a xenophobe *manage*, in India?

The name 'Mahabalipuram', connects the place with virtuous King Bali, legendary conqueror of Indra and the other gods. The Vedic gods, like their Teutonic counterparts, were seldom averse to subterfuge to gain the upper hand, and prevailed on Vishnu to save their supremacy. Vishnu manifested himself as a dwarf and craved from Bali just as much groundd as he could span in three steps. The Great Bali, master of heaven, earth, and the depths below, lacked divine subtlety and conceded this request, whereupon Vishnu bestrode heaven in his first step, earth in his second but, in deference to Bali's goodness and his father Pralada's devotion to Vishnu, accorded Bali the lower regions, from which time Mahabali has been known as the ruler of the underworld, or king of the demons, paradoxically at odds with his life on earth and of course diametrically opposed to the Christian view of wilful, rebellious Satan.

Mamallapuram is divided archaeologically into three zones: the Shore Temple to the east; the Five Chariots to the south; and the main complex clustering on the slopes of the great holy rock. All date from the 7th-8th centuries, comprising the earliest monumental architecture and sculpture in South India, and require at least one long day, starting at dawn if possible for the wondrous effects of light, and resting during the zenith of the day in one of the friendly restaurants sympathetic to Western taste-buds, such as the vegetarian Mamalla Bhavan near the bus station, or the Rose Garden on Shore Temple Road which specialises in fish.

The pace of life in Mamallapuram is light and easy, for it lies well off main road and rail routes, and its idyllic beach resorts are situated well outside the town, to the north. And where other South Indian temples predictably portray gods and goddesses to the exclusion of everyday life, here the rock sculptures and freestanding temples hum and throb with the preoccupations of the ordinary citizen, and sculpture remains (albeit dully and repetitively) the activity of hundreds of local people today. It does not do to labour the point, for kings and gods, sacred and symbolic images, the arcane and the majestic, hold sway over the rocks, but one has only to find the milking of the cow with attendant calf in the Krishna Mandapam or grooming monkeys near the Descent of the Ganges to

*Mamallapuram. 7th-century sculptures in the round: monkeys grooming*

realise the proximity of these figures to daily work and symbolism. Why should we separate fact from idea? Indians don't.

I couldn't resist exploring the ramshackle temple near the bus stand marked Sri Sthala Sayana Perumal, with its white pillars and columns, and the Recumbent Lord of the Vijayanagar period. 'Sthala' is a holy place, 'Sayana' means recumbent, and 'Perumal' denotes 'Lord', usually as here Vishnu. I loved the place, with its grinning priest, because elsewhere in the archaeological zone one feels a spectator as in a museum; here one becomes, if only by proxy, a participant in the life of the town. From the post-Pallava temple exalting Vishnu the nearest rock carving is a small columned hall of 640 overarching a scene showing Krishna lifting Mount Govardhana with a graceful movement of his left hand to protect the herds and their owners from being crushed. You can see traces of the original paint. The natural rock face is used ingeniously and the polygonal columns are carved too. Next is the contemporary Five Pandava Mandapam, for no known reason left incomplete after six columns had been carved. Last of this triad is the most miraculous bas relief in South India: the Descent of the Ganges, also of mid-7th century date, commonly known as Arjuna's Penance, Shiva Hunting with Arjuna, or Bhagiratha's Penance, depending on which scene you take as the key. It might be that the composition had no single inspiration, but achieves harmony by the near symmetry of the two boulder shapes separated by a narrow vertical cleft to represent the fall of the Ganges from the Himalaya through its plain to the sea. A cistern above indicates that water actually flowed down this cleft, possibly at times arranged by priestly accord, like the Delphic 'oracle' or the oozing Neapolitan 'blood' of St Januarius.

All the thronging figures face the cleft, giving an effect of confrontation. They include hunters (*kiratas*) and semi-human, semi-birdlike *kinnaras*, gods, heroes and saints. Scale is shown by the enormous figures of elephants on the lower right, and contrast by the ascetic figures in the more tranquil, less crowded reliefs on the lower left. A youth wrings out laundry, another carries water in sight of his ashram, beside which another worshipper stares at the sun in a self-afflicted horror that G.K. Chesterton would use (probably without knowing this antecedent) in a

*Mamallapuram. Detail from the bas-relief,* The Descent of the Ganges

Father Brown story. Shiva with his trident stands near an ancient ascetic – usually identified with Arjuna – who gazes at the sun while holding his hands above his head and standing on one leg, as thin and emaciated as the classic Buddha in the National Museum, Karachi. The moment illustrated from 6th-century Bharavi's poem *Shiva as Kirata and Arjuna* seems to be the harmony of birds and animals in the army of Shiva gathered to protect Arjuna. J.C. Harle questions this literary source, for he would have expected to find a boar, sent to destroy Arjuna, in a central position, but Nagaraja Rao affirms that the boar exists on the relief, wounded by an arrow. Whatever the scholarly argumentation, nobody denies that the composition is triumphant in ensemble and detail alike, from the deer scratching its nose, and the delicately observed baby elephant, to the amusing ascetic cat, doing penance by disregarding the playful mice, unharmed around its feet. Many flying figures in the upper sector are genuine masterpieces of light, movement and grace as fine as anything the masters Giambologna or Cellini would devise in their different media.

An unfinished version of the same mythological scene, obviously very close to the heart of the Pallava dynasty and to the Sanskrit poet Bharavi of Kanchipuram, is situated at the foot of the lighthouse on the shore side, near the Dharmaraja Cave Temple (early 7th century) with a tripartite sanctuary. The lighthouse may be visited every afternoon from two to four, when you can make out a nuclear power station, south along the coastline. It's probably not a good idea to bathe at Mamallapuram.

Behind the lighthouse, I found two cave temples: as at Petra, one 'finds' temples around hillocks and corners, sharing in the joy of discovery that the first Europeans would have felt here. The 7th-century Adivaraha temple has two extraordinary portrait reliefs of a Pallava king and his son, with two consorts or princesses. One of them is that Narasimhavarman known as Mahamalla, seated on a throne carved with animal legs. The women are seen three-quarter face, but the king, left arm akimbo, gazes steadily at us with the sober, righteous, granite gaze of a mortal teetering on the brink of immortality. End panels on the verandah depict Durga conquering the demon, seated Lakshmi between two elephants in the upper half, and female attendants in the lower. Within is the image of Vishnu as the first boar, his incarnation as Adivaraha, not to be confused with the Varaha Cave Temple to the north. Very close to Adivaraha is Mahishasura Mardini Cave Temple, where the huge buffalo demon is attacked by lion-borne Durga, her impetus sustained sculpturally by the leaning posture of the opposing forces, craven in sudden defeat.

Heading back north, you climb to the summit of the hill, where Olakkanatha Temple, dedicated to another of the multitudinous incarnations of Shiva, might be mistaken at first glance for the Athenian Acropolis; what a shame that time has so badly eroded the carvings of Shiva. Due north you see the Ganesha ratha. 'Ratha' can refer to a temple chariot or a temple model, and in this case the latter is meant: a monolithic shrine dated to 670-680, during the reign of the Pallava king Parameshvaravarman I, father of Narasimhavarman II called Rajasimha, who would commission the Shore Temple and at Kanchi the great Kailasanatha Temple, among many.

Kids bleated for their nanny among the rocks, and a little goatherd slithered up to me with a shy 'Hullo, Mister!', as I sauntered northwestward to the late 7th-century Varana Temple. The shrine has been robbed, but the wall panels preserve their original vigour: Three-stepping Vishnu; Vishnu with Bhudevi, the earth goddess he rescued; Durga (right) and Lakshmi (left). A small Archaeological Museum is situated east of Ganesha ratha.

Through the village square you take the Shore Road, where the only surviving Shore Temple is now protected from the ocean waves by a retaining wall: six other temples are drowned. Piglets snuffled by the sandy road, and vendors offered shell trinkets and clusters of dates. A shuttered missionary shack entitled 'Good News Book Centre' had the forlorn appearance of an unheeded haranguer at Speakers' Corner with the misfortune of being dumb. The Shore Temple itself seems to stand at the end of a processional way from Kanchi, with all the accomplishment of an architectural climax, though it may fairly be thought of as the beginnings of a structural temple tradition evolving from smaller, less confident, cave temples. The external walls teem with energy, bas reliefs in both niches and the spaces between. The larger shrine's wall is likewise covered, and numerous animals, such as bulls, elephants, lions and yalis protect the twin Shiva shrines and the central Vishnu sanctum, where the god is carved asleep on his serpent Ananta, on a granite rock. With the murmuring of the waves, sometimes reverberating like thunder, and a sea-breeze ruffling your hair, you might be back in the eighth century, were it not for the ruthless erosion by salt wind and water of the reliefs on the walls.

Returning by the same Shore Road, you bear left from the village square along Five Rathas Road, beside the tap tip tap of a legion of crouching, seated, haunched and bent stonecarvers, each using local stone to produce cloned Ganeshas, identical Shivas, with every hint of originality relentlessly burnt away. What is familiar is saleable. What is copied is comfortable. If the idol presents nothing but an outward semblance of reality, how can it matter what the carving looks like? A sanctuary in the Shore Temple centres on a many-sided basalt lingam, but the more prudish Hindus of the twentieth century do not commission or buy such obvious emblems of divine fertility. Coconut groves are planted on the shore side of the road, and when the thirsty traveller reaches the rathas nothing could be more deliciously welcome than coconut milk from a straw; after hacking open the top with his fearsome machete, the ancient vendor waited while I drank, then split the empty fruit in two and gouged out the moist white meat with the tip of the machete, all for two rupees.

There is no historical justification for the popular names given to any of the five rathas, which date to the 7th century. They are monolithic shrines, and for some reason remained unfinished, like three other along the beach, except for the smallest, dedicated to Durga and usually called the 'Draupadi Ratha'. Even the word 'ratha' is surely misleading, because although this means a temple car drawn in procession (the kind that can be seen in all the great temple courtyards in South India) and

*Mamallapuram. Five rathas*

39

any representation of such chariots, these monoliths were probably never intended for that purpose. They were carved from living granite boulders, much like the example at Kalugumalai in Tirunelveli district, and it is tempting but fanciful to view them as an architectual pattern-book, an 'Ideal Shrine' exhibition from which succeeding builders could draw inspiration. The northernmost shrine is Durga's, with a carved lion in front of the steps and bull behind, female guardians and a four-sided roof associated with Bengali tradition. All the others are Dravidian in style and incomplete. The adjacent Arjuna Ratha is adorned externally with Vishnu and his mount Garuda, Indra with his elephant, and Shiva with his bull. Its octagonal dome echoes that of the larger Dharmaraja Ratha, its elaborate roof and eave forms gracefully curved as if some-how botanic. Arjuna Ratha's sanctum is empty and the larger Bhima Ratha next door is incomplete on the lower level, except for the friendly lions. The vaulted roof gives an appearance of a stone barn's.

Lion bases also feature on the Dharmaraja Ratha, named for the eldest of the Pandava brothers, also known as Yama. Though the sanc-tum is incomplete, there is a splendid array of side reliefs: Shiva and King Mamalla, Shiva, Brahma with Harihara who is both Shiva and Vishnu in one form, and Brahma with Shiva as both male and female, in the manifestation called Ardhanarisha. Early Pallava art deserves your camera's close attention to detail in the Chandra and Surya and the lyrical shapes of worshippers. A stone ladder admits to the upper level.

Isolated from the group is the Nakula and Sahadeva Ratha, named for two more of the Pandava brothers. It sums up the Dravidian technique, which will linger in South India almost as long as the Classical Greek orders have survived in the West: the pilaster and base, neat corbelling, well-proportioned entablature, and a dome. European and 'Indo-Aryan' bias towards North India has traditionally obscured proper appreciation of Dravidian art in the West, and here at Mamallapuram – or at Mandagapattu and Trichy – cave temples and their bold, innova-tive successors can help to broaden your view of the Indian genius.

I was ready for a rest, and walked along the coast road north, pausing to buy moonstone earrings on Five Rathas Road and dining on grilled fresh fish and banana lassi at the Rose Garden Restaurant, where 'sixties-style hippies with long hair, beards and T-shirts spoke in slow, laid-back rumours and listened to Western pop music. I strolled out three km along the highway parallel with the sea as seagulls flapped lazily overhead, and booked in at the Ideal Beach Resort. Crows cawed their displeasure at an unfair universe, where nightingales enjoy all the best tunes.

P.M. Dharmalingam, from Sri Lanka, suffered the seizure of his tea plantation and other assets, so sought refuge in India and in 1979 founded this charming complex, with tall oleanders in radiant flower

*Mamallapuram. Ideal Beach Resort. Cottage rooms*

and coconuts ready to drop. A woman swept the sand paths with a
pandan brush, moving some sand and rubbish into a palmleaf basket
with holes in it large enough for the sand and smaller rubbish to fall
straight through again. Everyone looked mildly satisfied at this
arrangement.

My plush room near the beach had a kingsize bed and bathroom with
a bath, not just a shower, en suite. I fell asleep over my basic Tamil
wordlist which includes the equivalents of 'slum', 'prison', 'gur',
'tamarind' and 'horsegram'. I couldn't sleep for excitement, so padded
out in sandals (against broken glass) and called out to the half moon
across the expanse of sky and ocean: 'I wouldn't change places with you
for all the tea in India', and raced into the ocean like a mad Crusoe,
delirious with the ecstasy of living.

Next morning, after breakfast of papaya and coffee with toast and
honey in the company of a caged green macaw offering raucous advice
and encouragement, I headed back to town for the Pondicherry bus,
which I had been told was supposed to leave at 8.30, 9 and 9.30: I split
the difference. But nothing mattered about time, for the sunlit bus stand
of Mahabalipuram presented a spectacle as varied and grotesque as any
funfair. Bright-eyed urchins leapt and shouted, two backpacking tall
bigboned Swedish blondes attracted goggling attention already familiar
to them from tiny, dark men in sandals. A raving madwoman pranced

and let out a stream of oaths at the male gender whom she abominated, then got on a bus headed for Madras. When asked for a fare she pouted then cursed again, and when the conductor remonstrated with her a policeman suddenly arrived from the corner and beat her out of the bus with his truncheon, that iron-tipped bamboo stick called a lathi. Foaming at the mouth now, she rolled around the ground, uttering howls and mewls, like a cat-and-dog fight. A blind beggar shuffled up through the kerfuffle, stretching out his palm. A vendor of stuffed chipmunks paraded his wares on a bench to the silent wonderment of two scrapping urchins, at last transfixed. Crouchers awaited the bus – or possibly inspiration. A youth of 18 in a clean shirt and freshly pressed trousers leafed through one of the numerous glossy film magazines with unattainable beauties smiling decorously from every page. 'They are more available buses more than they are show on the timetable', a grinning Tamil consoled me. But there were fewer, for the first bus eventually ground to a halt at 10.15, packed to the doors and all aisles congested as cells in a brain. Luckily, most passengers alighted here, and I managed to get a seat all the way to Pondicherry, next to a Tamil with such glittering brown eyes that I should have cast him as Sindbad in the *Arabian Nights*.

Gingee

The highway south from Madras to Trichy passes through Tindivanam, where I left the bus for a connection to the abandoned fortress above Gingee, an hour's busride away, that is roughly 28 km. Its Tamil name Senji refers to Senji Ammal, the mother goddess assimilated here to the Hindu goddess of learning and wisdom Saraswati. A prehistoric settlement, easily defensible, was adopted by every power in the land in succession, though the first ambitious fortifications were erected in the 11th century by the Cholas against the Pandya dynasty ruling from Madurai. The fierce local Kurumba people captured the Chola fortress, only to lose it again, but in the 15th century the Pandyas of Tanjore seized Gingee and strengthened it with the triple-hill walls that we see now, and new forts on each of the three hills. The strongest and highest citadel is Rajagiri, 'Royal Hill', 215 metres and eight hundred stone steps above the sprawling little town; the other two are Krishnagiri (90 m above the town) and Chandragiri (85 m), between which an outer gate barred access to the whole ingenious complex. It all looks impregnable enough, but... If human ingenuity can devise defences, it can overcome them, and Gingee fell in 1638 to the Sultanate of Bijapur, who succumbed to an attack by Shivaji, the hero-ruler of the Marathas, in 1677. After the Mughals had taken the then Maratha capital of Rajgarh, Raja Ram made Gingee his Maratha capital and held out against the

Mughal general Zulfiqar Khan for seven years until 1698. The French took Gingee in 1750, losing out to the British after a desperate five-week siege in 1761: the last French outpost to fall in the Seven Years' War.

It is only when you stand on the citadel, among circling birds, that you appreciate the strength of Rajagiri, centred within three defensive lines, each with massive gateways. Seven gates hamper one offensive surge after another, the first with a moat and drawbridge, then ample court-yards where defenders can mass against onslaught. On entering the triple gate to the inner fort, one is first impressed by the ruined Kalyana Palace intended for the Governor's headquarters, with surrounding lodgings for his entourage, and a seven-storey building so excellently designed that spring and reservoir water could be pumped up to the sixth storey. A 16th-century Hindu temple is devoted to an aspect of Vishnu called Venkatarama, 'Lord of the Venkata Hills', who is wor-shipped also at Tirupati and nearby Tirumala in Andhra Pradesh. The clash of Tamil and Northern forces is symbolised by Tamil inscriptions on the temple, and Persian inscriptions on the Mosque of Saad Atallah, built in the 18th century. Crows rise like vultures from surrounding rice-fields to nest in the niches of Kalyana Mahal, bringing their own black immortalities to a tower long deserted by the men who built it and inhabited the citadel above. Krishnagiri I found even more bereft below the pitiless sun: the Hindu temple sits helpless, deconsecrated as it were, disconsolate among empty granaries and echoing audience hall.

### Tiruvannamalai
Tamil Nadu possesses five major temple cities: Srirangam near Trichy, Madurai, Chidambaram, Kanchipuram and Tiruvannamalai, the 'Holy Crimson Mountain', so called from the colour of the hill above it before sunrise. Sunworship here dating from ages immemorial is echoed in the Kartikeya or Subrahmanya festival in November or December each year. Legend recalls that Parvati completed her penance here and was reconciled with Lord Shiva, who showed his forgiveness by appearing as flames atop this sacred mountain to revoke the darkness covering the world. The Kartikeya festival continues for ten days and ends with the Dipam ceremony just before the full moon rises on the last evening. Brahmins in the Arunachaleshvara Temple, dedicated to Shiva as Lord of the Eastern Mountain, take a vessel from the holy of holies, revealing in the courtyard blazing camphor which is then poured on the ground in front of Lord Arunachaleshvara's image, placed for the occasion in the mandapam. On seeing this, Brahmins on the mountain summit light up a great vessel of camphor and ghee presented in preceding days by pil-grims, who rush from the temple up towards the summit to view the spectacle.

The three eastern gods have tirthas or tanks devoted to them throughout the town: Agni Tirtha (south-east) near the Salem Road, Indra Tirtha (east) near the main temple, and Ishana Tirtha (north-east) near the Vellore Road.

Tiruvannamalai is thus a place for the seeker or spiritual adept, and I find the town even more congenial at less busy times, before the pandemonium of the festival, when it is easier to find accommodation at the ashram – open also to non-Hindus. The slow train between Vellore and Villupuram across North Arcot takes three hours and the express two hours to get to Tiruvannamalai from Vellore. My 1926 *Illustrated Guide to the South Indian Railway* notes that 'there is a refreshment room at the station where light refreshments and aerated waters may be obtained, and the butler in charge keeps a small stock of travellers' requisites for sale,' and suggests sport about two miles south of the station, where 'hare, partridge, quail and antelope can be shot.'

Between 1753 and 1791 Tiruvannamalai was besieged ten times, and six times taken, thrice by assault. The temple walls show marks of cannonballs to this day.

Arunachaleshvara, or Temple of the Eternal Sunrise, has an eastern entrance gateway 66 m high, its lower storeys built at the expense of the Vijayanagar ruler Krishnadeva Raya (1502-29), and the higher of the eleven storeys being later renovations. Evidence of paintings can be seen: the more durable sculptures are splendid. The plan is triply rectangular, with courtyards gradually decreasing in size from the '1,000-column' mandapam of Vijayanagar age recognisable by piers flaunting majestic yalis, those composite animals nightmarishly at once horse, lion and elephant, each with its superb rider. Look in this first courtyard for the contemporary shrine to Subrahmanya, Shiva's son. There is a separate temple to Subrahmanya or Kartikeya opposite the temple to Durga north of this great complex.

As we approach the sanctum, the buildings date back and back, as you might imagine, beginning from an original nucleus. For instance, four smaller gopurams date from the 14th century, while the unassuming gateway to the sanctum enclosure is of 11th-century date, and hence we emerge into the Chola period, when the shrine itself was wrought. But its four surrounding corridors are of 17th-century Nayak date, to judge from brackets and piers. By one of the smaller shrines close by – which must have been pre-14th century – a small woman wrapped close in a brown and yellow sari muttered prayers to a divinity, confiding, eyes closed and palms lightly touching, the expression of her inmost being, its woes, worries, hopes and tribulations. She did not need to wait for Kumbh Mela in Prayag, or for the chance to visit Varanasi; even nearby Kanchipuram where Shiva and Vishnu are worshipped as two and one seemed unnecessary for these words to strike home. Her life, uncircumscribed by birth, ritual, marriage, ritual, death, ritual, and reincarnation, entered into the stream of cosmogony like monsoon rains into the rich soils of Tamilnad. For these deflecting moments she had ceased to become and had started to be. She turned from a wizened grandmother into a shining apsara, that seductive consort of the gods.


## Pondicherry

Liquor is not prohibited in Pondicherry, as it is in surrounding Tamil Nadu, for this is the hub of once-French India. What is left? The whole town plan is left, neatly boulevarded like modern Paris, and the policemen wear kepis. You can find an excellent Librairie Française, called Kailash, at 87 Lal Bahadur Street, and statues to Dupleix and Jeanne Darc. Retired soldiers of the French army mull over drinks in small bars, and barred windows could step straight out of Nantes or Arras. Dupleix's Palace has become Raj Niwas, residence of the Indian Governor of the Union Territory which also incorporates Karaikal (an enclave farther south in Tamil Nadu), the port of Mahé north of Calicut, on the Kerala coast, and Yanam in the Godavari estuary of Andhra Pradesh.

But Pondicherry, also known as Poduke, Puduchcheri and Vedapuri, has settled comfortably into its Indian motherland after it was merged with the rest of India in 1954; the majority of the people speak Tamil and by religion are Hindus. Agastya legends on the aryanization of South India skilfully summarized by Professor K.A.N. Sastri indicate that a soldier-hero-sage might have come from the north, bringing *rishis* or Hindu theologians capable of introducing Vedic lore to the Pondicherry area, where a Sanskrit university aimed to introduce northern studies to this Tamil area, dating back to at least the 9th century. The 10th-century Shaivite temple of Vedapuriswara has inscriptions suggesting the presence of Agastya, though it may be going too far to claim with G. Jouveau-Dubreuil that Sri Aurobindo's ashram stands on the site of Agastya's ashram, for there are too many claimants to that honour, among the Western Ghats alone. But the sacred connections of Pondicherry led Aurobindo to found his Auroville here and, as this is the single greatest attraction (like the Osho Commune in Pune), one must be aware of the historical or crypto-historical dimension. 'Poduke' was known to Greek and Roman geographers as a trading post on the route to the Far East in the 2nd century: a Roman emporium has been excavated at Arikamedu; some of its contents are now in the town museum. After the collapse of Rome, the area fell under Pallava and then Chola, Vijayanagar and Nayak rule, until in the 16th century the Portuguese arrived, followed by Danes, and in 1674 by the French, who were disturbed and for some years dislodged by the Dutch, who finally left in 1699. Then the British started meddling as well, often with greater government backing than the desperate French. Dupleix, having thirty years of experience behind him, took over from Governor Dumas in 1742, and built up a town demolished between 1761 and 1765 by the occupying British, except for a couple of Hindu temples unconnected with their rivals. Dupleix now energetically set about rebuilding Pondicherry and accomplished it in three years, a ring boulevard surrounding a flat grid plan bisected roughly north-south by the canal splitting the town into Ville Blanche (east of the canal) and Ville Noire, reflecting the division in Madras, for example. The administration of the town centred on White Town, with its parade ground in the centre and Governor's Palace. White too are the buildings, glittering in the tropical sun.

An eager rickshaw-wallah pedalled me to the Hotel Aristo at 36/E Pandit Nehru Street, where the roof garden restaurant full of foreigners persuaded me that I had come to the right place. The menu, only in English, confessed that a 'minimum of 20 minutes will be taken for preparation after order has been placed', so I placed an order for vegetable soup, Malay chicken with rice, and a pot of coffee, then ran down the stairs again and into the Central Market nearby. Indian women have a passion for jewellery and textiles, so that if you want to study their fluttering hand movements, their swift changes of mood and expression, their sense of colour co-ordination and flirtatious haggling style, you just hang around textile shops or, in the case of Pondicherry, pavements shaded from the midday sun by corrugated-iron overhangs. Women with bangles and nose-studs, earrings and necklaces, showed just too little interest in crimson and turquoise saris to fool the laconic moustached salesman. What Pondicherry streets lack in roaming cattle, they compensate for in cycling men and ambling women with the deportment of Greek goddesses, bearing baskets on their heads like amphorae. Many shops were shuttered for siesta like any French boutiques: Leo Photo Work and Muthi Silk House would yawn then eventually open again till ten at night. White lines were painted on the road to encourage traffic to stay on one side or the other, a suggestion blithely ignored by those to whom a traffic violation is an excuse for chaffing a bobby. 'I won't do it again' (under his breath: 'while you're looking').

After lunch, I prowled the Central Market, avid to identify mounds of spice and mysteriously twisted vegetables never seen in Europe. Where London is brown and grey, Pondicherry is red, white and green, flippant with prodigality like the cornucopia in Flemish paintings of Bacchus and Silenus, Dionysus and the maenads. *Heat and Dust* is Ruth Prawer Jhabvala's succinct view of one season, and the Deccan plateau monstrously upholds her description, but in Pondicherry *Heat and Colour* dominate the balmy winter from October to February. It's *Heat and Rain* from August to November.

As a devotee of Pepys's *Diary* and of his library at Magdalene Col-

*Pondicherry. Women shopping at midday*

lege, Cambridge, I was anxious to find the home of French India's
greatest diarist, Ananta Rangapillai, at no. 69 in the eponymous street.
Nainyappan, his uncle, was an agent used by the French in their dealings
with the Indians and Dupleix selected the young Ananta as his protégé,
to the jealous fury of Jeanne Dupleix. Rangapillai's diaries have all the
immediacy of gossip, as he rides in his exclusive palanquin to the French
enclave and entertains distinguished visitors in his Indo-French mansion, now a fascinating museum of the mid-18th century.

The ex-Government Library houses the Government Museum,
entered from Rue Romain Rolland, after whom a French library of
60,000 volumes was called, having been established in 1827 on the
opposite side of the main square. The museum, open from 10 to 5, is as

usual crowded with schoolchildren who are given no quizzes, explanations or orientation and seem totally bemused by the whole rushed operation, like a painless visit to the dentist. They clearly have no preparation, and no homework; nor do the museum staff make any effort to link one object with another or issue chronological guides or souvenirs such as postcards. In the sculpture gallery, a 10th-century stone Buddha demands attention, and there are notable images from Mathur in Karaikal. The French style typifies the museum's main hall, with an eye-opening *salon, salle à manger* and *chambre à coucher* that might have been flown in from early 19th-century Rouen; a four-poster bed, mirrors and clocks recall the homes of wealthy *colons*. No bitter Algerian War taints the memories of the French who left India.

Archaeological highpoints include neolithic tools and finds from Arikamedu, proving distant trade links by Roman lamps and Chinese ceramics found among local glass beads. A geological department has examples of sands, shells, rocks and minerals, with fossil wood from Thiruvakkari, South Arcot, known as the Cuddalore series, 20 million years old. As usual, it is the bronze sculptures which stand out: a Chola-period Shiva Nataraja from Thiruvandarkoil 16 km away, the site of a Sanskrit academy, a Chola Tripurantaka (Shiva as slayer of Tripura, or three cities, a name given to the demon Bana) from Karaikal. The usual depressing selection of arms is unimportant, but a French handpress accompanies rare examples of early local printing from 1817 in both French and Tamil. The handicrafts are nondescript, except for pleasant bronzes from Uruvayar and woodcarving from Pondicherry. The art gallery includes typical Tanjore work, but nothing of note.

The most important Hindu temple is Varadaraja, dedicated to Vishnu in the 12th century, sited just west from Gandhi Road off Thyagaraja Street. But francophiles will hire a rickshaw to tour the churches, still well attended by a minority: Nôtre Dame de la Conception (1691-1765) and the Chapel of the Sisters of Cluny are the most evocative of times past, and the Sacred Heart of Jesus at the south end of Gandhi Road the most elaborate, in its mimicry of Gothic, even to its stained glass and twin towers. Nôtre Dame des Anges, off Dumas Street, was designed by Louis Guerre in 1865 and might be in Cannes whereas the central monument in Government Park mimics the Paris Arc de Triomphe.

Pondicherry and the allied town of Auroville 10 km north are dominated by the movement centred on the life and teachings of Sri Aurobindo Ghosh, a graduate of King's College, Cambridge who abandoned his position in the Indian Civil Service in 1910 to cultivate in Pondicherry spiritual and physical discipline through yoga. 'The Mother' is the designation given to his best-known disciple, a painter born in Paris who guided the other students of Aurobindo when he retreated into deep meditation in 1926. Around her the ashram grew from a few students to several thousand, and the facilities in Pondicherry itself were considered inadequate, so Auroville was developed. Local resentment runs high between the prosperous ashram and the rest of the community, who feel that all the best land and property has been taken away from them.

More than fifty ashram locations are numbered on the map of central Pondicherry, including guest-houses, nursing homes, handicraft workshops, sports grounds and health services. If you are allergic to hotel Gideon Bibles in the West, then pictures of the Mother might detract from your enjoyment of rooms in the range of ashram-run guesthouses, but they *are* the best in town, and can be booked through the ashram reception office on Marine Street north of Government Square. Here too you can find the Reading Room and the samadhi (place of cremation in this case, though the term usually means 'ecstatic union with God') of Sri Aurobindo and the Mother.

Their teachings are noble, impressive, but extremely vague, like most aspirations. Any well-meaning poet or painter religiously inclined, like Cecil Collins or William Blake, might offer a similar vision of spiritual self-realization in the world, combining the meditative skills of yoga with manual work, the findings of modern science with the splash of paradox, the search for immanent form and structure free from prejudice about caste, gender, race or nationality. Regulations tend to be few, but smoking, drinking, free sex and political indoctrination are outlawed. There is not much to complain about, one might think, but of course any society with a hierarchy will suffer power struggles within, and envy or enmity from these human weaknesses. Auroville was seen as a spiritual city of the future, a religious equivalent perhaps to Chandigarh, and citizens of many countries lived in peace to some extent and a certain amount of harmony from 1968, when the project started, to 1973, when the Mother died and a conflict between the executive body and the members, who questioned expenditures and priorities.

The Indian Government had to intercede; then a truce was declared in 1980 and the central Matri Mandir, a great circular meditation hall, was completed amid lovely lakes and gardens. Fourteen settlements and at any one time up to a thousand foreign residents keep the place going. The buildings are clearly French in inspiration, but with post-modern ingenuity, by Roger Anger. The Information Centre, where you should begin, is at Promesse, and nearby are the International Guest House and the Hope settlement, producing organic fruit and vegetables for Auroville and the ashram in town. You can visit as many of the other enterprises as you like: some of the most interesting are the handicrafts community marketing such as incense and handmade paper called Harmonie, and if you want to explore the ways in which the local Tamil community's suspicions of their neighbours are lulled, you could visit

Udavi and Fraternité. In a cool season, you can bike round Auroville; in the hot season haggle with a rickshaw-wallah in Pondy for the day. My rickshaw man was of very small build, with calf muscles tough as whipcord; even when he walked he seemed to be checking the furrows for roadholding capacity.

At the bus station back in Pondy I was accosted by a quietly-spoken gentleman in a neat suit, who said, 'I am the Chancellor of the University of the Andaman Islands, sir, and if I were not in the most uttermost distress I should not trouble your good self, but the facts of the matter are that I haven't eaten for five days. All my things have been stolen, with more than eight thousand rupees. The police won't help me. I'm terribly hungry but I won't beg for food, just enough to send one telegram.' I gazed at him levelly. 'How much for one telegram?' 'Ten rupees'. I gave him twenty, and he vanished into the honking traffic and beyond the mounds of tempting watermelons. What could I have seemed to him: a six-foot, obese target bumbling in my shirt and trousers like a packed blancmange? I consoled myself with the idea that, even if I had been skilfully fooled, he needed twenty rupees more than I did. And if an alien from Arcturus tried to touch you with his story about feeling alone and penniless among strangers, I know you would do the same.

My bus to Chidambaram via Cuddalore swooped off, crowded as toothpaste in a tube. 'Chalo, chalo!' we whooped, 'Let's be on our way!' For me, it was the chance of a lifetime to see the most beautiful temples in all Hindustan.

### Chidambaram

How rhythmic a drumming is the name: Chi-dam-bar-am! Music and even more significantly dance are the essence of Chidambaram, where Shiva is worshipped in the form not of the usual lingam or phallus, but as the Celestial Dancer, victor in the great dance contest against Kali, his hair flying in the cosmic wind, his body in divine equilibrium in the tandava pose. The golden pavilion called Chit Ambalam celebrates the victory of Shiva and gives its name to the whole complex. The interpretation of Shiva's dance in verse 36 of *Unmai Vilakkam* is that the dance is for the world's welfare, and the demon Muyalaka, crushed under the feet of Shiva, represents evil, ignorance and the bondage of existence. Shiva's four hands show that He dances in all four directions and His oscillating belt shows that He dances without rest. The drum in his upper right hand holds a small drum, source of all music and the sacred sound *om* and all the sounds of all alphabets. The purpose of the dance is to free all souls from the chains of *maya*, and the site dates back at least two thousand years, though it attained wide renown only during the Chola dynasty, when Parantaka I covered the sanctuary in gold.

Thirumular observes, in his *Thirumandiram*, 'Chidambaram is everywhere, everywhere is His dance. The dance of the Lord takes place in the heart and self of each individual', always assuming the individual lets himself into the flow of this extraordinary sacred enclosure, without prejudice or preconditions. However, Gnanasoorian's statement that the temple 'is entirely devoted to Lord Nataraja' is misleading on two counts. Lord Shiva is also represented by a crystal *akasha* (space) lingam, and in the Govindaraja Shrine reclines a figure of Lord Vishnu dating to the 16th century, that is the Vijayanagar era.

But most of Chidambaram's great Nataraja temple is of late Chola date, that is to say 12th-13th centuries. It is said that Lord Shiva danced in a grove of tillai trees at Chidambaram, and the Chola dynasty's devotion to Shiva Nataraja and to Chidambaram has persisted in popular life and thought to this day: Bharata Natyam arising from the tradition. It is significant that Bharata Natyam as taught and practised throughout South India (with enthusiasts all over the country) has never been more popular than since World War II.

Chidambaram derives from the Tamil Chirrambalam, meaning 'little hall', a name peculiarly at odds with the Temple of Shiva Nataraja's beauty and significance. If you want to immerse yourself in the South India of the 12th and 13th centuries, then Chidambaram represents all that is finest, and indeed it is the only major temple complex of this Later Chola era. Three of the four enclosure walls are Late Chola and, though used for defence in times of war, despite appearances they were not designed for that purpose. The fourth is a 17th-century addition. I find the inner façade of the closure's east gopuram (early 13th century) one of the most harmoniously proportioned of all South Indian treasures, and the original granite sculptures filling almost all the thirty niches on each of the four gopurams intensely moving in their variety and immediacy. The upper sculptures are Shaivite, the best among them being the ascetic Shiva dancing on the demon, on the east gopuram. The lower sculptures on the south gateway portray the nine planetary deities or navagrahas: Surya the sun, Chandra the moon and so on, with on the north gateway Parvati as Durga, and Saraswati, consort of Brahma. The northern area of Chidambaram's Nataraja temple includes a late 13th-century temple to Subrahmanya, represented too on the west gateway, with an image larger than lifesize and paintings from the Purana or sacred text devoted to Subrahmanya, and splendid figures on the brackets. South of this, with access only from the Shivaganga tank, is a 12th-century temple to Parvati known here as Shivakumasundari, with 17th-century ceiling paintings.

Beyond the tank, with its majestic colonnaded gallery, is the late Chola Raja Mandapam with a Vijayanagar extension of the south side. Another of the so-called Halls of a Thousand Columns, this one actually totals 984. The temple's brilliant carvings form a pictorial encyclopaedia of dance and gesture, demonstrating 108 postures described by Bharata (2nd-3rd centuries) in his classic text the *Natya Sastra*, or 'Art of the Dance', as you can see in the early 13th-century Nritya Sabha in the southwest corner of the main complex, within the second enclosure, and on the two gopurams on the interior wall. Disappointingly, a lot of rebuilding has made a hodge-podge of the inner sanctum, but the atmosphere is heady with incense and history, noise and colour. Here is the vibrant Golden Hall, legend says, where the Lord of the Dance appeared in the middle of the tenth century, and here is his simulacrum in eternal metal – an alloy of five – dancing for all eternity, yet unmoving.

My feet still rocked with the dizziness of Shiva's shrine, but I wanted to find the intruder in Chidambaram's all-encompassing Shaivaism: the sanctuary of Govindaraja, 'cowherd-king' that is, or Krishna, eighth avatar of Vishnu. It dates from 1370, in the Vijayanagar epoch, when a Brahman general made his conquering mark on the town.

I wanted to spend more time in the Chola town of Kumbakonam, or in the once-Danish port of Tranquebar, sold to Britain by Christian VIII in 1845. But I had to reach Tanjore, and ruefully obeyed the first law of Indian travel: there is never enough time, so stick to priorities. Tanjore is inevitably a priority.

### Tanjore

What with stops for meals, mechanical breakdowns, poor roads, and slowing down for ox-carts and wandering cattle, buses in India seldom manage more than 20 km to the hour, so distances that seem vast on a map end up by becoming even more vast when you try to reach them on the ground. I always plan according to the law: 'Wherever you're going, you'll only get there after dark', and Tanjore obeyed that rule. Luckily, most of the hotels are in the zone between rail and bus stations; unluckily the Hotel Tamil Nadu on Gandhiji Road, and the nearby Rajaraja Hotel (formerly the Bilal) were full, so I fell back on the Rajah Rest House founded in 1981, a pilgrims' inn with rooms set back from a vast courtyard.

My room had its own shower-squat toilet area, with a lopsided tarnished mirror, a creaky ceiling fan, a topply chair and worn deal table, with a single bed covered with a mattress but no sheet. The view from the window, which would not quite close to keep determined flying insects out, framed a huge tree and the dirty Anicut Canal. In my bag I found one last mosquito coil, and lit it: the mosquitoes diminished sensibly in number and sound volume within ten minutes, and in fifteen I had showered, much to the amusement of a thousand bombarding insects, and fallen into dense sleep jungled with lianas and the roaring of

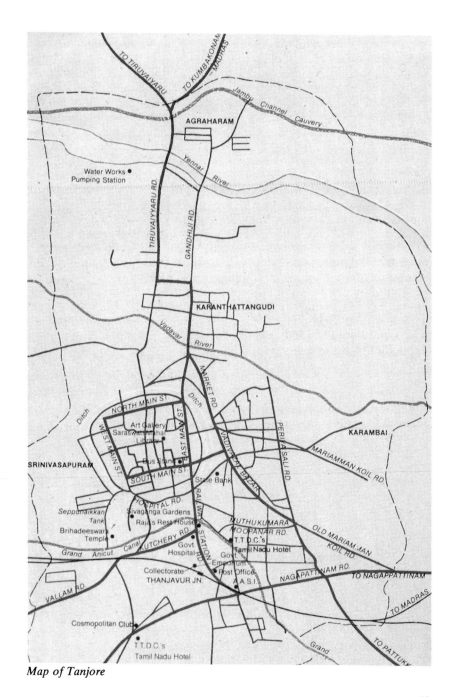

*Map of Tanjore*

torrents and tigers, rapids and crocodiles.

I was woken at dawn the next morning by dhobi-wallahs winning a hardfought struggle with the laundry by a knockout in the ninth round. Breakfast in the shabby Tamil Nadu restaurant next door consisted of burnt toast, a pot of overboiled coffee, and two mentally disturbed fried eggs. Tanjore is not the cordon bleu centre of India, which is a great pity for its Great Fort with the Rajah's Palace, and Little Fort with the Temple of Brihadeshvara or Rajarajeshvara – both epithets of Shiva – constitute two of the greatest sights in the world, befitting a capital of the Chola dynasty. 'Thanjan' means refuge in Tamil, so Thanjavur, anglicised to Tanjore, denotes 'a place of refuge'.

The Chola dynasty emerges in the Sangam Age – roughly the first four centuries A.D. – with King Karikala (c. 190 according to Sastri) victor over the Pandyas and Cheras at Venni, now Kovilvenni, 24 km east of Tanjore. This success proved to be a turning-point in Chola fortunes, celebrated in the long Tamil poem *Pattinappalai*, whose author is no longer known. The Chola revival began under Vijayalaya (850-71), and burned successively brighter under Aditya (871-907), conqueror of the Pandyas near Kumbakonam; Parantaka (907-55), who burnt the Pandyan capital Madurai and rebuilt many earlier brick temples in stone; and Rajaraja (985-1014) overlapping in rule the first two years of the reign of his son Rajendra (1012-44), who moved his capital from Tanjore to Gangaikonda.

### Brihadeshvara Temple

The Rajarajeshvara Temple vimana, 65 metres high, is the tallest in India, and dates from about 1010, near the zenith of Rajaraja's rule (985-1012), a fair apotheosis of a great school, which should be seen in relation to the Brihadeshvara temple at Gangaikondacholapuram constructed by Rajendra I (1012-44), successor to Rajaraja, almost in direct emulation, accessible southwest from Chidambaram or northeast from Kumbakonam, a site with neighbouring Darasuram also important during Chola times.

The courtyard's proportions are wide and open, almost like a sacred field, for no later additions mar the artistic purity of this Chola masterpiece, unless you count the rebuilt Nandi mandapam sheltering the original great granite monolithic Nandi. Or you might view the various shrines within the temple rectangle as chess pieces on a board, with twin gopurams as White King and Red King, and the Subrahmanya Temple as advancing White Queen. Watching barefoot pilgrims dwarfed by the great shrines, it is easy to recall the Tamil saying 'Legs which have not walked round a temple are of no use'. Dark-skinned pilgrims wearing a single green garment for modesty's sake were crouching in a sociable circle, and cramming rice into their mouths from a communal bowl. A

*Tanjore. Brihadeshvara Temple. Gopuram*

*Tanjore. Brihadeshvara Temple. Shiva lingam in sanctum*

sign to baths (Rs 1 each) read 'Sarkarai Pongal, Lime Bath, Puliyodarai and Curd Bath'. I stepped across the bricklaid courtyard with a feeling of isolated reverence: it was 9.15 and there were no other foreigners. Watered lawns glittered below casual rainbows that vanished and revived. Beside the great bull of Shiva, pilgrims wafted burning incense up to their face and hair, a holy perfume. Chipmunks scampered skittishly away at my approach. The obsession of Rajaraja with the god of dance and his dancers led to his commissioning 108 dance karanas in different poses, of which 81 were finished.

Each painted panel in the cloisters, accompanying a lingam-reminder of Shiva, is at normal head height and thus more easily seen than the fantastic ranges of sculpture. A frieze of Nandis surmounts the surrounding wall.

All parts of the temple are open to visitors every day except the inner sanctum, where the polished black Shiva lingam is draped and worshipped as a manifestation of the deity. Even in this case a coloured postcard is available, yet one lingam looks very like another. Each side chapel has a sacred lingram too, but the sculptures on the gopurams are ecumenically Vaishnavite. The Subrahmanya temple, harmonising as it does with the rest, is much later: a marvellous accomplishment of the Nayaka era (17th century), and dedicated to Subrahmanya or Kartikeya, son of Shiva and according to his designation protector of the Brahman caste. Nayaka paintings had been overlaid on Chola murals on walls of the internal ambulatory passage: the most interesting is a portrait of Rajaraja I with three consorts worshipping Shiva Nataraja. These are true frescoes, painted while the plaster was still wet. We shall come across much more evidence of Nayaka times in the Great Fort to the northeast.

Wherever you wander, among clusters of pilgrims overshadowed by the grandeur of all around them, you will come upon masterpieces of architecture, like the Shrine to Shiva, the sacrificial hall called Periyanayagi Temple. Do not miss the choice Archaeological Museum on the left of the inner courtyard. An elephant blesses worshippers by delicately touching them on the head with the tip of his trunk. Inscriptions relate the temple's prestige and wealth, endowments and rituals. Brihadeshvara was provided in perpetuity with flowers and ointments, agricultural produce to supply temple retainers, four hundred dancing girls, musicians, craftsmen, tailors and a complete administrative staff of functionaries, so that the temple city would never fail. However, a sacred play endowed in the mid-11th century was lost, and substituted by a dance known as the Kuruvanchik Kottu. Nowadays a drama is performed in the month of Visaka in Tanjore, and the Tourist Office near Hotel Tamil Nadu should be able to alert you to special events.

Beyond the temple gateway a seductive giant poster advertised the

*Tanjore. Main street from palace to rail station, looking back to temple*

movie *For a Night of Love* and someone had painted *Bagpiper Whisky* on the adjoining wall.

### The Nayaka Palace

The Nayaka Palace (1550), with a few later Maratha additions, is situated in the Great Fort, which looks impregnable from East Main Street even today. The palace museums and library open at 10 a.m., so it is advisable to spend the early morning and late afternoon, as elsewhere in Tamil Nadu, in temples, and reserve the hours from 10 to 5 for museums and galleries. The fascinating Great Fort compound includes the Rajah's Higher Secondary School (Tamil and English media) and a great art gallery founded in 1951, with an unsurpassed selection of Chola bronzes of around the 11th century, from Tanjore and environs.

The finest work is a Shiva and Parvati pair made in 1011-12 for presentation to the Svetaranyaswami Temple of Tiruvengadu just north of the Cauvery's mouth near the Bay of Bengal. They were uncovered by chance at Tiruvengadu in 1951. The tresses of Shiva's hair are arranged in fifteen locks, divided and swept into a turban effect at the front, while at the back eight are arranged in an elegant semi-circle just below the shoulders and two curl down. Shiva is manifested as a cowherd, so the haircurls are shaped into a kind of bahulamala: a shoulder decoration of bahula flowers. His other symbol, a crescent moon, is tucked into one of the higher strands of hair; a cobra is visible emerging from another lock on the right. A thorn-apple or datura flower on the left reminds one of Ovington's cautionary words in his *Voyage to Suratt* (1696) that 'mixing *Dutra* and Water together to drink... will intoxicate almost to madness'. Shiva's left ear has the patrakundala ornament, and his neck is adorned by three necklaces; a waist-belt and clasp holds in place a fine undergarment, with gracefully realistic folds. The right hand will have rested on a bull, now missing. Rings adorn each thumb and three fingers of each hand. Each fingernail and toenail is carefully finished, and the posture, with the weight on the left leg and the right leg crossed in front, might be considered as classical in Chola sculpture as the Metropolitan Museum's Stroganoff Caesar of the 1st century B.C. is classical in Greco-Roman sculpture. Shiva (here known as Rishabhavahana Deva) is matched by the sublime beauty of his Parvati, her posture in tribhanga (thrice flexed), her right hand half-closed in kataka, and her left hand drooping like a cow's tail. Her garments flow from waist down to a fine curved drape round each leg.

A four-armed Shiva as Beggar or Bhikshatana comes from the same trove at Tiruvengadu, but is marginally later (1040) and exemplifies that moment before the cosmic dance when Shiva and Vishnu entered the village of heretical sages whose ritualism and learning neglected the worship of Shiva. Shiva disguised himself as a beggar and Vishnu as a *mohini*, or seductive beauty; the handsome mendicant lured the brahmans' womenfolk and the *mohini* seduced the men. When the villages learned of the imposture, they realised how God will chase men to surrender their ego to Him, and abased themselves, thus restoring the central place of Shiva and Vishnu to brahmanical worship. The frustrated sages were represented by the young deer leaping up towards Shiva's lower right hand, their lower nature at once aspiring to better things but incapable of achieving Nirvana in their present form. The god is shown as restrained, immensely powerful yet compassionate, majestic yet capable of human understanding. His lower right hand points to an oval jewel on the pedestal representing Shiva's tears for erring mankind. Note how subtly Shiva's attributes are incorporated in this masterpiece, from the third eye on the forehead, crescent moon on the left, cobra on the right, and ornament on the left ear; the datura is shown as a bud, a flower, and blossom. The eyes, once jewelled, are now empty but easily visualised in their original splendour.

A myriad of other wonders dazzle the eye: a four-faced Late Chola Brahma from Karanthai; a rare Agni (Fire God) from Brihadeshvara itself; a stone Buddha from Pattiswaram; a great stone early Chola Durga as Slayer of the Buffalo Demon from Tiruvalanguli, and a 15th-century Vishnu from Kokkadi. Don't miss a wonderful Surya (Sun God) above his horse-drawn chariot from Mangudi dated to the 17th-18th centuries, or a sensitive 11th-century stone Buddha from Madagaran. A 12th-century Late Chola masterpiece from Darasuram depicts Chandikeshvara, the steward of Shiva's property.

The Rajaraja Chola Museum established to display the artefacts of the Chola period, with useful architectural photographs drawn from much of Tamil Nadu, specialises in copper vessels, inscribed copper plates, coins, palmleaf manuscripts, terracotta earrings and objects of carved bone. You ascend the tower – eight-storeyed like a vimana – and come to a whale skeleton, then views over the temple compound, to a 16th-century arsenal bell-tower, like an immense Iranian badgir, or wind-tower.

More bronzes shown in the Nayak's Durbar Hall, again far superior to anything in Madras, are presided over by a white lavatory-tile dais and a full-length portrait of Raja Serfoji II (1787-1832), one of the great Maratha patrons of art and culture.

He devoted a great deal of effort and money to building up the great Saraswati Mahal as a research library, with 37,000 Sanskrit MSS on palmleaf and paper, 3,000 Marathi MSS on paper, just under 3,000 Tamil MSS on palmleaf, and 800 Telugu MSS on palmleaf. A further 850 bundles of Marathi records in Modi script remain uncatalogued because of the paucity of Modi scholars. The book collection numbers 40,000 of which a quarter each are in Sanskrit, Tamil and English. The library is devoted to conservation, publication of more than 1,200 titles so far, and a display area, where Tanjore's school of art is best appreciated.

The Indian art of the book is exemplified by printing on paper, writing on palmleaf, engraving on copper. Serfoji's printing press, brought to Tanjore in 1805, was the first to set Devanagari type in South India. Samples of textiles, Johnson's English dictionary, and medical and botanical books and manuscripts acquired by purchase, or copied by Serfoji's own artists and scribes, can be found on display, though of course the main bulk of the collections are locked away in chests. Chipmunks skated down the wired windows to the hum of a printing press still in use. All the forty members of staff have had library training in Tamil Nadu: at Annamalai University in Chidambaram, or Madurai or Madras.

The Maratha Palace Museum is actually of Nayak date (c. 1550), but was amplified by the Marathas.

The Durbar Hall (1684) has a secret passage, recently discovered, thirty feet long, near the back wall, and yet more magnificent sculptures, with a polychrome decoration on its granite platform.

Two interesting churches are worth a visit. That of F.C. Schwartz near

*Tanjore. Nayak Palace, looking towards 16th-century bell-tower*

the Tank of Shivaganga commemorates a German missionary from Tranquebar, operating here for the S.P.C.K. as an ally of Serfoji II, who supported him for a decade, until Schwartz died in 1798: the monument by John Flaxman in the west end within shows his moving deathbed scene. Roman Catholic missions operated in Tanjore and elsewhere in the district from the early 17th century, and Protestant missions based on Tranquebar from the early 18th. The cemetery of St Peter's Church, southeast of the bus station, has several fine tombs, including that of Lord Hastings who succumbed to fever in 1875. Crows pestered the ground: what they would have given for the bones of Resurrection!

I took a horse-trap for one last drive around Tanjore: it bore the legend 'Jesus I Am Your Slave, St Joseph's Convent, Thanjavur', as though I or any passenger had some claim to be a Mother Superior; movie posters showed alluring women implying behaviour more shocking than anything voyeurs would be allowed to see on screen.

### A Train to Trichy
I paid Rs 38 for a first-class ticket to Trichy at the deserted booking-office, handing over dubiously-creased notes to a moustachioed booking-clerk blinking up at me from the Kipling era, his stiff back ready to bow to a lordly passenger, and the whiff of a conspiratorial

*Tanjore. Rail station*

smile in his mahogany eyes. He was the kind of babu who loved his job so much that, five weeks after being given his pension, he would waft into the oblivion that knows no Rameshwaram Express leaving at 5.09 a.m.

On the platform I checked the time and destination with one D. Robert of the Kannara Bank in Madurai, who introduced me to his brother, D. Jayaraj, who would continue on this Nagore-Quilon express as far as Madurai. Hordes of women crowded the platform as though it was open harem day: the sightseers' special. Like all good Westerners, I looked away; like all good Indians, they stared back at me in undisguised amazement. How can anyone look so white, so odd, so bald, so strange, so European? I was beginning to wonder myself, and yearned for the illusory privacy of a first-class compartment with its ceiling fans and space to stretch my legs. The train pulled in half an hour late, by which time the most ecstatic of the brightly-hued female throng had speculated about my ancestry, race, nationality, family and friends, information that I fed them through my slightly embarrassed interpreter, D. Robert. In my comfortable compartment I sat and shared oranges and bananas with S. Murugaiyam, Station-Master. The carriage seated 30 and slept 20, hours of rest being bureaucratically specified by the company: 'Please pull up the backrest cum bed during 6 a.m. to 9

*Tondamanpatti. Rural rail station*

p.m. to avoid inconvenience to sitting passengers'. Locomotive 6309 chugged at an easy 20 km an hour through paradisiac rural landscapes, stopping at Budalur, Aiyanapuram with its variegated green padis, and quiet Solagampatti. The corridor windows are set low, so that one looks out only when seated, not when standing as on European trains. Tondamanpatti station could have passed for a small inn, with hopeful mangy dogs waiting for leftovers, and an off-white shirt hanging on rickety railings, the whole shaded by massive trees that local custom would have hallowed long ago. Every ten minutes or so we chugged into a little station exactly like the last: Manjattidal with a Christian church just west of the village, Ponmalai and then increasing urbanism towards Trichy Junction, though cows grazed on ample pasture between the tracks, sure that Hindu drivers would brake in time. We were, in any case, travelling so slowly that we were at one point overtaken by a cud-chewing cow.

## Trichinopoly

I emerged into the wide expanse of the station forecourt, blinking against the sky's scintillation. Tiruchchirappalli, abbreviated to Tiruchi in Tamil or Trichy in English, is nowadays a city dominated by heavy industry, especially electrical, with a population just below half a million, mostly south of the Kaveri river. The name might denote 'City of the Holy Rock' or 'City of the Three-Headed Demon', depending on which etymologist you consult, the former implicit in an inscription of about 1520, which is the first record of the name we have. Its rock fort was a moated rectangle of half a mile by one mile, but the moat has been filled in and the walls levelled. The Chola town was situated at Wurayur or Uraiyur, now a suburb west of the Rock, but the Muslims under Malik Kafur displaced the Cholas in 1310, until the Vijayanagar dynasty conquered Madurai and Trichy in 1372, giving way to the Nayak dynasty from about 1559. Viswanatha Nayak fortified the town and expanded the Vaishnavite temple at Srirangam from its modest Chola beginnings. The eighth Nayak Muthu Krishnappa appointed Trichy as his capital, but Tirumala his successor understandably preferred Madurai. Under Muthu Virappa, Muslim invasions increased in number and ferocity, so Trichy fort had to be reinforced and later the Nawab's Palace was built there, partly from Tirumala's demolished palace in Madurai. Struggles for the succession allowed the Marathas, enlisted by the enemy of the last Nayak's widow, to seize Trichy in 1740, after marching through Karnataka, and it took three years for them to be dislodged by the Nizam of Hyderabad. The British and French took opposing sides; finally the French capitulated, retreating to Pondicherry. Another long confrontation in 1752-54 which resulted in a treaty allowing the French to stay in Srirangam broke out again in 1756.

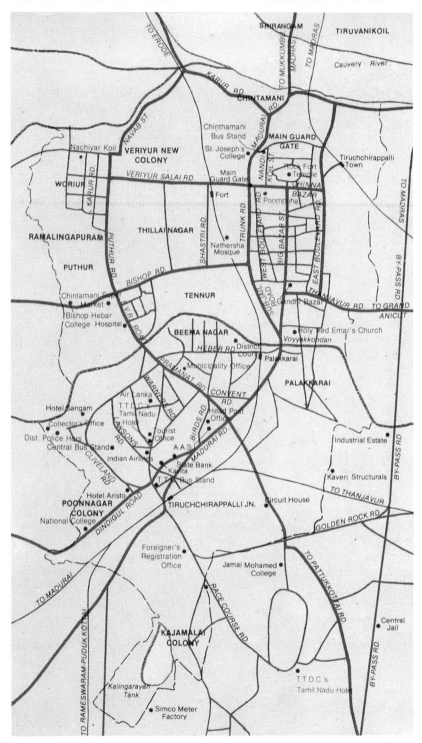

*Map of Trichinopoly*

Tipu Sultan marched on Trichy in 1790 during the later Mysore War and ravaged Srirangam.

The densely-populated city lies on the right bank of the Kaveri, dominated by the granite rock soaring 84 metres into the skyline. The pilgrimage area lies on a verdant island on the left bank of the Kaveri: its atmosphere is as different from Trichy City as Pollok Park from the Gorbals or Central Park from Harlem.

First thing in the morning, before the heat assails you on all sides, climb the worn steps near the crossroads where China Bazaar meets Main Bazaar, through a gateway flanked by protecting stone elephants. The Lower Cave Temple is of Pandyan age, the eighth century, when ecumenism prompted the dedication of temples to many divine aspects: on the rear wall of the mandapam Brahma in the middle flanked by Ganesha and Subrahmanya on one side, and Surya and Durga on the other, while the two side shrines are devoted to Shiva and Vishnu. You can then climb the rest of the 437 steps to the top of the outcrop, with its breathtaking views over plain, river and Srirangam, pausing to visit the Pallava-period Upper Cave Temple, of the early 7th century, which will remind you of shrines at Mamallapuram, its Lord Shiva absorbing in his hair the river Ganges as it descends from Himalaya. At the foot of the west side of the Rock stands the local Teppakulam, or sacred tank, with a graceful pavilion, but the moat round the ruined fort has been drained to provide a French-style boulevard; there are few traffic jams on this

*Trichinopoly. Rock fort*

thoroughfare. East of the Rock is Trichy Town rail station and west lies the Fort station, connected to the south by Trichy Junction: but forget these complications, and use an auto-rickshaw like the local people do. Between the Rock itself and the Fort station look for St Joseph's College, occupying since 1883 the buildings near Main Guard Gate, and St John's Church, of the early 19th century, where Reginald Heber is buried, having died suddenly at Trichy in 1826. Bishop Heber's hymn 'From Greenland's Icy Mountains', which continues 'From India's Coral Strand', stands as a missionary symbol of the early nineteenth century, when British India formed one huge, unwieldy diocese, and the white man's burden plainly extended from exporting indigenous products for fuelling European industries, to indoctrinating the foreign and hence benighted masses abroad in such delights as cricketing Christianity and the consequent overthrow of all other systems of thought and belief. The Bishop of Calcutta's notable hymn continues – as we all ruefully recall from school assemblies –

*What though the spicy breezes*
*Blow soft o'er Ceylon's isle,*
*Though every prospect pleases*
*And only man is vile,*
*In vain with lavish kindness*
*The gifts of God are strown,*
*The heathen in his blindness*
*Bows down to wood and stone.*

*Can we, whose souls are lighted*
*With wisdom from on high,*
*Can we to men benighted*
*The lamp of life deny?*

Most assuredly not: and many thousands like Heber have laboured across India 'to deliver their land from error's chain', with dubious success. If I felt uncomfortable with the communion table in St John's Church and the Heber brass plaque in the floor nearby, I felt even more disturbed by the later Roman Catholic Cathedral (1841) built eight years before the impressive Kaveri bridge designed by Captain Edward Lawford. The little churches of Kerala and the fine Portuguese basilicas of Old Goa seem historically resonant, but in the vicinity of Srirangam so potently sacred to Hindus there is very little place for these intrusions, any more than for a Hindu temple in Vatican City, say, or a Jain shrine at Mecca. The earliest church in Trichy is Christ Church (1765), a British military expense erected by the missionary Schwartz. And while we are looking at non-Hindu structures, the Nadir Shah Mosque near the Fort station catches the eye: it was once a Hindu temple, but a Muslim faqir called Sayyid Baba Nadir Shah took up lodgings hereabouts and so impressed the people that he became a saint and was buried in the converted mosque.

## Sri Ranganatha

But we are in Trichy for the temple of the reclining Lord Vishnu, Sri Ranganatha, and a Shaivite counterpart a couple of km to the east, Sri Jambunatha or Jambukeshvara. Both probably date from Chola times or earlier, but the present structures were begun by the Pandyan kings in the 13th century, ravaged by Muslims in the 14th, and expanded under the Vijayanagar and Nayak dynasties in the 16th and 17th centuries, though it is obvious that rebuilding has never really come to an end, and probably never will, for both resemble small towns in their colour, noise, bustle, and life. If you think of a temple as a place to meditate in silence, then Sri Ranganatha will come as a stupendous shock. The Raja gopuram at the southern entrance teems with polychrome figures and columns at every level or nilam as it sweeps up to 235 feet, and is said (locally!) to be the tallest temple tower in Asia.

The temple's seven enclosures are rectangular, with the shrine to Sri Ranganatha (closed to non-Hindus) just north of centre. A variety of self-appointed 'guides' competed for my custom: evasion was useless, since I had been totally surrounded from my first entrance at the fourth wall, which is where shoes are removed and guarded until your return. I dutifully paid my Rs 2 in the Museum to climb the roof (*Hurry Mister it closes at 5.30!*) and ran up the dark steps to the sudden brilliance of the cloudless sky, the golden shrine of Vishnu, its dome visible from the roof, and the ever-transforming glitter of the Raja gopuram. 'Indian Bank Welcomes You' announced a banner. I strolled oblivious to myself and my history among an India that Kipling and Clive would have recognised, except that the buckets are now plastic. Housewives were examining pots and pans for flaws, a lady of a certain age patted and shifted her arm-bangles as she scolded a silk merchant, and ash-covered sadhus dozed in the last heat of the sun. A police outpost painted with brick-patterns stood untenanted: I found the eagle-eyed officers at the entrance to the sanctum, waving away Westerners as though they knew we could not be Hindus, any protestations to the contrary inconceivable. A temple shop offered a tray showing a gaudy palm-fringed sea with the legend 'Success is to flow like water through a road of stones'. Brass figurines of Shiva Nataraja were aligned like a regiment. The time flashed up red 5.48 (we haven't reached the 24-hour clock at Sri Ranganatha) and nearby stalls purveyed plates of food-offerings: puja to Lord Vishnu. Lottery tickets exchanged hands briskly: if you have no luck here, then where? Children reached up for plastic pink trumpets, blue spinning tops, multi-coloured images of Ganesha. A moustachioed white-dhotied fatman, barefoot and wiggling his toes, gesticulated with

*Trichinopoly. Srirangam. Sri Ranganatha Temple. Raja Gopuram*

practised fingers towards a dozen varieties of nut in pyramids of brown shingle and pebble.

If you can drag your senses away from the extraordinary vivacity of secular and religious life here intermingled, and concentrate on the monuments, the fourth enclosure surges with majesty: ahead of the southern gopuram is the Rangavilasa Mandapam, its long columns carved with enough figures to fill a museum of oriental art. To the left is the Venugopalan shrine, in Chola style but of Nayak age, late in the 16th century, its high relief carvings possibly not achieving the excellence we have seen at Chidambaram, but exuberant and charming, with exquisite portraits of women: one demurely raising her hands to cover her nakedness, another coquettishly gazing into a mirror, a third conversing with a parrot, and each dressed differently, with ornaments enough to fill a pattern book.

Sauntering anticlockwise in this enclosure, one comes to the Sesharayar mandapam, each of its eight monolithic pillars alive with rearing horses and riders above hunters fighting wild beasts in an unforgettable riot of noisy struggle, reminding one of the Vijayanagar scenes contemporary with Trichy at the Jalakanteshvara temple in Vellore.

Then to the 'Thousand-Columned Mandapam' of nine hundred and forty or so columns, the balance made up to the sacred round number at the December festival called Vaikunta Ekadasi, lasting twenty days. At the climax of the festival, a pandal or decorated bamboo structure comprising the missing number of pillars is added to the great mandapam, and the image of Sri Ranganatha attired in rubies proceeds in pomp to the mandapam in the presence of thousands of worshippers, where Lord Vishnu is addressed as King and Lord, Sri Rangaraja. Sacred Tamil hymns are recited, and dance dramas evoke divine and heroic figures from living myth and legend which are so real to the Tamil devotees that film stars as deities have become members of parliament on the strength of their popular appeal: the analogy in the United States might be Ronald Reagan's popularity as film star and president. But the analogy is totally misleading in this atmosphere of incense and veneration, fasting and the clash of cymbals, where the senses are assailed on all sides, and vigil is kept throughout the night.

At dawn an elephant is brought to face the image of Lord Vishnu and a cow to face in the opposite direction, while soft music on the vina serenades the half-sleeping Vishnu, culminating at 6.30 with the first public adoration of the presence of Vishnu, or darshan, when the curtain protecting him from public view is briefly drawn back. Worship or puja takes place from 7.30-8.45, 11.45-12.30, 5.30-6.30 and 8.45-9.15, while seva occurs at 8.45-9.00 (Pongal seva), 9-11.45, 12.30-1.30, 2.45-5.30, and 6.30-8.45. Food offerings are brought at 9.15 to 9.30

*Trichinopoly. Srirangam. Sri Ranganatha Temple. Sculpture of a maiden*

p.m., followed by vina music as the Lord goes to his half-rest once more. Much of the temple is denied to non-Hindus, but the small museum which may be visited in the fourth enclosure offers some stone and bronze figures as well as coins and weapons; nothing here, however, equals the wonders without. I was invited to visit the Garuda mandapam in the third enclosure, with Nayak-era donors and well-formed temple girls, alluring to the point of distraction. The gilded sanctum, protected by railings and a low stone wall, has rounded arches framing a standing Vishnu, but this is out of bounds to non-Hindus.

### Sri Jambukeshvara

It is a short distance to the Shaivite temple of Sri Jambukeshvara, but a very long walk, because of the tempting stalls and myriad activities, because so many visitors are keen to greet you and while away the time of day, and because the buzz of eager anticipation will inevitably pass as you finally arrive. Or will it?

The seven great gopurams of Sri Jambukeshvara rise from their ebullient defence of five great walls and again one is reminded of a city more than a religious shrine, for the tumult seems never-ending, even at sunset. I crossed the road to Madras, being skimmed by a weaving cyclist with a tiny granny curled up in his basket like an overgrown brown kitten. A patient elephant waved his trunk in my general direction as I paid out Rs 5 rent for my camera and Rs 2 to buy a pamphlet by N. Shanmugham concluding 'Let everyone... visit the temple every year, why, every month and every day and receive the blessings of Sri Akilandeswari and God Jembunatha'. 'Jambu' is the guava tree, and 'iswara' means 'lord', the compound denoting one of the manifestations of Lord Shiva. Architecturally, the ensemble is Nayak, or 17th-century, in its present form, with numerous restorations, some as recent as 1963. In origin it is known from Chola times, and was early sanctified to Shiva's aspect as the Lord of Water, a lingam being worshipped below the surface of the water gushing out from a spring in the sanctum. Graceful palms and sandalled women seem to move in reciprocal undulation. Then the loudspeaker relaying popular devotional songs is switched off, and a light glimmers from a darkened temple cart: it is a man lighting a cigarette. A bevy of urchins demanding 'pen your country, pen pen' clamours as one. Garish neon bulbs detract from the mandapam of a thousand columns whose decorated pillars pulse and bulge with life and passion: beautiful women, lotus buds, princesses, dancers. Shiva's bull repeated as a protective device surmounts the perimeter wall, in an endless chain. I took an auto-rickshaw to the Femina Hotel at 14c Williams Road in the Cantonment area, and night fell on the hundred thousand twinkling lights of Trichinopoly.

If you arrive in Trichy during the monsoon, you might not cower from the rain as you would in Toronto or Antwerp. It is warm, and welcome: the fields guzzle it down and ask for more, rice-padis absorb it like sponges, and the gleaming brown earth sends up steam signals in gestures of appreciation. Sadistic torrents slap broad banana leaves but the banana palm masochistically raises its arm for more punishment. I walk in such hot showers for the delight in truancy: 'nobody willingly gets wet in India' is the unspoken reprimand, but I do.

## Madurai

'Do you not feel the southern breeze blowing from the city bringing the fragrance of holy black akil and sandalwood?' urged Prince Ilango Adigal, referring to Madurai in his Tamil poem *Shilappadikuram* of the second century A.D. 'It is laden with scent of musk and chives and saffron, passing near water-lilies across champaks in blooms, through jasmine and madhavi, and touching the mullai buds. The zephyr brings us the aroma of pancakes sizzling in the great bazaar, sacrificial smoke, and perfumes from the great royal palace of the Pandyas with his golden necklace offered to him by the greatest god.'

Canto XIV of the *Shilappadikuram* is devoted to the 'Sights of the City', by which Prince Ilango knows that his listeners will understand great Madurai. Ptolemy refers to 'Modoura basileion Pandionos', or Madurai of the Pandyan kings, and since the fourth century B.C. at least it has drawn respectful praise from visiting envoys and pilgrims whether bent on secular or religious business or – most usually – both at once. For the Vaigai river, often called simply the Madurai river, has attracted millions to Madurai much as Ganges has drawn them to Benares, and Sri Minakshi ('The Fish-eyed Goddess') evolved from pagan prehistoric worship into another manifestation of Shiva's consort Parvati. Shiva himself is here worshipped as Lord Sundareshvar ('The Lord of Beauty'). The 1981 census awarded Madurai 817,000 in population, a figure which bears as little relationship to the pulsating truth as the population given to Allahabad at the time of Kumbh Mela. The people of Madurai claim to be the purest Tamils in race and in speech, in culture and in religion, and they display a reluctance to speak English (or Hindi for that matter!) which can only augur well for the proud independence of this ancient Pandyan capital. Yet with the traditional Indian disregard of earlier dynasties, little in the great temple goes back before the 16th century, and most derives from the exuberant, not to say megalomaniac Nayak ruler called Tirumala (1623-60).

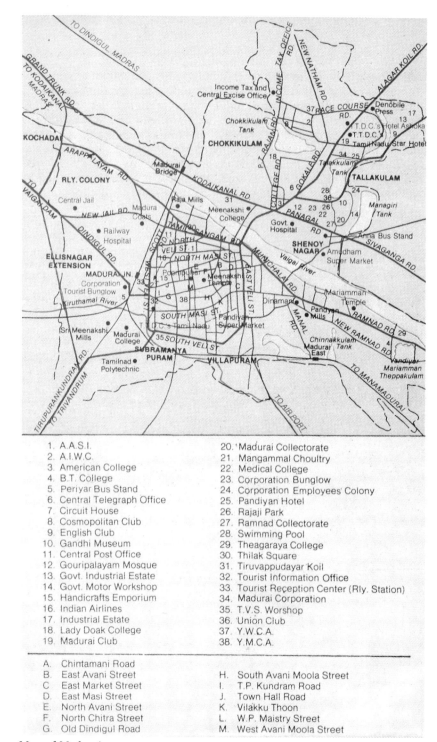

1. A.A.S.I.
2. A.I.W.C.
3. American College
4. B.T. College
5. Periyar Bus Stand
6. Central Telegraph Office
7. Circuit House
8. Cosmopolitan Club
9. English Club
10. Gandhi Museum
11. Central Post Office
12. Gouripalayam Mosque
13. Govt. Industrial Estate
14. Govt. Motor Workshop
15. Handicrafts Emporium
16. Indian Airlines
17. Industrial Estate
18. Lady Doak College
19. Madurai Club

20. Madurai Collectorate
21. Mangammal Choultry
22. Medical College
23. Corporation Bunglow
24. Corporation Employees' Colony
25. Pandiyan Hotel
26. Rajaji Park
27. Ramnad Collectorate
28. Swimming Pool
29. Theagaraya College
30. Thilak Square
31. Tiruvappudayar Koil
32. Tourist Information Office
33. Tourist Reception Center (Rly. Station)
34. Madurai Corporation
35. T.V.S. Worshop
36. Union Club
37. Y.W.C.A.
38. Y.M.C.A.

A. Chintamani Road
B. East Avani Street
C. East Market Street
D. East Masi Street
E. North Avani Street
F. North Chitra Street
G. Old Dindigul Road
H. South Avani Moola Street
I. T.P. Kundram Road
J. Town Hall Road
K. Vilakku Thoon
L. W.P. Maistry Street
M. West Avani Moola Street

*Map of Madurai*

## Sri Minakshi Temple

The massive rectangular temple is surrounded by broad, busy streets made wide enough to accommodate the numerous chariot festivals which dominate the city throughout the year. Rectangles blossom from Sri Minakshi like ripples in a pool: Chitra Street, Avani Street, Masi Street and Veli Street, so you find your bearings by heading from the airport (say) across South Veli Street to South Masi Street, then South Avani Street and South Chitra Street till you find yourself at the temple wall. Around this wall, street stalls with lamps and lanterns tempt goggle-eyed bumpkins with the extraordinary wealth of India's crafts and manufactures far into the night. The finest silks are fingered by a cluster of three saried ladies avid for new finery. Trinkets are set out beside a little boy of eight or nine who reads a comic by a lantern. An old man with a drought-wrinkled countenance squats beside a tower of popcorn. Vivid devotional prints in tin frames portray Saraswati, goddess of learning, Ganesha, Shiva, and Parvati. Sizzling samosas quenched my hunger, and I entered the great temple through the Eight-Goddess Portico near the southeast corner, finding myself instantly swallowed in a swirling vortex of clamour and incessant motion. Opening hours are 5 till noon and 4 till 9.30, photography being allowed only between noon and 4, for which you pay a fee in the temple office near the south tower. You leave your footwear at any of the four entrances, but remember which one: it can be a long and tortuous trail to recover them if lost! All but the inner sanctum is open to non-Hindus and priests are well adjusted to the bemused wonder of foreigners, so do not be afraid to talk to them if something puzzles you. Licensed guides are available, but as they range in expertise from the wellmeaning and partly knowledgeable to gobbledygookish speedmerchants, it is probably as well to visit on your own. But if you want to climb the giddy southern gopuram (buy a ticket nearby), you must be accompanied by a fleet-footed guide, who may possibly demand a further tip for so doing: it is however included in the ticket-price. At the top, the adventurous climber suddenly finds himself 180 feet up at the apex of the gopuram, with stunning views over Madurai city behind and Sri Minakshi in front, each tower spitting colours that burn and change with the drifting cloud as the sun exposes each sculpture and finial in turn. These are not the subtle forms and shapes that our conventional lectures on Western art have led us to believe are 'beautiful'; they drum on our retina as cymbals might clash one after another in a scene from *Mahabharata*, insistently and loudly. There is no escaping from them: they derive from the same background that will chant for hours *Hare Krishna!* and repeat the Nandi bull on protective walls surrounding a Shaivite sanctuary. One is convinced not by reason or logic, but by an assault on the senses, and at Madurai as at Srirangam or Benares that too is appropriate. I did not resist.

*Madurai. Sri Minakshi Temple. Aerial View*

The temple museum and art gallery closes at eight, giving you ample time for its many treasures. Situated in the immense Airakkal mandapam, in the north-east corner of the temple, it contains almost a thousand columns (985 at one count), built in 1569 at the expense of Ariyanatha Mudhaliar, a mathematician and minister of four Nayak rulers, shown on horseback at the entrance to the hall. This mandapam measures 250 x 240 feet, and the space for the 15 missing columns is taken up by two small temples. Magnificent black granite figures on the twelve-foot high pillars distract one from the museum's actual exhibits. The pillars themselves are exactly of the same size and shape: a miracle of Dravidian building technique, because echo has been reduced to the negligible, and whichever way you look, you can see 16 colonnades in any direction, and the central divine image.

Tamil texts show us that each temple practised the triple form of music: *gita* (vocal), *vadya* (instrumental), and *nritya* (dance) as well as the inculcation of meditative trance. One original feature of South Indian temple music lay in its use of musical pillars, beginning in the Vijayanagar period at Hampi, and spreading south to Lepakshi, Madurai, Tirunelveli, Suchindram near Kaniya Kumari and Trivandrum. Resonant types of stone (a pinkish biotite granite or granite gneiss found near Hampi) were deliberately selected by architects and incorporated in such a way as to vary the sound by varying pillars' length, diameter and shape, experimenting over a century to achieve their greatest success at Suchindram in the 17th century.

The art gallery begins with an exposition of Hindu faith and learning, symbols and iconography. Black denotes malice, and yellow the highest intellect; each branch of learning has its own path (mysticism has jnana yoga), its own precious stone or metal (emerald), and animal (elephant). Ganapati is the most popular god of Hinduism, says one caption: in South India he is the elder brother of Muruga, with an elephant's head and a tundila, or pot belly. As the god of wisdom and remover of obstacles, he is invoked at the beginning of any undertaking, such as the writing of a new book.

His vehicle is the bandicoot; he usually has four arms, but when dancing he has eight hands, and in his manifestation as Heramba ('Boastful'), he has five faces and ten arms.

The museum's centre-piece is a Shiva Nataraja, performing the cosmic dance. The marvellous lions and elephants on pillars which you pass, with polychrome levels above, make one long for western galleries to be so located: in vibrant surroundings instead of arid barns like the British Museum. What can Sri Minakshi have looked like to mediaeval pilgrims, before the iconoclastic Muslim invasions of the fourteenth century? I mused as I strolled among cross-legged beggars, vendors of toy drums and trumpets, and stalls purveying framed portraits of Minakshi herself. Spice-stalls and cosmetic-stalls proffered damrik (a facial cosmetic), henna, cardamom, sandalwood paste. A temple elephant extended its leg so that his rider could step down smoothly from his back to the ground. Children tugged at their mother's sari, whining to go away after a hard day at the temple. An infant was blessed on the head by a delicate tap from the tip of the elephant's trunk. Alongside Hindu worshippers I circumambulated clockwise the shrine of the planets, then walked on into lengthening shadows of flickering lanterns past begging sadhus with bare chests, past girls with garlands in their hair. Inside the shrine the same endless excited commotion, at the other pole from yogic inwardness, reminded me of the popular excitement of Lourdes or Fatima. A potbellied priest explained in Tamil that the high-relief polychrome full-length image portrayed Maharaja Manyaraja Sri Tirumala Nayak, reconstructor of this temple and builder of the Madurai palace, flanked by his two wives. Worshippers come to pay

*Tirumala Nayak. A 17th-century ivory carving made in Madurai*

their respects at this shrine too. An old man spread grey ash on the altar upheld by two stone elephants. A discreet policeman ensured that no non-Hindus filtered into the shrine of Minakshi. I sat in deep shadow near groups of chattering men along one of the cloisters surrounding Golden Lotus Tank and watched the rust-stained sun burn itself out, below the level of the opposite cloister wall. The following day I returned at dawn to study the cloister's murals showing the sixty-four miracles Lord Shiva is reputed to have conjured at Madurai, vigorous works in ochres, oranges, browns. The 16th-century tank has a brass lamp-standard in the centre, and the verses of Tirukkural are inscribed on the walls of the south cloister.

I suppose there must be more than two thousand columns at Sri Minakshi. They comprise four types in the main: one square and simple; another with a dragon or hippogriff; a third shows a portrait, often of one of the many Nayak donors; and the last depicts a deity, usually Shaivite. While we are accustomed in Greek architecture, as at the Parthenon, to find figures structurally significant, as in the caryatids of the Erechtheion, at Madurai they are though fully rounded simply attached to the shaft. Some lend a little support, but many enrich already intricate architecture, so that one feels entwined in jungle lianas rather than in any manmade edifice. I feel this keenly at the entrance to the shrine of Lord Sundareshvar, where riotously-carved pillars offer permanent refuge to superb sculptures of Shiva standing or dancing. A priest told me that within – where I could not enter – the Lord stands in the form of a lingam. East of Sundareshvar Shrine is a pillared hall called Kambathadi Mandapam, with divine images of the eight pillars around the Nandi, one of them portraying the wedding of Minakshi. Below the floorslabs, separate conduits carry sewage and drinking water. East of the Kambathadi mandapam stands the five-storey tower about 66' high built around 1600 by Visuvappa.

Outside this enclosure is a 46-pillar hall called the Viravasanta mandapam commissioned by Muthu Virappa Nayak (1609-1628), elder brother of the great Tirumala. Next is the kalyan mandapam, where figures of Lord and Lady are brought together at their marriage festival. Incidentally, priests allow the Lord to 'visit' his bride every night in a special bedchamber within the Minakshi shrine area.

East of the eastern gopuram is the Pudu mandapam, with 124 pillars in four rows, another work of Tirumala datable to 1628-35; in the middle you will find figures of fourteen Nayak rulers, including the donor. At most hours you will find pilgrims bathing in the tank, and vina, tabla and other instruments being played at the temple's own broadcasting studio. I chatted to Mr Chookalingam, a bookseller with a range of devotional books in Tamil and a few in English, then bought K. Gnanasoorian's *The Meaning of Life in Saivite Hinduism* (1985), advocating the theistic philosophy of Shiva Siddhanta originating from Tamil Nadu, with its own epistemology, metaphysics and spiritual disciplines. Nearby a games stall stacked up toys and boxed games, plastic windmills, tops and kites. Sweets of all types, fruits and vegetables, noodles and popcorn, balloons and transistor radios. A constant wave of human traffic pours relentlessly around shopkeepers perennially alert, waggling their heads in a range of replies from astonishment to good-humoured bantering. I never felt alienated, for the blatant tolerance of Hindus is there to be basked in, if you will allow yourself the luxury. Two Australians slept in a corner. I conceived the bizarre notion that I could explore the whole temple again and yet see none of the same sculptures or pillars twice. I bought a printed paper snakes-and-ladders board for Rs 0.50 from the SNKV Toys lock-up: it was festooned with mythical beasts, gods and goddesses, a row of lucky elephants at the foot, and a fierce snake at square 106 that would drop an unlucky player back to square 1.

I eventually dragged my weary feet to Hotel Kannimara (the Connemara familiar in Madras) on Dindigul Road and found a seat beneath the one ceiling fan that was working. Chicken soup, egg fried rice and egg custard, followed by a pot of tea: I quickly revived, then passed a night peopled with roaring gryphons and pawing bulls at the New College House on Town Hall Road, occupying a single room with bath for only Rs 35 with airconditioning.

### Tirupparankuntram

Early next morning I hailed an auto-rickshaw for the 10 km ride to the cave temple of Tirupparankuntram, dedicated to Muruga. Itself only of Nayak age, the temple is clearly on the site of much earlier shrines devoted to fertility gods, and a Subrahmanya Cave Temple, with images of Durga flanked by Ganesha and Subrahmanya, has been dated to 773 A.D. Their architectural style is related to those of Trichy and Mandagapattu. Legend states that the great rock temple is the site of Muruga's marriage to Devayanai, daughter of Indra. The entrance portico has 48 stained and blackened pillars with notable carvings, gradually picked out as you approach along the wide main street towards the mountainside. The massive gopuram is dwarfed by the bare rock until you are very close up. Around the temple gate, stalls of garlands and fruit-offerings for the gods are set out seductively: coconut slices and whole bananas. An elderly woman with a charming smile kneels watchfully by her Castrol tin as the paisa drop in; a sadhu in an orange robe bows *namaste* to me, his palms together, and I reciprocate; a street-cleaner in a creased dhoti vainly attempts to stem the litter-tide with a twig-broom just too short to be comfortable. 'I'd no idea this was here', muttered a German to his American wife, 'it's not in any of the

*Madurai. On the way to the cave temple of Tirupparankuntram*

guidebooks.' But if one were to cover everything worth seeing in a guidebook to India, nobody could carry the ton-weight round. Festival chariots in a courtyard represented the sacred serpent, naga, horses and cockerels. Down by the rock pool pilgrims were bathing below hens pecking nervously. A grinning man showing off his gold teeth sold salt to visitors, who would wave a pinch three times round their head for good luck. A priest pressed incense ash on the centre of my forehead: a grey mark to show my allegiance to Lord Muruga. I squatted cross-legged to watch the pilgrims pass, looking up to the brilliant, newly-painted gopuram, and across to a row of patient sadhus with bowls, as absently curious as I about the habits and temperament of passers-by. How can we live together? How could we live apart?

### Mariamman Teppakulam
My auto-rickshaw wallah unfolded himself from the shady seat of his vehicle at my discreet cough, and sped off, towards the opposite end of town, to the Mariamman Teppakulam, a reservoir or tank situated between the Ramnad Road and New Ramnad Road, a mile east of Madurai East rail station. The enormous tank laid out in 1646 has an island in the middle with gardens and a white temple; it is fed by an underground

81

channel running from the Vaigai and was yet another attractive idea of Tirumala Nayak. The tank is the scene of one of the most colourful of Madurai's many festivals: in January-February the figures of Sri Minakshi and Sri Sundareshvar are brought to the Mariamman Teppakulam, and floated to the Maya mandapam, to the acclaim of hundreds of thousands of pilgrims. The betrothal of Shri Minakshi on Chitra Purnami day is only one of the numerous festivals, which also include the procession of Alagar (Minakshi's brother) to the Vaigai, and brilliant street festivals when chariots are hauled through the broad streets around the great temple. The little temple above the tank's parapet was crowded with visitors: women preponderated, as it is clearly used for good luck with childbirth, children, and marital problems. A priest invited me into the sanctum, asked my name, and when I gave it invoked blessings on my head and smeared my brow with grey ash. Beside the tank Nandi bulls flanked the steps and women had set up fabric strands like looms along the pavement. I exchanged Rs 3 for Gold Spot orange drink and nibbled biscuits while the rickshaw driver revved up and we headed for the Tirumalai Nayak Palace. I dismounted and paid in a side street nearby, amid wandering cows seeking whatever they could devour before wending their way home at dusk, roaming goats, bikes laden with rice, a communist hammer-and-sickle painted in red on a whitewashed grainstore, and seductive film posters with hero and heroine as close as the censorship allows.

**Tirumalai Nayak Palace**
The palace is open from 9 to 1 and 2 to 5, with an English-language Son et Lumière show at 6.45. The original palace complex of the 1630s was enormous, taking Mughal pointers unusual in this Hindu city, but Tirumala's grandson ransacked the palace for his new capital at Trichy and beginning in 1665 reduced Madurai's palace from its grandiose beginnings to a quarter of the area, enclosed by walls on all four sides but sadly neglected to the point of virtual dilapidation. Then in the 19th century even the defensive walls were removed. The British used the area as a barracks, and a paper factory was organised, run by convict labour. Lord Napier, Governor of Madras from 1866 to 1872, wrote a stirring appeal for the protection of ancient monuments in general and Tirumalai Nayak Palace in particular, and after R.F. Chisholm came from Madras to report on the need for work to be done, iron ties were put in to hold the weak structures together, ruins' rebuilt, and plasterwork and paintings restored. The District Courts functioned here till 1970, when they moved into a purpose-built complex, and since then the palace has been preserved as a state monument.

Ten stone pillars forming part of the Ranga Vilas courtyard are all that remain of that area, but the Swarga Vilas, or Celestial Pavilion, remains largely intact. This was the ceremonial throne-room where Tirumala would receive in state vassal rulers and dignitaries, and measures 75 metres by 52, with a large central dome supported on twelve pillars. Swarga Vilas is approached by steps adorned with equestrian figures now badly damaged. I visualised the annual Sceptre Festival inaugurated by Tirumala to validate his sovereignty on the eighth day of Chitra, when the image of Sri Minakshi would be decorated at the temple and 'present' the Nayak king with a royal sceptre encrusted with jewels. The sceptre, thus blessed, would be brought to his palace nearby on a royal elephant, and be placed on the throne the whole day, to be worshipped by the king and returned the following day, symbolising the rule of the Nayak empire by the goddess through her servant Tirumala, a festival enduring into the 18th century reign of Rani Mangammal. Or in September the Navaratri 'Nine Night' Festival might capture one's imagination, the Celestial Pavilion alight with handheld torches as the richly-jewelled monarch sat in pomp giving audience to his subjects. Nowadays only irritable crows populate the pavilion, pestering the ground for suspected crumbs.

A museum has been established in the cathedral-like Natakasala, a hall 22 metres by 42, with a pointed-arch brick roof, above an upper gallery. Rumour said that an Italian architect had been involved at some stage, an assertion easy to support by conjecture. Could this have been the sleeping apartment of Tirumala as the guide claimed? It seems unlikely, but the lurid tale is worth repeating. A thief made a hole in the roof one night, swung down the chains which held the royal swinging bed, and robbed his sleeping lord of his priceless gems. The following day Tirumala announced that he would award hereditary land and its rent (*jagir* is the Persian term used in much of India) to anyone who would bring him the thief. The thief himself claimed the reward. Tirumala thereupon kept his word, awarding the thief his due *jagir*; then as the gleeful criminal left the palace he was arrested for his crime and executed at once *pour encourager les autres*. It all sounds a very useful rumour in times of civic upheaval. The trouble is that this hall is known from Tamil records to have been used as a theatre and dance hall where the court would be entertained by musicians, dancers, and actors performing sacred dance dramas based on the *Ramayana* and *Mahabharata*.

The museum is strong in stone sculptures, such as a Late Chola Brahma (12th century) from Darasuram near Tanjore, and a Nayak king (*c.* 1700) from Pattisvaram, also in Tanjore district. Pride of place on the platform is given to a superb Narasimha (Vishnu as lion-man) of Pandyan age, about 800 A.D. but my preference is for a full-length Vishnu of around 900 from Kizhmattu, Madurai district. Microliths of 4,000 B.C. and larger hand tools of 2,000 B.C. indicate Neolithic industry near Madurai, and Iron Age implements of the 1st century A.D. prove continuity of occupation – though that would never be in serious doubt in South India, with its fertile soils and permanent rivers. The palace is roughly equidistant between the Roman Catholic Church and the Anglican Cathedral of 1875, the latter designed by R.F. Chisholm while he was working on the palace. On the other bank of the Vaigai, the Friday Mosque can be seen near the American College; eastward is the 17th-century palace of Queen Mangammal (10-12 and about 2-4.30 every day except Wednesdays), rather incongruously used to display the life and labours of Mahatma Gandhi, apostle of the poor. Accessible by buses 1, 2 and 3 from the bus station, it shows books and other memorabilia of the Father of the Nation, including the dhoti he was wearing when gunned down by a Hindu extremist on 30 January 1948, an act from which the fundamentalist fringe is only just now beginning to recover, with the emergence of chauvinist groups like the Bharatiya Janata Party, and banning the use of English from Uttar Pradesh's government offices from 1990. Gandhiji would have been inexpressibly saddened by the dictum of Mulayam Singh Yadav, Chief Minister of Uttar Pradesh, that as long as India continues to rely on English 'no villager can lead a better life'. An attempt to impose Hindi on Bihar in the mid-1960s achieved scant success, and we can only hope for the sake of Bengalis, Tamils, Marathis, Gujaratis, Malayalis, Punjabis and every other linguistic minority that this provocative and divisive move will be rescinded as early as possible. If you stroll back from the Gandhi Museum along Tamukkam Road, you can pick up bus 44 near the Central Telegraph Office for the 19-km ride to the Vaishnavite temple of Sri Alagar at Alagarkoil village. Alagarkoil Road is your destination if you want some of the most expensive hotels in town: the Madurai Ashok, the cheaper Pandyan, and cheapest of all the Tamil Nadu, not to be confused with the hotel of the same name on West Veli St which is better value still.

### Rameshwaram

Just as Madurai is an early site transformed by Nayak grandeur, so Rameshwaram dates from the collapse of centralised rule from Vijayanagar, and the rise of Nayak viceroys, now independent kings, at Vellore (North Arcot), Gingee (South Arcot), Tanjore, and Madurai. The greatest architectural achievements of this era have been seen at Kanchi, Vellore (Jalakanteshvara Temple), Srirangam, Madurai, and now at Rameshwaram, where the magnificent corridors are formed by closed ambulatories flanked by continuous platforms, with massive pillars on each side of a sunk pathway, and brackets corbelled to the point where they almost join. Executed like Madurai's Sri Minakshi on a unitary plan, Rameshwaram offers an awesome spectacle of corridors

84

*Rameshwaram. 17th-century pillared corridor*

varying in width from 17 to 21 feet with a height of 27 feet, and a length of 671 feet.

For a couple of rupees, I obtained benison from the temple's elephant's trunk, and watched Hindu families praying to Ganesha for family trust and happiness, and bachelors praying to Kalyana Sundareshvar for a blessed marriage.

Festivals at Rameshwaram occur throughout the year, but the greatest include Thai Ammavasai in January, Masi Shivaratri in February-March, Thirukalyanam in July-August, and Mahalaya Ammavasai in September.

Rameshwaram seems the grandest of all Dravidian conceptions because it is literally at the end of your journey: your next landfall would be Sri Lanka. It was completed in the 18th century, at a time when Wren, Hawksmoor and Vanbrugh were transforming the English view of architecture, yet the continuity with Pallava and Chola aesthetics is there for all to feel, to see, to touch. Behind every column hovers the living legend that Rama, having killed his enemy Ravana in his island fortress of Sri Lanka, returned here victorious to worship the lingam of Lord Shiva, purifying himself. A temple nearby is said to protect a footprint made by Rama on that return journey, and another temple, the Kotandara Swami at Dhanushkodi, is where Rama bathed before praying. There is still a bathing pool at Dhanushkodi, accessible by bus from Rameshwaram. (Dhanush is Rama's bow.)

The island of Rameshwaram is joined from Mandapam to Pamban (on the west) and Rameshwaram (on the east). If you find Hotel Tamil Nadu full as usual, it is as well as to try the Railway Retiring Rooms on arrival, especially if there is a special festival or you strike a weekend or public holiday, because Rameshwaram is to the south as Benares is to the north: an All-India Hindu pilgrimage.

As at Madurai's Sri Minakshi, the main shrine for the male deity adjoins a smaller shrine to the female goddess: Shiva always accompanied by Parvati. Non-Hindus may not enter their sancta, but then the marvel of Rameshwaram is the astonishing perspective of corridors, and the details, such as damsels, soldiers, animals on the pillars of the Chokattam corridor from the western gopuram towards the centre. The tank in front of the Gandhamardana Temple is a constantly shifting scene of bathing pilgrims. Paintings on pillars and ceilings have faded, but some medallions have recently been restored. The western corridor is penetrated at five points by earlier shrines, dating back in some cases to the 12th century, clearly out of context but adding in their unexpectedness another dimension to this great masterpiece of Dravidian craftmanship, so alien to eyes accustomed to identify Indian architecture with Mughal inspiration. Even the traditional Dravidian gopuram is exemplified by a superb example here: the eastern gopuram forming a gateway to the second enclosure, begun in 1640 but only finished in modern times. Its eleven storeys soar 150 feet into a radiant aquamarine sky.

## Kaniya Kumari

Mystical union of sea with land and air at Rameshwaram finds a parallel at Cape Comorin (Kaniya Kumari in Tamil), at the southern tip of the Indian subcontinent, on a latitude close to that of Sigiriya in Sri Lanka. You can reach Kaniya Kumari on any one of six buses daily, taking eight hours via Tuticorin, once a Portuguese port, and Tiruchendur (whose district has a substantial Roman Catholic minority), but most visitors will reach the cape from Madurai via Tirunelveli and Nagarcoil. The daily Madurai bus is reputed to take six hours, but in fact normally takes seven and is usually crowded, so book early and take your seat for the final run south. Do not be surprised to find yourself sitting near a worshipper of Surya, the Sun God, for you can see at this cape both moonrise and sunset simultaneously. Ptolemy's *Komaria Akron* was named for Kumari, 'the virgin', a manifestation of Shiva's consort who in one incarnation did penance here but failed to win her beloved in matrimony and so vowed to remain celibate. Another legend has it that Parvati was to marry Shiva on an auspicious day before the demon king was to be attacked. However, as the demon could be slain only by a virgin, the gods tricked Shiva by imitating a cock-crow before dawn, so persuading him that the auspicious day for the wedding was past. Parvati remained a virgin and as such was able to slaughter the demon king.

In her shrine at Kaniya Kumari, Parvati as Virgin Queen is covered by white sandalpaste, and her two diamond noserings – given in the early 20th century by the Maharaja of Trivandrum – glitter in the lamplight. Pilgrims enter the shrine through the north gate because the usual eastern entrance is unlucky: it was through the east gate that some British thieves stole the original *naga mani* nosering after their shipwreck. Likewise her bathing pool nearby is sacred, which is odd and depressing because the once-holy beach and village has been reduced to a litter-infested, popmusic-wrecked festival of bric-a-brac stalls where shoddy merchandise takes precedence over natural wonders. I walked away quickly from the cries of 'Hey, mister!' to find a lonely spot where I could dwell on the Upanishads, composed more than two thousand five hundred years ago yet addressing the same questions that would vex Kierkegaard or Cioran in our time.

Brahman, the ultimate reality, the spirit of the universe: 'All is Brahman', it is written in the *Chhandogya* Upanishad, 'let men and women meditate on the visible world, for they are born in it, die in it, and have their being in it. As a human being is a creature of will and belief, whatever his or her will is in this life will shape what he or she is to be on departing this life, so let him or her will as follows:

> Sandilya the sage said the Brahman is the intelligent being, whose body is spirit, whose shape is light, whose thought is true, whose nature is ether, who never speaks improperly and is never surprised, who originates all actions and desires, all scents and tastes. Brahman is myself within my heart, tinier than the least rice-grain, the least barley-grain, the least mustard-seed, the least canary-seed. Brahman is myself within my heart, greater than earth itself, heaven itself, the universe itself. When I depart this life, I shall obtain that Self. He who has this faith has no doubts, affirms Sandilya.'

The Gandhi Memorial commemorates the place where his ashes were brought for viewing. It is said that the Arabian Sea, Bay of Bengal and Indian Ocean commingle at Kaniya Kumari, and his words are inscribed on the memorial: 'I am writing this at the Cape in front of the sea, where three waters meet and furnish a sight unequalled in the world. For this is no port of call for vessels. Like the Goddess, the waters around here are virgin.'

Vivekananda Rock nearby can be reached by ferry. Here the Swami meditated in 1892, and here Vedantists meditate beside the inscribed *Om* and before the statue of Vivekananda. The little fishing village of white houses and red-tiled roofs is dominated by the Roman Catholic Church of Our Lady of Ransom: behind it green palms swish in sea breezes; behind them rise misty distant mountains curved like camel-backs.

### Suchindram

Far more wonderful than any temple in Kaniya Kumari, or its Gandhi Memorial or Vivekananda Memorial, is the Sthnanunatha Temple to Lord Shiva at Suchindram, a 5-km ride away by auto-rickshaw, yet another demonstration of Nayak glory, begun in 1545 but dating mostly to the 17th century. You will recognise from Madurai the rectangular enclosure and surrounding broad streets of a dimension convenient for large-scale chariot festivals, but the original shrines to Shiva and Vishnu date to the 9th century, and further12th century shrines are devoted to Vishnu, Ganesha and Parvati as Durga. Moreover, the main gopuram was clearly finished in the nineteenth century, but the overwhelming sensation is of Nayak grandeur, as at Srirangam, Madurai and Rameshwaram, the last evoked by a solemn corridor with donors and damsels greeting you before the main temple. Within the rectangle, a small pavilion has high-relief figures of the heroes Karna and Arjuna, the God of Love as Manmatha, and his consort Rati. Another magnificent colonnade surrounds the shrine: sculptures here include the fantastic lion-like yalis on large brackets below the ceiling, while the great pillars are ornamented with a range of figures divine and human. Very few foreigners seem to reach Suchindram, or to be aware of its importance, possibly because Nayak art has still not found its popular champion, while the Mughal art of Northern India has found so many. But who could resist the Chemparakaman mandapam, with its painted friezes of Krishna lore, or the Shaivite carvings of the Chitra Sabha?

We have heard musical pillars at Madurai, and more can be heard here, in the Alankara mandapam, where a sixteen-foot figure of the monkey-god Hanuman is covered in rice-paste, facing Rama and Sita. Long Dravidian-style corridors are flanked by divine handmaidens, or *devadasis*, holding lamps that once burned to illuminate temple festivals. Nowadays the main festivals are Chitra Purnami in the first week of May and Navaratri in the last week of October.

A civil engineer from Nagpur shook his head at such wonders, confiding in me, 'What for we go to foreign? I am thinking we have here in India itself too much good to see.' 'Right you are,' I agreed, and invited him to tiffin. 'So sorry,' he apologised, 'but my stomach is out.'

## Nagarcoil

Deshnok in Rajasthan has the leading Rat Temple in India; Nagarcoil in Tamil Nadu 18 km from Kaniya Kumari has the leading Snake Temple, with serpents protected inside a small thatched hut at the back of the shrine. I wondered whether the reptiles would be let loose among the worshippers, as rats are at Deshnok, but my apprehensions were quickly set to rest: the only cobras one can touch are carved in stone. Nagaraja the cobra-king may be worshipped now at Nagarcoil, but the temple must originally have been Jain, for tirthankaras are carved on the pillars of the inner temple. A non-Hindu is welcome to pass through the pagoda-like gate and circle the sacred pipal tree, with its shrine to Nagaraja with stone cobras sprinkled by pilgrims with turmeric. The main Nagaraja image is garlanded and plated with silver.

## Padmanabhapuram

Past Nagarcoil, on the road to Trivandrum, Tamil Nadu offers one last delight before the state border with Kerala, and that is the Kerala-style 17th-18th century Palace of Padmanabhapuram, once capital of the State of Travancore. Here is the apotheosis of the curved and drooping pendant on bracket capitals, proceeding from wooden buildings later to stone; here are dormer windows and long corridors reminiscent of religious antecedents. You will be told that some of the structures at Padmanabhapuram date back to 1335, but most are much later. I liked best the entrance hall or *pumukham*, the theatre hall (used mainly for dance drama) and the council chamber.

In the oldest part of the palace surviving, and dating roughly to the mid-16th century, a one-piece wooden pillar rises from base to capital supporting the ceiling in a kind of tree-like growth expanding to branches near the top, with leaves, flowers and a delicate lotus-bud. Equally notable woodcarving is found in the wood-house or Nerapura in the palace grounds, dated to the 18th century and entirely of wood except for its tiled roof: it has been restored during the recent crafts revival. Those interested in woodcarving should make a point of seeing the 45-panel frieze around the Ramaswami Temple dated to 1744, in the reign of Maharaja Martanda Varma, demonstrating a high technique deriving from many generations of masters. But it is for its paintings on the four walls of a room on the fourth and highest storey of the palace that most visitors will remember Padmanabhapuram. Some fifty scenes from the Hindu epics and scriptures rival those of the 17th century in Cochin's Portuguese-built Mattancheri Palace. See how Ganesha's form and line reverberate with energy, every inch covered as at Cochin with colour and movement. The palace is closed every Monday.

### Kodaikanal
Three hill stations are strategically situated in Tamil Nadu. Most celebrated of all is Ootacamund, in the Blue Hills or Nilgiris in that enchanted triangle where northwest Tamil Nadu meets southwest Karnataka and east-central Kerala. Yercaud rises gloatingly above the steel

*Kodaikanal. Sunset and clouds*

plant of busy Salem on the road from Bangalore to Dindigul. But my favourite, unspoilt and breathtakingly beautiful in the subtle shades of twilight or the brisk chill of dawn is Kodaikanal, accessible either from Dindigul or a four-hour bus-ride from Madurai; it is so much smaller than Ooty that most spectacular views are within easy walking distance. The climate is congenial throughout the year, but probably best from May to October; it can be quite chilly in January, after the main rains of November-December. The observatory, brought here from Madras in 1899, stands 7700 feet a.s.l. Local flora and fauna are exhibited in a museum at the College of the Sacred Heart, and there is a botanical garden: Bryant Park. Citrus fruits are cultivated locally; so are spices such as cinnamon, pepper, and nutmeg. The waterfalls are natural, but Kodai lake is manmade with a three-mile perimeter walk ideal for relaxing and the leading hotel, the Carlton, on its shore. You can hire a boat on the lake, or a horse for hill-riding, but hiking is my chief pleasure around Kodai, with the view from Coaker's Walk (off Club Road) a spectacular bonus at any time of year, especially just before sunrise. The Zum Zum Lodge just off Club Road was the choice of one independent traveller, an Austrian who had nearly run out of rupees, but if you are still in funds you might prefer the Hotel Jaya, nearer the bus station than the comparable Hotel Tamil Nadu on Fernhill Road. In the other direction I explored a number of interesting restaurants near Hospital Road, the best being the Tibetan Brothers opposite Kodai School.

If your nostalgia threshold remains fairly high, the British period in Kodai is perpetuated in cottages with herbaceous borders and meticulous lawns in a temperature you might compare with midsummer South Downs flecked with a touch of Grampian hauteur at the edges. Accents are frankly Home Counties, clipped like the shrubs for neatness. But the days of the Raj are over, and the British are few in number. It may not be literally true, but I always remember Sir William Hunter's bald assertion in *The Old Missionary* (1895): 'The Englishman in India has no home and leaves no memory'.

### Yercaud

The most convenient hill station from Madras is reached from Salem Junction, a stop 207 miles from Madras Central and 3 miles from Salem town. The bus up to Yercaud takes a couple of hours and more to negotiate 33 km and 19 hairpin bends of hill climbing into the coffee plantations. The Shevaroy Hills vary in height from 3600 to 5400 feet, Yercaud itself stretching out from about 4200 near the lakeside to 4800 at Shevaroyan Point. Accommodation is divided between Hotel Tamil Nadu (with its own dormitory-style hostel in addition) and the more expensive Hotel Shevaroy. High season is April to mid-June but off season is equally recommendable. Sights include Anna Park and the lake, with boating; the State Agricultural Farm (its roses must be a state secret, for photography is forbidden there!), and the Botanical Survey of India gardens. You can find hibiscus and dahlias, eucalyptus imported from Australia and casuarina. The Grange is a fortress-like home built by M.D. Cockburn, once Collector at Salem. Shevaroyan Temple is one of the highest viewpoints in Yercaud, its major festival occuring in May, when hill-tribes converge there. Lower down is the Rajarajeshvari temple, with a striking yellow gopuram. Granite quarries crash and thump with activity. Beginning at Yercaud Church, it is a 2-km hike to Bear's Hill, or to Prospect Point, or to Ladies' Seat; and between 3 and 4 km to Kiliyur Falls or Pagoda Point with its ruined temple. The best guided excursion is the 8 a.m. round trip called in ninety minutes at surrounding villages and coffee estates: Semmantham, Periakkadu, Manjukuttai and Velakkadai. Citrus trees, jack trees and plantain ensure a plentiful supply of local fruits throughout the seasons.


## Coimbatore and the Way Up

With a population of around 400,000 (all census figures from India are to be treated with caution), Coimbatore is the third city of Tamil Nadu after Madras and Madurai, though with much less to see, if you are not excited by textile mills and timber mills. Sri Muruga's Marudhamalai Temple is situated on a hilltop, and the Shaivite Perur Temple built by Karikala Cholan some 7 km away is worth visiting for the beautiful sculptures in its Kanagasabai Hall.

If stranded for the night, your best hopes are Hotel Sri Shakti, Hotel Zakin and the government-run Hotel Tamil Nadu on Dr Nanjappa Road, all near the bus station but a long way from the rail station, where you might try Hotel Anand Vihar on State Bank Road. Coimbatore has a small airport for internal flights to Bangalore, Bombay and Madras. You'd go to Madurai, Mysore, Nagarcoil, Trichy and Pondicherry by bus. Good rail services exist across South India to Rameshwaram (14 hours) and across Deccan to New Delhi (38 hours).

Frequent buses to Ooty make sure you don't have to wait too long, but anyone will recommend the rail trip from Coimbatore to the Nilgiri Railway departing Mettupalayam at 7.45 or 9.30 a.m., reaching Ooty respectively at 12.10 and 13.55. If you want to take the bus as far as Coonoor, itself an attractively cool hill station, you have the option of an 8 a.m. or 5.30 p.m. departure, arriving at Ooty either at 9.15 or at 7 p.m. Connections are always available from or to Madras on the Nilgiri Express: allow $4\frac{1}{2}$ hours to ascend the 46 km of rainforest track up to Ooty, or $3\frac{1}{2}$ hours to descend. I took thali on a banana and a glass of tea in a coconut grove at Mettupalayam, waiting for the train to Coonoor.

At this level, the luxurious tropical jungle and plain looks as Indian as the Kerala coastline, but shortly the train will puff its way through temperate-zone bamboos and acacias, beside coffee plantations, and end up through tea gardens to a landscape combining the rugged Cairngorms of Scotland with the Blue Mountains of Australia, from which the eucalyptus and wattle were introduced.

Eleven miles of plain railing end in a seventeen-mile mountain section as far as Coonoor, which was not completed to Ooty until 1908. The track from Kallar to Coonoor rises 5,500 feet in 13 miles, with a maximum gradient of 1 in 12.5, necessitating the Swiss rack system. Special rack bars are laid between the track rails on 'chairs' and form a ladder along which the engine climbs, taking the train with it. The rack-teeth are spaced 4.72″ centre to centre, corresponding to the pitch of the pinions of the driving-wheel fitted to the locomotive. The racks are laid in a double row 1¾″ apart and 2½″ above the running rail, so the tooth of one lies opposite the gap of the other, as in a zip fastener. There is no rack on the Coonoor-Ooty stretch. The train has no toilet, but each station has facilities, and a sympathetic guard can be prevailed upon to stop in emergencies.

## Coonoor

Switchback bends brought us eventually to Coonoor, where I wanted to explore the bazaar. I found heaped cardamom, women bringing flour to a miller, and a butcher in a cool white-tiled roofed enclosure hacking mutton with a cleaver, dogs scavenging earnestly for bones. A muaddin called to prayer: the tall clock-tower pointed at 4.15. I bought a packet of a hundred joss-sticks, and sat on my haunches beside a Hindu shrine and a friendly khaki-clad policeman looking up above the market towards a mosque and church. Goats enquired of my pockets and shopping-bag; pigs rootled around in the refuse-strewn rivulet, and a dog lay fast asleep in the middle of the road, where he had felt the urge to curl up. Buses, auto-rickshaws, mango lorries and pedestrians alike swerved to avoid the snoring animal. I guiltily bought and chewed a bit of jaggery: a lump of solid sweet palm-sap, brown as honey.

Coonoor is milder than Ooty, and has grown enormously from a population of eight thousand in 1901 to 50,000 or more in 1990, mainly due to the return of many Indians from Sri Lanka. The great traveller Richard Burton wrote of the Coonoor peak called the Droog, 'The rock upon which we tread falls with an almost perpendicular drop of four thousand feet into the plains. From this eyrie we descry the houses of Coimbatore'. Ask your auto-rickshaw wallah for Pakkasuran Kottai, the name of the ruined 16th-century fort there at one time used in a campaign by Tipu Sultan himself. Easier of access for picnics is Lamb's Rock, 5 km from Coonoor on the way to Dolphin's Nose. Lamb's Rock,

*Coonoor. Wayside Hindu shrine and policeman near the bus station*

overlooking the railway and the town of Mettupalayam, is so-called because a Captain of that name hacked a path through to the viewpoint. Lady Canning's Seat is another belvedere 3 km farther on, where Charlotte, Lady Canning, enjoyed painting the terrible, sublime landscapes so fashionable in her day. A further four km brings you to Dolphin's Nose, where the views are even more tremendous, down to St Catherine's Falls one way, and the other down to Coonoor Stream and the Kotagiri stream, which will meet as tributaries in the Bhavani river.

Sated with grandeur, you might prefer the more domestic pleasures of the Pomological Research Station (1920), specialising not only in apples but also in pomegranates, plums, peaches, persimmons and apricots. Sim's Park in Upper Coonoor has expanded since its beginnings in 1874 to incorporate roses and shrubs that do less well in Ooty. The annual flower show in Ooty is followed by the rival fruit and vegetable show in Coonoor: can you believe that these luscious tomatoes, pink radishes, small potatoes, succulent peas, fresh lettuce and tiny Brussels sprouts are really Indian grown? Any money goes so much *further* than back in Blighty.

At 5.30 I boarded the first-class compartment at Coonoor rail station, and took my seat in the front row, with only the driver between me and stupendous views to Wellington (5.40), with its soccer pitch below the station, the mountains rounding into a dramatic amphitheatre where every noise reverberated several times. Families walked along the track ahead of us, till parped out of the way. A Ministry of Defence gunpowder factory by Aravankadu (5.50) provoked the driver to remind me not to take a photograph of this military installation while we halted for a tea among great stands of eucalyptus at a Vegetarian Tea Stall. I had time to ask to see the four beds available in the retiring rooms at Aravankadu station, but was told that nobody there had the key. 'One vegetarian tea', called out an American student with a mauve T-shirt marked UCLA, but it was too late: the wind resumed its blaring through the open windows, and panoramas again changed and cavorted, though we were travelling ever more slowly, and the driver, Mr M.S. Narayanan of the Railway Colony, Mettupalayam, told me of his ten years on the line, with another eight to go before he retired. What could be more enchanting than to spend your whole life in any schoolboy's dream: chugging up and down on a miniature railway amid sensational mountain vistas?

### Ootacamund

We pulled into Ketti at 6.15, then strained every mechanical sinew to reach Lovedale by 6.40, the southern edge of Ooty proper. Ooty station now reads 'Udagamandalam', a name you need to remember if looking up Ootacamund in Indian books or gazetteers, though the form 'Udhagamandalam' is also prevalent. It was darkling as our little train pulled into Ooty at 6.50, and the temperature dropped suddenly. Overnight a frost solidified the diesel in a lorry parked outside the Fernhill Palace Hotel, where I had been booked into Room 105, a palatial suite with four-poster bed, hunt photos on the walls, and a crackling log fire in the grate.

Fernhill was built as the summer palace of the Maharaja of Mysore, its Grand Ballroom nowadays the restaurant, thirty-three rooms each individually designed, and views from the rear over the hillside. The smaller Palace Hotel is a former summer home of the Nizam of Hyderabad, and I can also recommend the atmospheric Savoy and the new Lake View Hotel. But nowhere beats the beautiful Fernhill. The first Fernhill bungalow was built by Captain F. Cotton in 1842; he sold it in 1855 to Major-General Stratton, and it passed in 1861 to Major W. Wapshare and in 1870 to Lt. Col. Campbell, before the late Maharaja of Mysore acquired in 1873 for Rs 10,000 a total of 400 acres, of which only 44 acres remain. It was the Maharaja who added the Burmese carved teak reception desk and the Grand Ballroom. It was renovated in 1975, and is under the management of the former Mysore Royal Family, with a sales arrangement connecting it to the Welcomgroup. The current prince of Mysore is H.H. Srikantha Datta Narasimharaja

Wadiyar, who comes here for a few weeks at least every summer.

I was anxious to find the first European home in Ooty: the legendary Stone House that gave its name to the district between Charing Cross and Old Ooty. Oddly enough, Mollie Panter-Downes, whose *Ooty Preserved* (1967) is a charmingly nostalgic account of the Victorian Hill Station, 'gave up' her hunt for the original British residence built for John Sullivan, Collector of Coimbatore. But my auto-rickshaw man had no difficulty, apart from a fruitful misunderstanding that took me first to the Government Arts College where one student said that the Sullivan House had been incorporated into the College fabric. Another student said that what I really wanted was the College Principal's Residence, on the hilltop close by. Sullivan's 1821 bungalow still stands, windows and doors painted grass-green, with two outside staircases to the upper floor, and stands of trees to deflect the iciest of mountain winds. Sullivan wrote to Fort St George in Madras: 'your readers will be surprised to learn that frosty regions are to be found at no great distance from the Presidency and within eleven degrees of the Equator.' At that time there were no hill-stations: for relief from the heat, servants of the Raj took to the Cape or Mauritius, neither as salubrious as Ooty or Coonoor or Kotagiri.

Of course, Sullivan was not the first to find Ooty. Early Nilgiri graves are the subject of a special display in the British Museum, thanks to donations by Mrs S.M. Breeks (1879) and Sir Walter Elliott (1882). Dated expansively to the epoch from the 3rd century B.C. to the 6th A.D., the varied graves (dolmens, barrows, cairns and cists all occur) contain large flat stone slabs covering cinerary urns. Such urns were found to preserve bronze bowls, iron tools, gold jewels most interesting of all, jars with lids bearing human or animal figurines, usually of buffalo. A site of such excavations was Kambhatti, in Toda country, though the artefacts predate Toda occupation in the Nilgiris.

In Sullivan's time, Ooty was native territory to the local Toda hill-tribe, then pastoralists relying on herds of hill-buffalo, of a species different from plains-buffalo. Their typical village or *mund* consists of about six thatch-and-bamboo domed huts, with only one door. The Todas practise polyandry but a price for their sexual freedom has been exacted in venereal disease and sterility. They used to expose female babies to stampeding buffaloes until the British Government prohibited the practice in 1856, as if the Martians had dropped in and stopped World War I. We cannot say whether the Todas paid any attention: very little of the strange ways of the outside world seem to have impinged on them over the centuries, despite the Indian Government's attempts to settle them. Anthropologists have written widely about them, but cannot solve the riddle of their ancestry. Some of the more lunatic theories involve their descent from Macedonian infantry misplaced by Alexander the Great, or from the Lost Tribes of Israel, or from a Roman colony sacked by Dravidians. More plausibly, they may be an offshoot of the original Dravidians forced south by Aryan invaders in the north. Early in the 17th century, a Portuguese priest named Jacome Ferreira led a party of missionaries from Calicut on the Malabar Coast into the Nilgiris. Some thirteen miles from Ooty, the Catholics encountered a group of Todas: a culture shock something akin perhaps to Captain Cook's with the Maoris. To the peaceable but amazed Todas, Ferreira distributed hanks of cotton and looking glasses; he attempted to explain something of the Christian faith to them, but they displayed ignorance and indifference so convincing that Ferreira muttered something about coming back at a later date and, shivering in cold winds unknown down

*Ootacamund. Toda settlement above the Botanical Gardens, with Toda woman*

97

in Calicut, beat a prompt retreat. It was consequently more than two centuries later when John Sullivan, 'Father of Ooty', displayed such enthusiasm for the Nilgiris that within a few decades it was *de rigueur* for the British sweltering in the plains to buy land from the Todas at a rupee or so per acre and build on the plot a bungalow reminiscent of the Home Counties. Sullivan bought widely and wisely, selling on later to the Government or privately. He introduced hops – which failed – and flax, barley and hemp – which all succeeded. He brought out hollyhock seeds and potatoes, introduced apples and strawberries, and naturalised into these marvelling landscapes such oddities as fir and oak. He threw up a bund to create the present lake (actually a manmade reservoir) three km long and averaging 350 m wide, where boat races and boat pageants are still held.

Walks around Ooty, once the local bazaar has been enjoyed, include the Botanical Gardens with its nursery and Toda settlement at the top; Wenlock Downs near the golf course; Cairn Hill, on the road to Avalanche, with its sad cypresses over a century old; and along Upper Havelock Road, then from Nawanagar Palace to a Forest Department road skirting Marlimund Lake.

The Botanical Gardens (1848) are situated at the end of Garden Road, and near Government House, or Raj Bhavan. The first Superintendent was W.G. McIvor, from Kew, and he sensibly planned an informal garden, an Italian parterre with a lily-pond and bandstand, several little ponds, and 14 acres of neatly trimmed, lush lawns that would do credit in Wisley. Parkkeepers are supposed to enforce 'Keep off the grass' notices, but who would deny a family from the plains their chance to relax on a cool lawn in a mountain breeze when they are just here for the day from Coimbatore? Nobody: the parkkeepers nod pleasantly and chat among themselves. A delicate Japanese flowering cherry arrived in 1982, and a Bhutan cypress in 1891. One crow cawed balefully at me from a Himalayan Cedar (1885), and another from a pugnacious Dragon Tree imported from the Canaries. Above the casuarinas and Virginia junipers soared a Chinese Fan palm from Japan.

Almost anything can grow somewhere in the Nilgiris, because of the vast differential in altitude and microclimate. Average rainfall is 48 cm during the north-east monsoon which lasts for about a month from mid-October; the temperate winter months then continue until February, and the summer season lasts from mid-March to late May. The south-west monsoon brings about 95 cm of rain between June and August, giving relief to the parched and often drought-troubled hills.

Down Garden Road I came across the Lawley Institute, founded in 1911 as an Indian club to provide social and sporting facilities for those excluded by the rigorous rules of the Ooty Club and the Gymkhana Club. I was greeted by a tea planter, B.K. Nunjiah, who employs seventy-five labourers picking 4000 kgs of tea annually from sixty acres. 'Would you care to join me for tiffin?' The price of green tea fetches Rs 8 a kg now whereas a few years back it fetched only Rs 3 to 3.50, so tea remains a fine investment, like coffee down at Coonoor. The main crops are in March-April and September, he told me, as we sat down to idli sambar and Bournvita in the restaurant. The foundation stone was laid by the then Governor of Madras, H.E. the Hon. Sir Arthur Lawley, and the Bobbili Hall given by the late Sri Ravi Sri Ramakrishna Suratchilapathi Ranga Rao Bahadur Varu, 13th Raja of Bobbili, Chief Minister of Madras (1932-6), whose biography by Nilhan Perumal was published in 1960 by Topical of Coimbatore, celebrating the youngest Indian (aged 31) ever elected Minister of State. The reading room, called Abban Sait Hall, had locked bookcases with *The Indiscreet Limerick Book*, Salman Rushdie's novel *Shame*, *Adam Bede*, and masses of Victorian and Edwardian books by authors long forgotten. Life membership costs Rs 20,000, or just over US$1,800; ladies were admitted to full membership in 1988, though I saw no evidence of them during my visit; twenty rooms are available for residents. Tennis, badminton, squash, billiards and snooker are the most popular games, though there is a cards room.

In the Toda Handicrafts Sales Emporium near Charing Cross, I found cotton shawls embroidered in red and dark blue for Rs 137 and tablecloths for Rs 78 (less than US$5).

Spencer's Store was being besieged by trimly-uniformed schoolgirls stocking up with sweets; its barnlike interior smelt vaguely of Lily Langtry and colonels' wives 'staying on', the dull aroma of ancient spices exposed too long to the sun, and antediluvian mothballs: it was enchanting. So too in its own way was Higginbotham's Bookshop, a more leisurely version of its Madrasi heaquarters. Newly in were R.K. Narayan novels in English, *The City Atlas of India*, and an academic American study on the Todas. Next door the police station slept in the afternoon sun, like the notaries Gonsalves and Gonsalves. The only sign of life came from the gift shop of Mrs Adina Williams.

I enquired for the home of Kathleen Beulah Carter, widow of the tea planter George Carter, and was directed to a delightful bungalow behind Higginbotham's. The sign on the little wicker-gate was 'G.J. Carter', surely the acquaintance Mr Carter, 'sitting in a front pew' described at a service in St Stephen's Church in *Ooty Preserved*. A suggestion that I took note of the dog's ferocity was belied by the amiable tail-wagging of a few strays sunning themselves after lunch. I knocked at a door overlooking the valley view. Mrs Carter's ayah, Jane Mary, welcomed me in. 'Memsahib will be pleased to have a chat,' she smiled.

Kathleen Carter, ninety next birthday, perked up in bed and greeted me effusively. 'How nice of you to come and see me'. A Christ portrait framed above her head gazed at me absently. She had thought about going back to England (her daughter lives in Billericay), but she cannot stand the climate, and on a small pension, with income from surplus garden produce, manages to keep a household of an ayah who also cooks and stays with her overnight (Mrs Carter suffers from angina), a shopping servant, and a gardener doubling as a house coolie. Born in Devonshire, she made a life with her first husband John Smith in Ceylon as a planter of tea, rubber, cocoa and coffee; after the troubles there the Smiths moved to 'Snooty Ooty', where John died of overwork: he is buried in Coonoor. Kathleen then married George Carter, another planter, but survives him, and is now advised by her friend Colonel

*Ootacamund. Jane Mary, Mrs K.B. Carter's ayah*

Shindy not to leave her compound. She doesn't eat a lot of meat nowadays: just two eggs a day, a mild curry, occasional fish, and a wide variety of vegetables, especially peas, runner beans and broad beans. She loves the exotic garden, with its tropical and temperate plants, though rats gnaw her cabbages, and boys get up to all sorts of tricks, like stealing a rare black arum lily. Apart from enjoying her garden, she spends a lot of time reading, writing, sewing and knitting. 'As you leave, make sure Jane Mary shows you the burning bush!'

Next morning I strolled from Fernhill Palace Hotel down to the lakeside, above which I found George Carter's grave in the cemetery of St Thomas' Church, which could be any village church in Hants or Wilts, with 37 long wooden bench-pews, and windows set as if intended for stained glass which never arrived. St Stephen's (1829) is the oldest church in the district, its timbers having come from Tipu Sultan's Palace at Srirangapatnam. St Thomas' grimy exterior looks out on stunning views and graves evocative of imperial days: Daisy Spitteler died in 1977 at 89; the prolific Samson family, including George (d. 1987); a towering neo-Celtic cross to Rt. Hon. William Patrick Adam of Blair Adam, Governor at Madras who died in 1881 at 57. Inside the church, below its *infra dig* corrugated-iron roof, a board lists presbyters and missionaries who have served St Thomas' since 1874: their very surnames ring ecclesiastically: Paul, Barnabas, Samuel, Benjamin.

I had an appointment with Dr H.E. Eduljee, Vice-President of the Nilgiri Library, a subscription library organised in 1859, with a building designed by that well-known architect from Madras, R.F. Chisholm. The membership is restricted to 200, and there are 17 on the waiting-list. Every year a new library committee is elected, but very few new books are added; its wealth lies in the excellent collection of local South Indian literature: history, topography, folklore andd travel. The staff consists of three: Mr Raman Nair, Mr Francis, and a peon to go to the post office and bank. The main reading room has a churchy aroma of quiet mould, except for the newspapers and a handful of recent magazines. 'Papers must not be removed from the lectern' warns a notice. 'Mills and Boon romances are very popular among the ladies,' mused Dr Eduljee, 'then we have these *National Geographics*, and the *Encyclopaedia Britannica*.' The main library glows on its rosewood shelves with first editions of Trollope, standard works on the East India Company by Hunter, Elliott, Briggs and Smith, gazetteers of India, *Fauna of British India* and that obsession of the Victorians and Edwardians: hunting, shooting and fishing. The British view of India remains fossilised in this fascinating library.

What a contrast is the District Central Library, in the town centre, half of its stock in English and half in Tamil! 'Our motto in 1989 is to get free site for each and every library in Tamil Nadu.' It was full of Tamils reading newspapers in a barn-like room, but the books looked relatively unused, and there is a great gulf between the academic life and the rest of India. In 1966 the Collector of the Nilgiris suggested the amalgamation of the subscription library with the District Library, but in 1968 the Nilgiri Library eventually replied, 'I am directed to inform you that the members of the Committee have no wish to see this century-old private library merged with any other institution.' Thus was status quo preserved.

The most exclusive South Indian club outside Madras is the Ooty Club, built by a wealthy businessman from Hyderabad, Sir William Rumbold in 1831-2, rented by Lord Bentinck in 1834, and used as a hotel for five years up till 1841. In early 1842 a prospectus noted that 'the house as it now stands contains three elegant rooms, and bedroom accommodation for 11 resident members, all of the most substantial and comfortable description.' Sir Richard Burton, in his youthful *Goa and the Blue Mountains* (1851), related how 'The gay and gallant bachelors of Ootacamund entertained all the beauty and fashion of the station in the magnificent ballroom of the Club. The scene was a perfect galaxy of light and loveliness.'

Nowadays the lawns are just as beautifully kept as ever, the lounges just as sedulously cleaned, and the dining-room as well maintained, if the menus have changed to suit the changing tastes of the planting community. The four family suites, six double rooms and four singles remain in constant demand. Lt. Colonel I.P. Poovaiah (Retd.), of the Madras Regiment, is the resident manager, and the current President and Master of the Ootacamund Hunt is Vice-Admiral E.C. Kuruvilla. At St Thomas' I realised that the British devotion to God applied only to Sundays; the rest of the week was devoted to clubby activities like hunting and smoking, chatting and reading the papers. They served as administrators, and sweated if need be in the plains, but their heavy work was always meted out to the coolies, and when the British disappeared their neatly defined hierarchy was copied by the new Indian government, largely educated like themselves at public schools and the better class of varsity. Look at the Ooty Club's tell-tale reciprocal arrangements – with the Bengal Club, Calcutta, the Calcutta Club, the Poona Club, the Royal Bombay Yacht Club, and the Royal Overseas League in London. Look at the mania for weather records: rainfall received at Ooty Club *6.1.90* 0.6 of an inch; *7.1.90* 0.8 of an inch; *8.1.90* 0.8 of an inch. After Independence, the other Indian Hunts (Poona and Meerut) faded away, and only Ooty survives 'east of Suez' in the redolent phrase, kept going mainly by the Staff College at nearby Wellington. It was started in 1907, and the Governor in 1908 (Sir Arthur Lawley) duly won the Hunt Cup in a race over four miles. In 1910 the hounds hunted down a hyena, whose head still graces the Ooty

*Ootacamund. The Ooty Club. Main entrance*

Club. An *Ooty Almanac* memorably records how 'the hounds killed many pigs, and of course pigs killed many hounds.' A good time must have been had by some. The walls of Colonel Robert Jago's Room still groan under the weight of his innumerable hunting trophies. Jago acted as Master of the Hunt on and off from 1874 to 1887. The mixed Bar walls are lined with panels listing winners of the Peter Pan Cup, the Hunt Cup, the Ladies' Point-to-Point, and Ooty Hunt Races.

The billiard-room was opened for me by a discreet waiter. 'Excuse me, Sir, you from B.B.C.?' I disclaimed any such affiliation. 'B.B.C. man with camera came here ten years back.' I pulled back the brown cover from the baize and saw it: the table where snooker rules were first

103

applied. On the silent wall a framed letter from Col. Sir Neville Chamberlain, The Wilderness, Ascot testified in the words of J. Dunlop Watson, 'I was at Ooty, and a member of the Club there, where I frequently saw the game played and I have since then stated that you were the originator of the game', referring to the years 1882-4. Rival accounts claim that 'snooker' was played at Jabalpur in 1875, but the *rules* were probably first formulated at Ooty. During my silent visit nobody disturbed the slightly claustrophobic calm of the billiard room, with its prints, *Scotland for Ever!* and 'Napoleon in 1814 after Meissonnier', its three raised benches for spectators, its trophies of bear, gaur and tiger. The men's toilet has a swing-door of the Wild West variety; the ladies' cloakroom decked out in blue-green was fitted with three tables, mirrors, and a weighing-machine.

The British used to relax in Ooty for months, far away from the debilitating, sweltering plains, and I too felt like wandering far and wide around the peak of Dodabetta, to Kotagiri, and Mudumalai Sanctuary.

I found Ooty irresistible, as evocative in its way as Versailles or Regency Brighton, Karnak or the temple of Todaiji in Nara. Take for example the Gymkhana Club, with its eighteen-hole golf course, or 'Mr Brown's Assembly Rooms', the only venue large enough for society balls. The rooms were leased in 1873 for weekly concerts and the occasional amateur dramatics, serving on other days as a workshop for the maintenance and repair of horse carriages needed to transport Ooty's visitors. From 1902 to 1923 the Assembly Rooms became a police station, but then Lord Willingdon, Governor of Madras, acquired the land and extended the buildings as rooms for meetings and entertainment. In 1974, the Assembly Rooms, or Willingdon Hall, opposite the Lawley Institute, was turned into a cinema, but the foyer portraits of Lord and Lady Willingdon still waft their scent of comfortable patronage over expectant faces in the foyer gazing at movie posters of *Sphinx* with Lesley-Ann Down and *The Good, the Bad and the Ugly* with Clint Eastwood.

The best Chinese meal in Ooty is Shinkow's, at 42 Commissioner's Road, near the State Bank.

The hourly bus from Ooty to Kotagiri takes 1 hr 20 m to cover the 30 km across the Dodabetta-Snowdon col and down to Kotagiri, which is nevertheless higher and cooler than Coonoor. There's nowhere very special to stay in Kotagiri; I found the Ram Vihar Hotel cheap but acceptable, and anyway you spend all your time hiking with superb views of the Nilgiris at every fresh turn: Elk Falls and Catherine Falls are each about 7 km away and Kodanad a splendid taxi-ride 17 km away.

## Mudumalai Wildlife Sanctuary

If heading from Ooty to Mysore, make time for Mudumalai Wildlife
Sanctuary, for this – with Bandipur Reserve in neighbouring Karnataka
and Wynad in Kerala – is a reserve protecting not only the tiger but their
timid, gentle prey the jungle bison or gaur, whose head we have just
seen loppedd and mounted in the Ooty Club. Wild elephant roam
Mudumalai, which covers an area of 320 sq km at about 880 m a.s.l.
Some elephants sufficently tamed may be seen feeding at Theppakadu,
the reception centre where you can arrange accommodation at Sylvan
Lodge nearby, or in the Abhayaranyam Rest House in the village of the
same name. As usual, sightings are random, seasonal, and dependent on
good luck and good eyesight, as well as a knowledge of what you are
looking for, such as chital (spotted deer), wild pigs, and otters and
crocodiles. Sloth and panther are less frequently seen: don't go out
tiger-spotting at night! Buses between Ooty and Mysore will set you
down in the sanctuary, and the Wildlife Warden, Coonoor Road, Ooty
or Tamil Nadu Tourist Offices will book you advance accommodation
there, though it is more difficult to find rooms from January to April,
the most popular time. Avoid the rains in mid-October to mid-
December. The easiest way to see Mudumalai is on a guided tour out of
Ooty, but again you have to be fortunate in the moist deciduous forest
to glimpse the bonnet macaque monkeys, though they are tame enough
in the surrounding villages, and the darkfaced Nilgiri langur with its
whiteish ruffle. Watch out for crocodiles in the streams now cleverly
made permanent by astute management; you might even glimpse the
bat-eared Indian giant squirrel. If animals vanish at your approach,
console yourself with the sumptuous views as sunbeams illuminate spir-
als of gnats at their unwitting choreography or the penetrating scream of
peafowl.

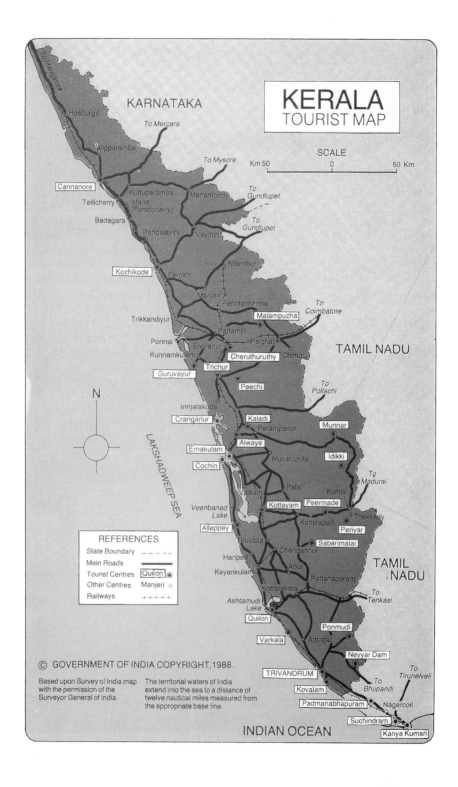

# KERALA
## TOURIST MAP

SCALE

Km 50     0       50 Km

KARNATAKA

To Mangalore

Hosdurga
Valipparamba
To Mercara
To Mysore
Cannanore
Kuttuparamba
Manantoddy
To Gundlupet
Tellicherry
Mahe
(Pondicherry)
Badagara
Pandalayini
Vayittiri
To Gundlupet
Kozhikode
Ferokh
Nilambur
Manjeri
Perintalmanna
To Coimbatore
Trikkandiyur
Pattambi
Malampuzha
Ponnai
Shoranur
Palghat
TAMIL NADU
Kunnamkulam
Cheruthuruthy
Chittur
Guruvayur
Trichur
Peechi
To Pollachi
Irinjalakuda
Cranganur
Kaladi
Perampavur
Munnar
Ernakulam
Alwaye
Muvatupula
Idikki
Cochin
To Madurai
Vaikam
Palai
Kumili
Veenbanad Lake
Kottayam
Peermade
Thekkady
Alleppey
Kanjirapaili
Periyar
Tiruvalla
Sabarimalai
Haripad
Chengannur
TAMIL NADU
Kayankulam
Adur
Pattanapuram
Kottarakara
To Tenkasi
Ashtamudi Lake
Quilon
Ponmudi
Varkala
Attingal
Neyyar Dam
To Tirunelveli
TRIVANDRUM
Kovalam
Bhupandi
Padmanabhapuram
Nagercoil
Suchindram
Kanya Kumari

LAKSHADWEEP SEA

N

## REFERENCES

| | |
|---|---|
| State Boundary | – – – – |
| Main Roads | |
| Tourist Centres | Quilon ⊙ |
| Other Centres | Manjeri ○ |
| Railways | +++++ |

© GOVERNMENT OF INDIA COPYRIGHT, 1988.

Based upon Survey of India map with the permission of the Surveyor General of India.

The territorial waters of India extend into the sea to a distance of twelve nautical miles measured from the appropriate base line.

INDIAN OCEAN

# II: KERALA: ALONG THE WATERS OF PARADISE

The southwesternmost state of India appears on the map to be escaping towards the Laccadive Islands in the Arabian Sea. It clusters in a narrow strip often narrower than a hundred kilometres from Western Ghats to palmfringed coastline, with a climate at once tropical, in the rice-planted plains, and temperate, in the tea-planted hills. The Anamudi peak in the High Ranges of Kottayam soars to 8,841 ft a.s.l., the highest point in India south of Himalaya. Between the coconut-palm lowlands and the dense forests of the highlands, Kerala possesses an intermediate landscape producing spices, cashew nuts, rice and tapioca.

After the neatness of Vermont or Sussex, the luxuriance of Kerala seems scandalous, as though a Puritan Sunday painter had suddenly let go, and emulated the Gauguin of Tahiti. But then Gauguin's flat colours are also wrong: there is nothing in art or literature to match the sheer exuberance of these coco-palms in deep grove after deep grove, these shimmering rice-fields, these banyans larger than life and twice as holy, these flowers shouting their colours in a tumult of effervescent joy. We are scandalised because the fruits of our northern soil are so worn-out, but Kerala coconuts are there just for the picking, Kerala flowers need no tending: the reckless sunlight spreads its preponderance over the land like a prince showering gold coins among the multitude. There is a prodigality in Kerala which in the west we know only in grand opera: *L'Africaine* of Meyerbeer, or the ardent panoply of Verdi's *Aida*.

Many scholars have declared dogmatically that Kerala's great distance from north Indian cities have left it culturally insulated; their opponents point to conquests by powers dominant in areas occupied by Tamil-speaking and Kannada-speaking populations. Neither school must be allowed to pass unchallenged. Polyandry and matrilineal inheritance are distinctively Keralan, but the customs of north Kerala show Kannada influences, while those of the south display Tamil traits. It is true that Aryan ideas, Buddhism and Jainism took longer to penetrate Kerala than elsewhere, but Christianity affected Kerala before the rest of India, and several Hindu temples to Sri Minakshi prove the impact of Madurai's religious cult. The Mughals of North India never tamed Kerala, but in early times Kerala was invaded by armies of Chalukyas, Rashtrakutas, Pandyas and Cholas, and in later times Vijayanagar and

Mysore rulers took up arms to subdue Kerala. Malayalam has become the literary vehicle of Kerala, but in its northern dialect it shows traces of Kannada; in its southern dialect hints of Tamil. The Jews of Cochin-Ernakulam have proved more tenacious than elsewhere in South India; St Thomas' Catholic Church atop Malavattur Hill in the taluq of Alwaye, near Ernakulam, is one of the most important centres of Christian pilgrimage in South India, corresponding to St Thomas' Mount outside Madras, yet it lies not far from Kaladi, birthplace of the great Hindu philosopher Shankacharya (788-838), whose Vedanta commentaries enriched Hinduism as the works of St Thomas Aquinas enriched mediaeval Christianity.

But perhaps everyone travelling in Kerala will remember it for the lapping of waters, from the lake at Periyar to the waves on the shore at Kovalam; from the preponderantly westward-flowing rivers (all forty-one of them!) to the three eastward-flowing tributaries of the great Kaveri; from the backwaters linking Alleppey and Quilon, to the busy harbour of Cochin; from the landfall of Vasco da Gama in 1498 at Calicut, to the European forts at Tellicherry or Cannanore. Only the flooding of the Periyar in 1789, after all, prevented the onward march of Tipu Sultan's armies towards Travancore.

Known from antiquity as the land of ivory and monkeys, peacocks and cardamom, cinnamon and ginger, Kerala achieved its greatest affluence exporting teak from its forests and the pepper that would be known there as 'black gold'. The Romans gladly offered gold for pearls and diamonds from Kerala. The Portuguese, Dutch, French and English paid almost any price, including life and limb, for pepper to flavour their food.

Overpopulation remains the chief economic problem facing Kerala, Hindus being reluctant to practise birth control, and Syrian and Catholic Christians theologically bound not to do so. Few major industries are attracted to distant Kerala and, though food may seem abundant, most families are locked within the poverty cycle despite their celebrated enthusiasm for education at all levels. Even many of the best graduates cannot find suitable employment, and migrate to Indian cities already overburdened, or emigrate as remittance men to the Arabian Peninsula, where their mastery of English serves them well in business and industry.

### Early Kerala

The British described Kerala as the Malabar Coast, so it is worth unearthing the origin of these names. Gundert's Malayalam dictionary derives Keralam as 'Cheram', the land of the Chera people, living between Gokarnam and Kumari. As to Malabar, *mala* means 'hill' and

Malavaram denotes the hilly country, or Malanadu, as the area was known in mediaeval Tamil. The Arab writer al-Biruni called the area Malabar as early as the eleventh century. Our knowledge of Keralan history is severely hampered by the lack of early annalists, for the compilations called *Keralolpathi* (in Malayalam) and *Keralamahatmyam* (in Sanskrit) can be dated by internal evidence to the British period. We can thus only piece together the story of Kerala from the archaeological record, and from literary sources in Malayalam, Sanskrit and Tamil. Malayalam broke off from its parent Tamil in the 9th century, but the first extant records of historical significance do not predate the 12th; they are suspect because they tend to eulogise ruling patrons, but incidentally they shed light on men, manners and places. Thus, the ballad of Iravikutti Pillai describes his courageous stand against Tirumala Nayak and his death at the battle of Kaniyakulam in 1634: it is reminiscent of the *Chanson de Roland*, perhaps, or the *Cantar del mio Cid* of mediaeval Europe.

In the 4th century B.C. the Greek envoy Megasthenes touches on the Chera kingdom; Pliny, Ptolemy, and the author of the *Periplus* in the 1st century B.C. refer to the ports of Malabar, such as Muziris (Kodungallur or Cranganore) and Kalaikaris (Kozhikode or Calicut). The Byzantine author Cosmas Indicopleustes (6th century) provides the first definite evidence of Christian worship in Kerala. The 15th-century Chinese Muslim Ma Huan relates the wonders of Cochin during his journey to India, and dilates on the bustling entrepôt that was Calicut. Ibn Battuta visited Calicut several times in the 14th century, and describes Quilon as 'one of the finest cities in Malabar with magnificent markets and wealthy merchants', standing amazed at the pepper trade and the great Chinese junks berthed in the dock.

If you wanted proof of the legendary toleration shown by the Keralan people to those of other races, faiths and nationalities, you could select any number of instances. There is the case of John of Monte Corvino, one of the first recorded Roman Catholic missionaries to China, who became first Archbishop of Peking. At the end of the 13th century he touched at Quilon, where he found Chinese, Christian and Jewish traders with a steadily increasing number of Muslims. Then, near Parur (between Alwaye and Cranganore), you enjoy the mindboggling spectacle in Kottai-Kovikalam (Chennamangalam) of a single compound providing hospitality to a Hindu temple, a Christian Church, a mosque and a synagogue.

Of course the indigenous religion of Kerala was the same animism informing the whole of India prior to its selective absorption and subtle transmutation into Hinduism. Totems and ancestor worship, tree worship (especially the banyan) and fertility rites all played a major rôle in the relationship of early Dravidian man to his milieu. Such universality

109

of awe enabled them to welcome fresh gods and fresh beliefs from Vedic sacrifice to Jain practices, from Buddhist rites to Christian worship without any feeling of conflict or paradox; my own view is that this instinctive pluralism derives in part from matrilineal dominance: the emphasis on what is gentle and enduring rather than aggressive, divisive, transient political advantage, though there is no shortage of political difference and debate. Katalamma, sea goddess, is never very far from coastal Keralan mind and attitudes, and underlies the classic Malayalam novel *Chemmeen* (1956) by Thakazhi Sivasankara Pillai, translated into many languages including English.

Pillai's own home might be seen as a microcosm of Keralan culture; he was named for his native village Thakazhi, 16 km south of Alleppey and came from a family involved variously in farming, scholarship, and the Kathakali dance drama, marrying a deep love of Sanskrit literature with the indigenous arts of Kerala. As a boy, Thakazhi would listen to his father reading at night from the *Mahabharata* (recently filmed in 91 television episodes of such popularity that India virtually comes to a standstill whenever an episode is transmitted) and the shorter and more popular *Ramayana* and by day go to school in the heart of the fishing community. He trained as a lawyer in Trivandrum, thus coming into contact with city life and the National Movement for Independence, and read widely in French and English authors, as well as Marx and Freud. Comfortable bourgeois literature of the time was invigorated by Thakazhi's new working-class stories and novels with a realistic approach, to be tempered in *Chemmeen* by romantic and superstitious elements more in keeping with the rural Malayali temperament.

The Cheras who gave Kerala its name cannot be traced to their origins; we merely know that the first Chera dynasty to rule as such was founded about 130 A.D. and traded with the Roman Empire for its lifetime of about a century, occupying a vast territory known from inscriptions near Karur in the Trichinopoly district to have incorporated parts of present-day Tamil Nadu, including for some time Salem and Coimbatore districts. Their contemporaries were the Pandyas in southern Tamil Nadu and the Cholas farther north. It is from this time that the southern Keralan cave temples date. Chera power seems to have fluctuated and weakened till the eighth century, when the second great dynasty was formed, beginning with Kulasekharavarman (*c.* 800), until 1102. Contemporaries of the second Chera dynasty were the Pallavas of Kanchi and the Pandyas of Madurai. This is a period of political stability and economic vigour, with the revival of international maritime trade, especially with China and the Muslim world. The Cholas, envying this prosperity, launched attacks on Kerala during the reigns of Rajaraja I (985-1016) and his son Rajendra (1012-44) but the so-called 'Hundred Years' War of Kerala' that ensued merely fragmented Kerala, rather than destroying it, and one of these fragments actually survived independently (as the State of Travancore) until as recently as 1956.

With the growing demand for spices and other tropical products in the interior, the ports of Malabar rose to eminence, but unevenly. Calicut, before the arrival of the Portuguese in 1498, was ruled by a so-called Zamorin, probably a Malayalam corruption of the Sanskrit word for sea, still used in the Indonesian *samudera*. It was he who controlled the traffic in ginger and cardamom, pepper and cinnamon for which Europe and the Arab World would pay so dearly. Lesser rajahs occupied Quilon (the Kulasekharas, from 1102) and Cannanore (the Kolatiri line). They felt threatened by the Zamorin of Calicut, and with the rise of Cochin in the fifteenth century, Calicut found itself isolated by the alliance of Cochin and Cannanore with the Portuguese. The Zamorin naturally sought alliance with the Arabs against the Portuguese, a conflict by land and sea which continued throughout the 16th century. Then the Zamorin made a treaty with the Dutch in 1604, and a similar accord with the British in 1615, hoping to use one foreign devil to oust another. By 1663 the Dutch had conquered the Portuguese strongholds protecting the harbours of Quilon, Purakkad (near Alleppey), Cochin, Cranganore and Cannanore, thus effectively removing Portuguese control from Kerala. Invaders from the interior threatened Kerala thereafter, but the British threat to Mysore in the 1780s demanded that Tipu Sultan return from his aggrandisement and annexation plans in Kerala, and he abandoned plans to seize Travancore, gradually releasing his hold on other Malabar towns to the British, whose control by direct rule began in 1800 and continued until 1956, when the new state incorporated with British Malabar and Cochin the former State of Travancore and a part of the former district of South Kannara, Karnataka.

The greatest concentration of Shaivite cave temples can be found northwest of Kaniya Kumari in modern Tamil Nadu just across from the Kerala border, but the finest rock-cut temple in Kerala proper can be seen at Kaviyur, a site inland from Alleppey well worth visiting, not only for the small pre-950 shrine, but also for the Mahadeva Temple of the 8th century restored in the 18th. The former comprises an ardha mandapam, pillared façade and lingam shrine all facing west. Figures include dvarapalas or guardians, a standing chieftain probably to be identified with the donor, a bearded sage or *rishi*, and a seated four-armed Ganesha. The latter, located 1 km away, is a monumental temple with a square shrine with lingam contained in a circular mandapam. Typically for Kerala, the shrine walls are of stone, and the circular mandapam of wood, with carvings in high relief, nearly in the round: these are of the later 18th-century period; beyond the temple proper a mandapam has a nine-panelled ceiling elaborately carved with divinities, while dancers and musicians cavort nimbly on the brackets.

111

It is their timber components which endangered the longevity of Keralan temples; if they were not replaced by later stone structures, even the best workmanship would perish, often several times. This explains the paucity of early Keralan temples, before 1000 A.D. Sloping roofs found in Himalayan temples against heavy rains are needed here in tropical Kerala for the same reason. Keralan temples in the middle phase, ending around 1300, are characterised by a new type of shrine with an internal circumambulatory passage called a *sandhara*, its sanctum becoming a separate building with its own superstructure and flight of steps: we have arrived at the Dravidian-Keralan temple style which certain scholars attribute to immigrant architects from Sri Lanka influenced by circular Buddhist temples. A typical middle-phase temple is the Shaivite temple of Tirunillai, near Palghat, which you can explore as a stop on the route between Trichur and Coimbatore. Within a complex now ruined, the brick-built sanctum (or *garbhagriha*) on a circular stone plinth has been made into a square internally. Compare this with Trichur's Vadakkunnatha *garbhagriha* in the temple of the same name, dated to the 12th century.

But of course most Keralan temples date to the Late Period, after 1300, even if constructed on an existing site, as at Trichur, and they rapidly evolve into temple compounds with main shrines, ambulatory pavements, cloisters, a lamp-house with its lamps, and a main votive platform or *balipitha* in front of the temple.

Interestingly, the spread of Islam on the Malabar coast seems to have produced very little distinguished architecture: by comparison with the supreme Mughal mosques in Agra, Delhi, or Fatehpur Sikri, Kerala's humdrum examples appear as crestfallen in style as they are numerous, a typical example being the two-storey edifice at Cranganore and the Mithqal mosque at Calicut. These reflect the Arab instinct for simplicity and humility, as seen in Najd and Oman, rather than the Iranian adoration of the complex, polychrome and grandiose, as seen in Isfahan or Tabriz.

### Kovalam

Many visitors, surprisingly, seem to obtain nothing more substantial from a visit to Kerala than the sand slipping between their fingers and toes at Kovalam Beach, admittedly as close to the waters of Paradise as you are likely to reach on the subcontinent. Take care when swimming because the undertow is deceptively dangerous, though the surface may seem as tranquil as it is blue. One bay after another, each palm-fringed and sunsoaked, will lure you to stay longer: the worst period for storms is the monsoon from June through August.

A curious feature of the Malabar Coast is the strange and unmistakeably separate identity of each coastal town or village: you could not confuse Quilon with neighbouring Tangasseri or Ambalapulai with Alleppey. It is as though each were an island, like those dotting the scratched and splintered coastline of Dalmatia. Kovalam has developed into a highly popular resort – some might think now too popular – with numbers of Indian men congregating as they do on Goan beaches to ogle the foreign girls. ITDC's Beach Resort designed by Charles Correa on the seaward side of the bus station is the most expensive place in Kovalam, and gives you a measure of privacy. I have enjoyed the Sea Rock Lodge, close to the beach, and the Blue Sea (with an attractive garden) on the Trivandrum Road, but there is a wide range of accommodation at the cheaper end of the spectrum which can be rented by the day, week, or month. A bronzed German family staying at the Hotel Orion had booked their room for the whole winter, and intended to do the same every winter. Uneven rocks, slippery paths and the sudden onset of night demand that you take a torch to avoid nasty falls: septicaemia could always become dangerous in the tropics.

From Kovalam Beach to Trivandrum town a combined taxi departs when full; even cheaper is bus no. 15 to the Fort bus stand.

## Trivandrum

Trivandrum is the capital of the former princely state of Travancore, and seems to participate only vaguely in the modern state of India, dreaming of its illustrious royal past in noonday heat casting a white glow. Travancore printed its own stamps, minted its own coinage of twenty-eight chakrams to the rupee, maintained its own solar time twenty-two and a half minutes slower than the rest of India, and started every year in August. I felt like Robinson Crusoe stranded on dry land. The Maharajas of Travancore (again legend neatly supplants any flailing attempt at history) are said to descend from Muna, explaining the matriarchal system of inheritance by which the heir to the throne was the eldest son of the Maharaja's sister.

For shopping, Mahatma Gandhi Road has Higginbotham's Bookshop, and such antique dealers as the Gift Corner and Natesan's. A Queenslander compared Trivandrum's town plan to most Australian provincial towns, with one main street, which is somewhat like comparing Pondicherry's town plan to Manhattan's. The Indian experience is overwhelming, with a rage of colour and hubbub washing over you at every street corner.

Covetable textiles include white cotton, with elaborate lungis and dhotis which you would dearly like to venture to wear in tropical Kerala, radiant silks, fashionable saris and handwoven textiles of rare beauty. I found a temporary bazaar set up by the local weaving society to market their wares direct to consumers. Sandalwood and rosewood carvings may be unmanageable on your flight home, but brasswork, lacquerware,

113

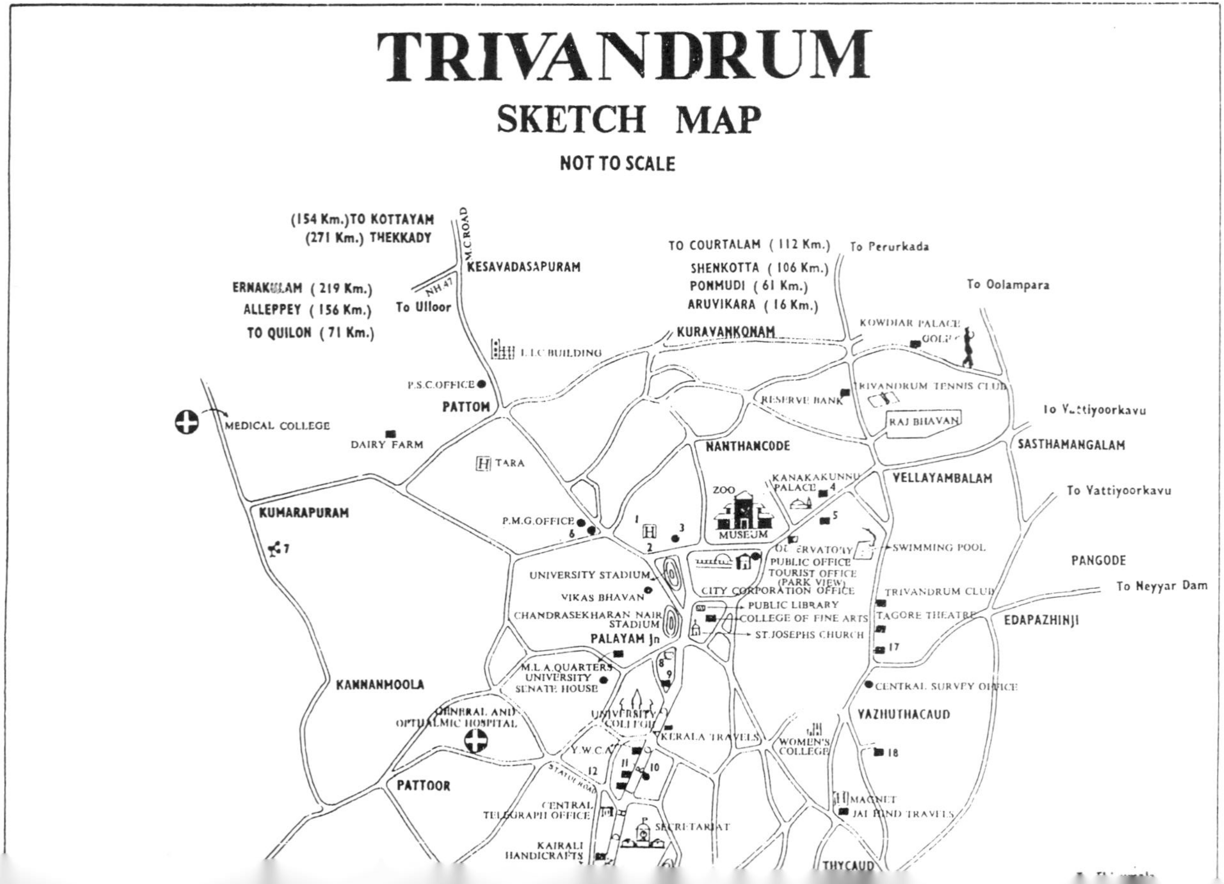
TRIVANDRUM
SKETCH MAP
NOT TO SCALE
(154 Km.) TO KOTTAYAM
(271 Km.) THEKKADY
ERNAKULAM ( 219 Km.)
ALLEPPEY ( 156 Km.)
TO QUILON ( 71 Km.)
To Ulloor
NH 47
M.C.ROAD
KESAVADASAPURAM
TO COURTALAM ( 112 Km.)
SHENKOTTA ( 106 Km.)
PONMUDI ( 61 Km.)
ARUVIKARA ( 16 Km.)
To Perurkada
To Oolampara
KURAVANKONAM
KOWDIAR PALACE
L.I.C BUILDING
P.S.C.OFFICE
PATTOM
RESERVE BANK
TRIVANDRUM TENNIS CLUB
RAJ BHAVAN
To Vattiyoorkavu
SASTHAMANGALAM
MEDICAL COLLEGE
DAIRY FARM
TARA
NANTHANCODE
KANAKAKUNNU PALACE
VELLAYAMBALAM
To Vattiyoorkavu
ZOO
MUSEUM
KUMARAPURAM
P.M.G.OFFICE
SWIMMING POOL
PUBLIC OFFICE
TOURIST OFFICE
(PARK VIEW)
CITY CORPORATION OFFICE
PANGODE
To Neyyar Dam
UNIVERSITY STADIUM
VIKAS BHAVAN
TRIVANDRUM CLUB
PUBLIC LIBRARY
CHANDRASEKHARAN NAIR STADIUM
COLLEGE OF FINE ARTS
TAGORE THEATRE
EDAPAZHINJI
ST.JOSEPHS CHURCH
PALAYAM Jn
M.L.A.QUARTERS
UNIVERSITY SENATE HOUSE
CENTRAL SURVEY OFFICE
KANNANMOOLA
VAZHUTHACAUD
UNIVERSITY COLLEGE
KERALA TRAVELS
WOMEN'S COLLEGE
Y.W.C.A
PATTOOR
CENTRAL TELEGRAPH OFFICE
MAGNET
JAI HIND TRAVELS
SECRETARIAT
KAIRALI HANDICRAFTS
THYCAUD

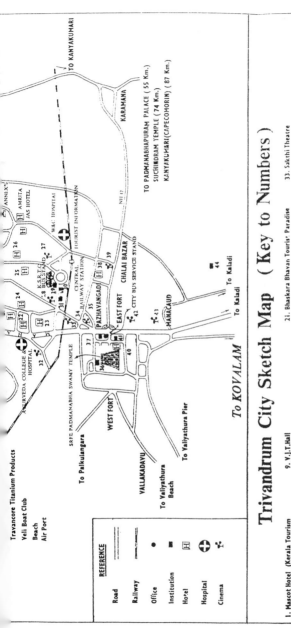

Travancore Titanium Products
Veli Boat Club
Beach
Air Port

TO KANYAKUMARI

KARAMANA

TO PADMANABHAPURAM PALACE ( 55 Km.)
SUCHINDRAM TEMPLE ( 74 Km.)
KANYAKUMARI(CAPECOMORIN) ( 87 Km.)

ANNEX
AMRITA
JAS HOTEL

WAC HOSPITAL
TOURIST INFORMATION

CENTRAL
RAILWAY STATION

K.S.R.T.C.
BUS STAND

CHALAI BAZAR

CITY BUS SERVICE STAND

PAZHAVANGADI
EAST FORT

AYURVEDA COLLEGE &
HOSPITAL

SRFE PADMANABHA SWAMY TEMPLE

WEST FORT

To Palkulangara

VALLAKADAVU

To Valiyathura
Beach

To Valiyathura Pier

MANACAUD

To Kaladi

To KOVALAM

# Trivandrum City Sketch Map ( Key to Numbers )

| | | |
|---|---|---|
| 1. Mascot Hotel  (Kerala Tourism Development Corporation) | 9. V.J.T.Hall | 21. Bhaskara Bhavan Tourist Paradise | 33. Sakthi Theatre |
| 2. AIrIndia | 10. Accountant General's Office | 22. Baba Tourist Home | 34. Ajantha Theatre |
| 3. Indian Airlines  Booking Office | 11. State Bank of India | 23. Sivada Tourist Home | 35. Central Theatre |
| TOURIST INFORMATION OFFICE (Park View) | 12. State Bank of Travancore | 2A. Sunder Tourist Home | 36. Varma Travels |
| 4. Jawahar Balabhavan | 13. Central Stadium | 25. Keerthi Hotel | 37. Ganapathi Temple,Pazhavangadi |
| 5. Handicrafts Research-cum-Design Centre | 14. Trivandrum Hotel | 26. Paramount Tourist Home | 38. Gandhi Hotel Chalai |
| 6. Foreign Registration Office | 15. Y.M.C.A.& British Council Library | 27. New Theatre | 39. Chitra Theatre |
| 7. Simi Theatre | 16. S.M.S.M. Handicrafts | 28. Sreekumar Theatre | 40. Rajadhani Hotel |
| 8. Mosque,Palayam | 17. Srimulam Club | 29. Tourist Information | 41. Karthika Tirunal Theatre |
| | 18. Yoga Centre | 30. Corporation Rest House | 42. Sree Padmanabha Theatre |
| | 19. Guest House Complex | 31. R.M.S | 43. M.P. Theatre |
| | 20. Antiquarts(Handicrafts) | 32. Sreekanth&Kasturi Theatre | 44. Attukal Bhagavathi Temple |

REFERENCE

Road
Railway
Office
Institution
Hotel
Hospital
Cinema

wooden toys and Kathakali masks all invite inspection.

Trivandrum's charming red-tiled roofs and winding lanes are reminiscent of Old Panjim in Goa: in each, a local administrative headquarters bred discreet mansions for those involved in business of the court, and diplomatic residence. The headquarters of the Travancore Government demanded a comparable residence for the British Resident for Travancore and Cochin, a military government, and a civil service, with offices in the former Maharaja's Palace, which is within comfortable walking distance of the Napier Museum (1880), Sri Chitra Art Gallery, and Botanical Gardens. Two rooms in the palace are open to visitors.

The city's name derives from three Malayalam words: 'thiru' meaning holy; 'ananta' meaning the infinite, often applied to Vishnu or his couch and canopy the Naga King, who causes earthquakes every time he yawns; and 'puram' or city, hence 'City Sacred to Lord Vishnu'. The mother temple, within the fort, is consequently that of Sri Padmanabhaswami or Anantasayanam, an incarnation of Lord Vishnu. Doubly unluckily, this temple has been totally renewed in the last two hundred years and, even had it survived in its original form, non-Hindus are prohibited entrance. I found it disconcerting to see even Hindus stopped by the gate and made to change into a new dhoti, which reminded me of the ceremonial garb enjoined on Muslims at Makkah al-Mukarrimah. Legend is convinced that around 200 B.C. there was a Buddhist stupa on this site; unfortunately we shall never know, as living Hindu temples are not excavated. I rely on Srinivasan's standard *Temples of South India* for the information that the central stone-built two-storey shrine is oblong in plan to display the reclining image of Lord Vishnu, the eastern gopuram and open-pillared mandapam are in Tamil Nadu style, and a subsidiary entrance north of the gopuram has a Kerala-style gabled roof and a parrot-beak entrance, to give the projected arched opening its usual Keralan designation.

The bus stand opposite the Vishnu temple is only local; for long-distance buses there is a stand near the rail station which cannot be recommended for the faint-hearted. Scrapping for seats require several weeks of commando-style training-camp, for diplomacy and tact have no place here, and only a slight benefit may accrue if you have acquired a 'priority ticket'. The ticket-vendors understand English but there are no signs to help you except in Malayalam. Long-distance buses to Madras or Mysore or Thekkady (for Periyar Wildlife Sanctuary) are an authentic Indian experience similar to long immersion in a hot bath with seventy strangers who believe in the saving grace of decibels from tapes, horns and shouting as loud as possible. The drowsy backwaters of Kerala seem a million miles away even as you drive parallel to them. So if you intend to get to Cochin, step off the bus after a couple of hours at Quilon and take the ferry. Rail buffs will miss a lot on the line running

116

north to Mangalore via Ernakulam or east to Tuticorin via Nagarcoil and Tirunelveli. Those in a hurry will want to know that Trivandrum Airport links with Sri Lanka, the Maldives, Cochin, Goa, Bombay, Delhi, Trichy and Madras. The small aquarium (closed on Mondays) is situated near the airport, accessible on a 14 bus.

The best bazaar for keen photographers and shoppers overflows into all the side streets near the rail station, and cannot be overpraised for its spicy aromas, fantastic colours, and a spiral and plume of extraordinary noise which ebbs and flows but never stops. An Arts and Crafts Emporium lies behind the southeast corner of the Secretariat, halfway along Gandhi Road. Proceeding north along Gandhi Road you pass the Indian Coffee House, the Victoria Jubilee Town Hall, a mosque, St Joseph's Church, and finally the Napier Museum.

The Napier Museum, by Robert Fellowes Chisholm, has been quietly renamed the Government Art Museum, but give the British their due: this extravaganza could never have been built without the example of Regency Brighton as well as the Kerala-Chinese connection in architectural eclecticism, and even a quick nod to Mughal style. Colour as the key to Kerala infects the museum with its rainbow mimicry: yellow arches, yellow and red stripes, pastel pink and pastel blue declaring an unashamed delight in banter. The Sri Chitra Art Gallery displays highlights of the former Travancore royal collections, with Mughal and Rajasthani paintings, 19th-century Bengali pictures, folk-art from Tanjore, and works by the ever-popular but overrated Raja Ravi Varma, whose portraits manage to convey neither artistic integrity nor a feeling of documentary accuracy. (This is lèse-majesté in Kerala, like deflating Sibelius' reputation in Finland, but when the emperor has no new clothes I fear I cannot admire them.) Powerful bronze guardians of the 17th century make a lasting impression, as do the lifesize figures of Kathakali dancers, who perform at the Kovalam Ashok several times a week if you cannot see a performance in Trivandrum itself. Well over a hundred Malayalam films a year are made in Trivandrum, which says more about quantity than quality: there seems to be no end to public demand for the formula of singing, dancing and overacting that coins millions or rupees every year. The pap that keeps the public entertained can possibly be justified for its employment value in keeping three hundred thousand Indians in jobs, but the 150-odd Tamil films made in Madras, the 170-odd Telugu films made in Hyderabad, and the 180-odd Hindi films vastly outnumber the few works of lasting value by world-class directors such as Satyajit Ray, Shyam Benegal, Mrinal Sen, Adoor Gopalakrishnan and Ketan Mehta. I cannot really recommend that you spend a couple of hours in a darkened cinema with all of India passing like a kaleidoscope under the glittering sun outside; masterpieces of the Indian cinema are for when you return home.

There is no point whatsoever in joining a city tour, because the visit to the Vishnu Temple is for Hindus only, the visit to Kovalam Beach is much better enjoyed in more leisurely fashion, and the same applies to the museum, art gallery and botanical gardens. Even less can I recommend the two-day tour to Periyar out of Trivandrum, since that offers too little time at Periyar, and the route back is identical. Go there on a single trip, stay as long as you like, then pursue your itinerary from there. I do however strongly recommend aimless wandering in the lanes and thoroughfares of the city, where you will be invited to see coir products being made from coconut husk fibre, offered a chance to see weavers at work, gaze at rosewood carvers crosslegged or crouching intent on their work in darkened rooms suddenly bannerlit by the sun, and examine a vast choice of the gold and silver jewellery that makes a princess of any burnished Indian woman it adorns. 'You are welcome', is the constant greeting, and exuberant colours make houses and even offices alive with green, red, yellow and blue made brighter by the substantial hours of light, then flickering candles and neon bulbs. Flowers twined into the hair of girls suggest a poignant commentary on their passing youth. If you're so captivated by Trivandrum and Kovalam that you need to stay here instead of continuing your trip (a perennial temptation in India that I suffered at Ooty, Vellore, Madurai, Chidambaram, and Halebid), a couple of days could be spent at Ponmudi ('Golden Peak'), a hill-station 70 km northeast of Trivandrum in the Western Ghats. Ponmudi is inhabited by the Kanikar hill-tribe, once nomadic cultivators of rice and tobacco. The guest-house at Ponmudi has 24 rooms, and there are ten small stone cottages for families, all bookable direct to Ponmudi or through Kerala Department of Tourism office: that in Trivandrum is situated opposite the Napier Museum.

## Quilon and the Waterways
I took the Cochin bus next morning along Highway 47, and after a couple of deafening hours, in which our bus driver failed despite all his heroic efforts to stun or maim all yoked oxen on either side of the road, alighted gratefully into the mid-morning hullabaloo at Quilon bus stand.

Quilon is a Portuguese form of the abbreviation 'Kollam', deriving probably from 'Kovilagam', meaning 'House of the King' or 'Royal Palace' from its ancient dignity as a principal port of Malabar. In 1343, the great Arab traveller Ibn Battuta reached Quilon ten days after leaving Calicut. 'The city of Kaulam is one of the finest in Malabar', he noted. 'Its bazaars are splendid and its merchants are known as Sali. They are so rich that one of them may buy a ship with all its fittings and fill it with goods from his own warehouse.' Though clearly not the first of the kings after whom the town was named, King Ramavarma Kulasekhara moved to Quilon from Cranganore in 1102, and the name

Kulasekhara was preserved as a dynastic name among later rulers of Travancore until the last Maharaja surrendered his claims to the nation in 1949.

Quilon has given up all majesty and grandeur these days: it has gradually relaxed as a characteristic Keralan town of 15,000 which seems smaller because the population is spread over a relatively wide area.

The Arabs and Chinese traded with and through Quilon, and the Romans are likely to have come here too though we have no evidence proving that assumption. It is probable, on the other hand, that three Syrian Christian missionaries were permitted to build a church by King Chakravarti in 823. The Chinese knew the town as Kiu-Lan, for in the 1280s it sent an ambassador to the Mongol Court to present precious gifts and a black monkey. The Portuguese opened a factory in 1503 and defended it by a fort called St Thomas you can still see in ruins 3 km north at Tangasseri. A mournful bell-tower presides over the Protestant cemetery. The Dutch chased out the Portuguese in 1653, and then Quilon fell into the hands of the British, who founded their usual Gymkhana Club, Social Club, Memorial Club, and free reading-room. The Maharaja's Palace, the Thavalli, stands on a promontory overlooking Ashtamudi Lake on the bank facing the former British Residency, now an eight-room guest-house which can be booked through the tourist offices in Alleppey or Trivandrum. The grand residency is two centuries old, and the flavour is dusty-nostalgic, the view 'a living map of emeralds' as Emily Eden might have described it if she had lived in the south instead of the north. Chinese-style fishing nets on the lake resemble those at Cochin. Local industries include coircraft, silversmithing, cotton-weaving, lacemaking and fish-curing; the leading products are aluminium, cashew nuts, coconuts and their derivatives. Don't miss the daily market of fruit, flowers and vegetables.

In the months of Meenam-Mesham (March to May), traditional religious festivals involving mock-horse shows are held at Trikadavur and Mulankadavu. This is the period, too, of festivals in Quilon at the temples to Lord Shiva and Lord Krishna; if you miss these there is a Lord Vishnu Temple festival at Mukuthalay, about 8 km from the rail station, but then India is a perennially vibrant festival for the senses even if no specific celebrations are in progress.

Wandering in Keralan towns like Trivandrum and Quilon makes a unique experience: equally extraordinary in its different way is the ferry leaving Quilon at 9.45 a.m., chugging through the backwaters with numerous stops (and you *can* get off for drinks and toilet intervals!) to reach Alleppey around nine hours later. Of course it is possible to make shorter backwater trips from Quilon, such as that to Guhanantapuram, but I recommend total absorption in the Keralan experience, a long tropical Venice, talking to students and office-workers, and observing the schoolchildren in their smart uniforms 'commuting' to school in a way that they find entirely normal but we consider ineffably romantic. The boat is not comfortable, so bring a cushion; there is no food service aboard, so bring a bottle of mineral water, bread and bananas. Then the adventure can begin. In my case I was surprised to see the captain drop a lighted match on the cabin floor, but I trusted like any Hindu in my ineluctable destiny and the match sputtered wispy-grey then black. My travelling companions found me of surpassing fascination, touching my white skin as if it were talismanic and uttering English words as if – and this might one day be the case – they were their open sesame to a starry career in business or commerce. A red-tiled white church shimmered up from its reflection in the waters; we puttered from narrow canal to widening lake. Old women impossibly burdened with vegetables made the boat rock as if Moby Dick were nosing it abaft. I felt guiltily worried for a couple of Norwegians trusting to the boat's roof. Palms leaned out of the wind, their branches shady umbrellas over the straggling villages, with waffling pigs, scratching chickens, and shouting brown infants as kin to the water as mermaids.

Dugouts with sails unfurled cruised past like a fleet carrying Marco Polo himself, who tells us that the waters of Keralan rivers were hot enough to boil an egg. Marco travelled in Kerala in the late 13th century, and clearly enjoyed his time on the Malabar Coast, taking in good part the tall stories, and adding some of his own for the reader's astonished pleasure.

'Everything there is different from how it is with us', he noted with satisfaction, 'and excels both in size and beauty. They have no fruit the same as ours, no beast, no bird. This is a consequence of the extreme heat. They possess no grain but rice. Their wine is made from sugar, and very good it is, making a man drunker than wine from grapes. Everything a human needs to sustain life is there in abundance and very cheap. They have no lack of adept astrologers, and many physicians who are skilled in maintaining the body healthy. Both males and females are black-skinned, and stark naked but for the brightly-coloured loincloths. They consider sinful no form of sensual indulgence.'

I fell into conversation with a Carmelite monk, Brother Augustine Stanley, who lived at a monastery 2½ km from Varapuzha, near Cochin; he invited me to visit him there at the terminus of a regular ferry service from Ernakulam. A straw-hatted man and his son in shorts were baling out a rough canoe below a palmtrunk that curved out drunkenly above our ferry. A barge chugged past loaded to the gunwales with coir fibre. Amid so much natural wealth and such hardworking people, why oh *why* is there so much unemployment and poverty?

After three or four hours of drifting through canals and lakes the millions of cocopalms had literally entranced me: I felt drugged by the endless filmstrip unrolling before me like a Sesshu painted scroll, perhaps, but with technicolour vividness. A dragon-shaped prow darted past. Cashew-filled dugouts paddled out of our wash, the boatmen ignoring us in their placid concentration. Ripples on the watery roads sway away in immemorial symmetry, a duality unthinking like Shiva's congruence of creation and destruction. A civil servant was returning to Ernakulam from the backwaters: how could he abandon his paradisal home near Kayankulam? 'I don't like roads', he said, 'but I am finding the open sea much of a scare also.'

Constant paddle ferries carried passengers from one canal bank to the other: there are few bridges in the backwaters. The civil servant explained that the matrilineal law of inheritance in Kerala had been misunderstood, because it used to extend only to the Nairs and some Muslims of Cannanore, while the patrilineal system applied to Brahmins, Kammalas, Tiyyas and Mukkuvas. It is likely that the reason for matrilinear inheritance was to prevent the alienation of family property. As to polyandry, the fraternal type existed in South Kerala till the early 20th century, and the non-fraternal type preponderated in North Kerala. The Nairs were the martial caste among the southern Hindus, corresponding to the Kshatriyas in the north. The Brahmins formed the highest caste, the Nairs joined the military or took occupations such as clerkship or accountancy. Next in rank came the Tiyyas, mainly working as toddy-tappers, the Kammalas or artisans, and the Mukkuvas or fisherfolk. Untouchability infected Keralan society as an integral part of the caste system prevailing elsewhere in India, but here unseeability and unapproachibility added to daily inhibitions, One of the Pulaya caste had to stay at least sixty feet away from a Nambudhiri Brahmin and attendants would precede him calling out *po! po!* (away! away!) to protect the distance. If a lower-caste person dared approach within view, they could be murdered without redress from the authorities.

These events of the 16th and 17th centuries and other abuses made such an impact on Keralan history that eventually, in 1958, it became the first Indian state to elect a communist leadership; landownership and wealth are more equitable in Kerala today than any other state. Communism is not the only cause of social and economic advancement, of course. Other factors, dating back in some cases to the British administration in the 19th century, include the abolition of slavery, the abrogation of hereditary offices, and the purging of some corrupt officials. The introduction of the rule of law regulated by Western-style courts and civil and criminal codes permitted an increase in civil liberties; the cancelling of feudal taxes and compulsory government labour allowed greater economic freedom to the individual. Vigorous Christian missions underlined Western mores, egalitarian principles, and a stress on education for personal advancement; the opening of factories allowed promotion by skill and hard work instead of by birth and caste, influence and corruption. Caste as a blight on human rights was attacked by the Theosophical Society headquartered in South India, by the Ramakrishna Mission, by Arya Samaj, and locally by Chattampi Swamikal (1853-1924) and Sri Narayana Guru (1856-1924) who declared 'One caste, one religion, one god for man'.

Temple entry, reserved throughout Kerala, was defeated first in Travancore by the Maharaja Sri Chitra Tirunal Balarama Varma, who proclaimed in 1936 that 'there should henceforth be no restriction placed on any Hindu by birth or religion on entering and worshipping at the temple controlled by Us and Our Government'. In 1947 this edict was supported by legislation covering Cochin and Malabar. Comparable measures have been taken to redistribute land to ameliorate the direst poverty of the past. This has led to a descent of the upper classes and a rise from the lower classes into a greatly-expanded bourgeoisie of professionals and officials where expectations have perhaps risen faster than reality, and abundant qualifications have not always earned their appropriate reward. I spoke in fact to one graduate journalist who admitted that colleagues of his would commit petty larceny in order to live more comfortably in jail without working than they would be able to outside. I found the same distaste for manual labour among the educated that appears in accounts of Brahmins three centuries earlier.

### Alleppey

Alleppey is a westernized form of the Malayalam Alappuzha, meaning 'wide river' and its life is to a great extent water-borne. The main local industries derive from the coconut palm: copra (the meat), the delicious milk, and above all the fibre or coir which is made into matting, and brought from the backwater villages roundabout for processing in Alleppey. Alleppey bursts into life for the Snake Boat Race in mid-January and the more lavish boat races for the Nehru Trophy every August. You can rest here after the trip from Quilon and before the trip to Cochin, but there is also a great deal to see locally, though you are not allowed to enter the main Hindu temple. Cross Lake Vembanad by one of the many daily boats on the 2½-hour cruise to Kottayam, with its many churches, a printing and rubber town colonised long ago by the Syrian Christians. The Vallia Palli (Great Church) and Cheria Palli (Small Church) are said to be seven centuries old, and the Bishop of Travancore and Cochin still resides in Kottayam, with its long main street full of spices, textiles, bookshops, and pavement knick-knacks that gleam and dazzle in the afternoon sunlight.

Some useful tips in Alleppey: the Kerala State Road Transport Corporation bus station is just east of the boat jetty, past two lodgings (the

Mahalakshmi and Krishna Bhavan) which are not recommendable. Try instead the top-grade but by no means extravagant Alleppey Prince Hotel on Highway 47, or you could stay in Kottayam at the Kumarakom Tourist Complex, with only four rooms overlooking a lotus pond. This is located on Lake Vembanad in woodlands that become a well-populated bird sanctuary during migration time every autumn. Alleppey is not served by trains, but numerous buses will take you southward or northward. The beach is long and luxurious, you won't believe the excellent value and friendly service in St George's Lodging, with clean bathrooms, but it is quite a way from the jetty, for which the Hotel Kamala is the obvious logistical choice, with a copious choice of meals.

Your overwhelming recollections of Alleppey are likely to remain those from every other town of its size in Kerala below 200,000 people. Colour, vivacity, a tendency of the people to giggle at you in embarrassment, and a subcutaneous pride in the beauty surrounding everyone and everything; then the benison of relaxing warmth, which provokes open houses, open hearts and an open expression of welcome on their faces. Whether I lunched at a vegetarian restaurant near the Raja Tourist Home or dined at the non-vegetarian Indian Coffee House near the hospital, I found both waiters and fellow-visitors inclined to chat. Alleppey is too often treated as a transit port, but it has all the potent attractions of a place brimming with its own special excitement. But then I had just been reading the writer Kamala Das's evocative *My Story* (1988), so much of it set in Kerala: so scandalous, so direct, so controversial! In the lanes of Alleppey I felt, with Van Gogh at Arles, that 'night is even more richly coloured than day', with swinging lanterns, bulbs framing stalls like a film-star's mirror in her dressing-room, and neon flashing trumpery messages below the velvety absolution of the sky.

### Kottayam

It was Kottayam that I first tried cold fried bananas and Cadbury's Very Nice Biscuits. An American pointed to my Thums-Up cold drink in the Cakra Restaurant and Cool Bar; 'They just found out that can give you cancer', he informed me helpfully. 'Just this bottle?' 'Naa, Limca, Gold Spot, any of them. They're supposed to be banned by the government, but can you see any government closing down these soft drinks factories?' 'No', I said uneasily. 'Damrye', he nodded, chewing my biscuits and mopping his ample brow. I left my Thums-Up unfinished, and he swigged the dregs with a sigh of satisfaction. It was hot as geysers. Kottayam is to all intents and purposes a Christian town, so the shops close on Sundays. Queen Mary's Public School gives you the flavour of the place, so to find a Chinatown there might be disconcerting. But there it is.

I wanted to explore the Old Seminary at the limits of Kottayam, founded in 1815 by the Metropolitan of the Syrian Orthodox Church. English was taught in Kerala here first but these tactics of propagation of the Syrian gospel by educational incentives were quickly copied by the (Protestant) Church Missionary Society, who competed – all too easily – with the traditional Sanskrit-based ancient literature, and its limited competitor, modern Malayalam, neither of which could match English for administrative and commercial vocabulary or international connections; Henry Bailey's introduction of the first Keralan printing press at Kottayam might be seen as the last nail in the golden age of traditional Keralan culture.

### Ettumanur and Vaikom

Just north of Kottayam we resume the Shaivite series of Hindu temples, first at Ettumanur, and then much nearer to Cochin, at Vaikom. Both in their present form date to the 16th century, but Ettumanur's Mahadeva shrine is circular and Vaikom's temple to Lord Shiva has a square sanctuary. I implored a temple priest to allow me to see the outer parts of Mahadeva, and he silently beckoned me in with a ghost of a smile, like an executioner with a willing victim to the block. West of the temple proper, an open mandapam with a pyramid-shaped roof had a wooden ceiling covered with twenty-five panels portraying gods of the Shaivite pantheon. Outside the temple, a wooden screen is carved with figures connected with the Ramayana and the Loves of Krishna. Outside the temple a crouching middle-aged man in shorts tugged sweet bananas from a sawn-off branch and extended the bunch to me. I shared them – all three rupees worth – with an emaciated woman clutching a shrieking baby, and hurried off into my half of the universe, ashamed of my revulsion against poverty. What is there to be ashamed of but shame itself?

I wanted to see Vaikom because of its associations with Gandhiji. The temple to Lord Shiva, 16th century in its present form, has 18th-century murals of Shiva Nataraja, Parvati, Ganesha, Vishnu with his consorts and Garuda, taking up the wall-space between doors and windows and protected by a metal roof. From the entrance gateway, even the non-Hindu will be allowed to see a separate mandapam with a pyramidal roof, and the usual brass lampstands. As one of the holiest sanctuaries in Kerala, Vaikom's Shiva Temple forbade untouchables and lower-caste individuals to pass along the street in which it stood. In 1924 a twenty-month struggle was pursued by progressive forces including some higher-caste Hindus led by Mannath Padmanabhan. Victory was achieved by the satyagrahis in 1925 after the intervention of Gandhiji, who suggested a face-saving compromise to the authorities, by which they should keep closed a token stretch of road for a limited period, and open the rest. By 1928 approach roads to all temples had been thrown open to all Hindus throughout Travancore, so as you stand outside Vaikom's Shiva temple give thanks for the wise mediation of the Mahatma, without whom the cause of liberal humanism in India would have been set back decades, as we shall see again at Guruvayur. I caught the bus at Vaikom, where a Frenchwoman's handbag was snatched and the urchin responsible dissolved like a puff of smoke into the milling crowds of pilgrims and passers-by.

## Periyar Wildlife Sanctuary
Back in Kottayam I took the long-distance Madurai bus as far as Kumily. As there is also a local bus-station in Kottayam, make sure you head

*Tea plantation 93 km above Kottayam*

for the right one, and don't be put off if there is no bus direct to Periyar, for it is an easy bus connection from Kumily to Thekkady on the beautiful route to Madurai over the Western Ghats.

I felt tempted to stop off at the tourist bungalow at Pirmed, but stayed on the bus, luxuriating in landscapes of gently waving palms, cooler air, and bottle-green to emerald-green tea plantations. At Kumily I changed to the Periyar minibus. A barrier across the road marked the entrance to Periyar Tiger Reserve, and the minibus jolted through black pepper and clove plantations in 'the most beautiful national park in the whole of India' according to Nagel's *India*, though others will prefer different sanctuaries, in my case Manas Tiger Reserve in Assam/Bhutan or the Narayan Sarovar Chinkara sanctuary in Gujarat's Rann of Kutch.

The minibus from Kumily stops near the two 'mainland' hotels: the cheap Periyar House, with singles, doubles, ten-bed dormitories and its own restaurant, then the lakeside Aranya Niwas, much more pleasant, like a weekend country-house. Best of all for those yearning for peace after the pandemonium of Madurai or Cochin is the Lake Palace Hotel, accessible only by ferryboat from the Aranya Niwas jetty. You are not so independent there, but more likely to be visited by monkeys knocking on the window for titbits. The most adventuous can try to hire one of the isolated forest bungalows, but these have to be booked far in advance, and from the lakeside landing stage it is a jungle hike of 2 km to the bungalow. This is your only real chance of seeing a wide variety of the wildlife for which the reserve is famous, and those nocturnal sounds give you a vicarious feeling of identification with 'nature red in tooth and claw'.

Surprisingly, there is no lack of excellent restaurant meals at Periyar: I dined off sweetcorn soup, grilled fish and vegetables, and butterscotch pudding at the Aranya Niwas (the 'Forest House' built in 1952), then melted into the jungle at dusk (with torch and anorak) to watch families of Nilgiri langurs feeding and leaping playfully, then watching me inquisitively as they munched, the infants squeaking not too far away from their long-tailed elders. A swoosh of a blackheaded oriole outlined against the setting sun. Sambar deer quietly moved down to the lakeside to drink, their ears and noses twitching nervously as the group of sixteen kept their eyes open for the deadly tiger. Monstrous dancing butterflies floated like bright petals. A langur turned round and aimed excrement in my direction, in contempt or warning, fear or anger, or perhaps a combination of all these. A family of lion-tailed macaques nibbled between banyans over a small range a few hundred yards away, their calls eerily reminiscent of the human voice, whereas the *ruf* of the langurs sounded more like a dog's bark. Three little Keralan boys sat fishing on the other bank, unaware of learning the talent for serenity early on. The lake petered away into pools and lagoons. Parrots chattered about nest-

*Periyar Wildlife Sanctuary. Lake at dusk*

time on the other bank, and a pair of black butterflies continued their zinking and zwipping overhead. That successful predator, the Indian darter, white as snow and just as motionless, poised its long thin neck and beak for the discreet fish-kill before nightfall. The temperature swam unnoticed, neither hot nor cold, the wind neither still nor tempestuous, in this mountain haven.

I woke at dawn for a lake cruise departing at 7.30, and found three otters tumbling and chasing by the landing stage. A ride on the *Ambuja* or the *Kripa* (15 passengers each) would cost Rs 75 each; the 125-passenger *Shakuntala* Rs 25, and the 250-passenger *Bhakthi* Rs 50. Almost immediately wild pigs scuttered out from the undergrowth on the far shore, and scared birds flapped off and out of sight. The paradox is that the visitors' eager chatter and the boat's engine-noise frighten away the very animals and birds that we have come to see, but binoculars will give you the chance to make out species habituated to the clamour of tourists. Elephants came to drink, the calf protected between bull and sow elephant as it gulped down soothing draughts. We didn't see bison that morning, but turtles sunbathed on the shore and dragonflies with diaphanous wings hovered like the balance on Judgement Day.

When the boat approached the bull threatened us, trumpeted, and

127

*Periyar Wildlife Sanctuary. Elephants come down to the lakeshore, early morning*

told his family to move away. The cow sniffed in disdain at his cowardly behaviour, staying to give herself a dust bath. A misshapen and broken tree-trunk protruding from the waters of Periyar's man-dammed blue lake and reflected in them reminded me of a glistening landscape by Dalí, perhaps his overcrowded *Swans Reflecting Elephants* (1937) in Geneva. Few tigers come down to the water's edge by day until the intolerable dry heat of May and June desiccates their watering-holes.

Herons imitating taxidermists' prize specimens sit on gnarled trunks or posts jutting out of the water as diving boards, only their beady eyes roving. A sparkling, iridescent blue kingfisher dived below the level surface of the lake, then just as quickly its russet head re-emerged up, clear, and away. A brahminy kite floated on the air-current, then we disembarked for a forest walk led by a ranger. Again, the larger the party the less likely you are to see any fugitive wildlife, so you can concentrate on trees in these Cardamom Hills, the rustle indicating monkeys, sunlight splintered by branches, the tinkling of a stream, unexplained voices of macaque or langur, a swathe of gnats like a cat's cradle or DNA helix, so that nothing is wasted.

Back at Aranya Niwas families of Indians were being given rides on tame elephants along well-trodden tracks. By the checkpoint out of the park the minibus stopped beside two performing sloth bears, for a Bombay wallah to take a picture of the degrading spectacle: he thought they were funny. The mandaris, street entertainers who train India's sloth bears to 'dance' for coins, are concentrated in the Katputli district of Delhi, and fear that the government will enforce the 1972 wildlife protection laws by repatriating the bears to their native Himalayan foothills. But they provide nearly four hundred families with daily sustenance and, once released back to the wild, there is of course no guarantee that they could survive in a long-forgotten environment, or that they would not be recaptured illicitly and made to resume their tricks. The conservationist lobby points to the fact that fewer than two thousand sloth bears remain in India.

## The Road to Madurai

The next town on the road to Madurai is Kumbum, where piled goods on both sides of the road threaten to make all traffic single-line. Practically nobody wears glasses: is it because their eyes are not as weak as ours, or not so strained with reading? Certainly, they screwed up their eyes in the dazzling sunlight yet I saw only one in a thousand wearing sunglasses. Crescent-horned oxen with bold humps and frilled silky dewlaps flumped their slow pedestrian paths in monsoon-saturated fields. Maize-fields and rice were growing around the village of Seelayampatti. Chinnamanur boasts a Sericulture Demonstration Training Centre. A Christian cemetery spread out as witness to missionary activity in Uthmapalayam. Near Putupatti women pumping waved cordially to our crowded bus. Yoked bullock carts mooched on the sandy roadside, parallel with the internal combustion engine but resistant as ever to change, like sempiternal India.

We explore the centuries-old temples for what has never changed, and then have the effrontery to criticise the Indians because they lag behind western technological achievement. But quick scientific enterprise can be achieved only at the expense of polluting the environment, readjusting values from the familial to the statal, making a man a worker or a professional first, and a father and husband second, and this Indians are notably reluctant to concede, rightly in my opinion. If you devote a great deal of time and money to the extended family, as happens all over the Middle and Far East, Latin America and Africa, you will not put first the Five Year Plan or the Gross National Product. In the West's urgent admonition for the East to industrialise, the implicit suggestion is that social cohesion and individual rights should be subordinate to the needs of the Government. But as Communist ideologies wither, and the rights of private ownership and individual freedoms return to the fore, we are beginning to see that the Government has more duties than rights, and the private citizen may have as many rights as duties. When

129

*Kumbum. Bazaar*

Stalin, Ceausescu and Hoxha called for greater sacrifices, sooner or later the people asked 'why?'. And they were right. If Indians don't want change, or want change at a pace slower than the rest of the world, why not assume that they are right? It is too easy to try to impose alien patterns on a country, instead of attempting to understand the people's own innate pattern. As Nirad Chaudhuri reminds us in his *Autobiography of an Unknown Indian* (1951, *p*. 503), 'So far no foreigner in India – Aryan, Turk, or Anglo-Saxon – has been able to escape the consequences of living in the Indo-Gangetic plain. His energy has been drained, his vitality sapped, and his will and idealism enfeebled.'

India has never thrown off its invaders by its own efforts, but by the

*Theni. Tamil Nadu. Main street*

gradual enfeeblement of the invaders. You have only to see the hordes of people sitting and *doing nothing* to understand this simple truth. An enervating climate, monotony of the great plains, dourness of the staple diet, repetition of seasonal labours, conservatism of temple and state, narrowness of educational aims: all seemingly unite in a kind of magnetism towards lethargy. Rajiv Gandhi's suggestion about reversing economic protectionism and state controls lost him the leadership of the country, though it might have gone part of the way to ameliorating the lives of six hundred million villagers lucky to have water from hand-pumps and bicycles instead of the old wells and ox-carts. As for change, vested interests in government and military circles would lose by it, and the poor at large might not gain a great deal. A Gandhiji with his handloom may have served India well as a saint and visionary, but the next visionary will have to be a completely different kind of woman or man, and must be supported by vested interests. Where could such a diplomatic genius be found?

Not in the town of Theni, decked out for the spring festival called Pongal, with a sentimental film called *Forever Mine* showing at the cinema, where another film almost indistinguishable from it will be shown next week as a means of passing the time before sleep, work, sleep, work. But the time would have passed anyway.

Not in the banana market of Usilampatti, an agricultural centre where methods have not changed significantly for generations.

*Usilampatti. Tamil Nadu. Banana market*

I had fallen asleep despite the rising volume of the bus-driver's horn as he approached Madurai, and at the long-distance bus-station I checked that my zipped shoulder-bag remained intact, then headed for Hotel Aarathy.

## Ernakulam

From Madurai (locally-pronounced Maj-rye) you can reach the Cochin-Ernakulam conurbation by a picturesque mountain road; equally beautiful are the alternative routes: southward from Cannanore or northward from Trivandrum. It is usual to spend most of your time in historic Cochin, and stay in modern Ernakulam, but the airport stands on Willingdon Island, equidistant between the two.

I found a room at Bijus Tourist Home on Ernakulam's Market Road because of its proximity to the Cochin jetty, along Cannon Shed Road. 'Listen, my friend,' urged a friendly Bihari, 'I want you please never use what they have these tea bags, these just dust only, you are wanting the high quality leaves. We have.' And he proceeded to induct me into the arts of buying tea: Darjeeling, Assam, Kerala.

I must say I found restaurants disappointing in Ernakulam: even the usually dependable Indian Coffee House seemed to be vaguely inferior, possibly because of the nature of its trade: quick transit passengers with their mind on the ferries across the road. All in all, the best meals I had were at the Sea Lord Restaurant, Shanmughan Road, handy for the Sea Lord Jetty and not far from the High Court Jetty for Bolgatty Island, with its sumptuous yet inexpensive rooms: do not be put off by a bland receptionist saying only the treehouse cottages remain available. But to make sure, book up well in advance (the apt telegraphic code name is 'Relax', and the telephone is 355003). Bolghatty Hotel was built by the Dutch in 1744, then used by the British as a Residency.

Two of the other three expensive hotels are on Willingdon Island, which is not a good place to be, except for the local airport. The Malabar Hotel on the tip of Willingdon Island, an artificial island built into the harbour on consolidated harbour silt dredged in the 1930s, stands on the tip and has been taken over by the Taj Group; it is reached by ferry between Ernakulam and Cochin (though not all stop there). The Casino Hotel dates from the 1950s and suffers from live western music and high prices. The newest de luxe hotel is in Ernakulam on Paramara Road: the Presidency Ashok is an Indian Tourism Development Corporation Hotel, and is handy for the rail station, with high prices on the Malabar's level.

For atmosphere, you can't beat Cochin itself, the nearest hotel to the ferry being the Seagull, strategically placed between the ferry to Vypeen and the one to Ernakulam, and the very cheap Port View Lodge, on the main coast road south of Fort Cochin on the way to Mattancheri Palace and Jewtown.

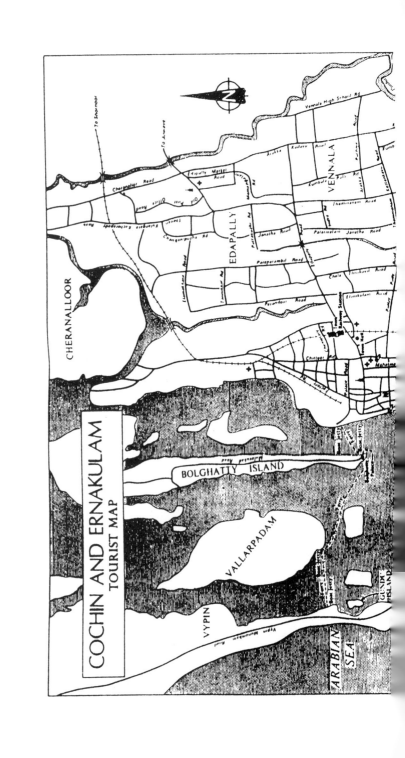

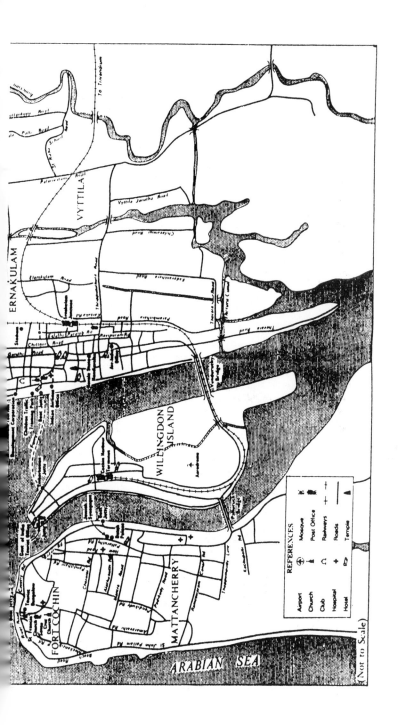

A poster announced the 'All Kerala Break Dance Competition & Body Beauty Contest of Babies' and the State Bank of India bore the admonition 'Please keep your cycle locked', the only bank I have found where the thieves prefer bikes. Crows stumped around a refuse tip like angry undertakers deprived of their just corpse. At the Indian Coffee House on Cannon Shed Road I breakfasted off mango juice, omelette and a pot of coffee, and requested three pieces of toast. 'Three no,' contradicted the dignified waiter consulting items, 'two or four'. 'I'll take a portion of two now, and half-portion later'. 'Achcha, sahib'.


## Cochin

To board the ferry, which leaves Ernakulam for Fort Cochin roughly every half-hour, I bought a ticket at the little booth which opens two minutes before departure. You can board without a ticket, but then the collector will charge double on board.

I chatted with Mr Ganesh, who still works for the British-owned Aspinwall coir company of Cochin, as proud of his firm as of his town and country. 'If you please have any problems while in Cochin, you come into me and I will tell you anything.' Once in Fort Cochin he showed me Aspinwall's charming cream building over a century old, its plainness flattered by climbing bougainvillea, and countrified by goats ruminating placidly on sparse slivers of grass surviving on the swish of sand outside. Opposite the New Ananda Bhavan restaurant trim, shining schoolgirls in red and white check gingham self-consciously paraded to school. Beside Aspinwall's extensive grounds (most firms have moved to Willingdon Island) I met a Keralan with a briefcase and more for the pleasure of a meeting than for information I asked the distance to the Church of St Francis. He considered for a moment and with the judgement of an English nineteenth-century arithmetician concluded 'It is barely one furlong from here.' The Chinese fishing nets are more properly 'dipping' nets, cantilevered to secure the biggest catch with the minimum effort and counterweighted for operation from the shore, but catches are down due to over-fishing. These curved nets, squareish but elegant as mainsails, can also be seen on the backwater around Cochin-Ernakulam, and between Quilon and Alleppey. They derive their name from the fact that their design was introduced from China during the Mongol ascendancy there.

The Vicar of St Francis of Assisi, the Rev. John Chacko, conducts services in both English and Malayalam for his Church of South India congregation of some two hundred families; Santa Cruz, the Roman Catholic Cathedral nearby, serves five hundred families. Christianity is known (from Cosmas Indicopleustes) to have flourished in Kerala from the 6th century, if we discount traditions of St Thomas the Apostle's landing here (and the Madras tales) in 52 A.D. Local Christians stoutly defend the Thomasian tradition, citing a Brahmin record in the *Keralolpatti* that a certain 'Thoman' became an opponent of all the Vedic teachings and converted 'many prominent people in the country' including the reigning king. This Thomas, whoever he was, is said to have lived in the Jewish quarter of Cranganore (then called Muziris) and to have converted four hundred Hindus and forty Jews. This view ill consorts with the Jewish account of their first landing at Muziris in 69 A.D., seventeen years *after* the arrival of the missionary. Syrian Christians converted high-caste Brahmins and Nair Hindus, as is proved by their tacit place in the oldest caste systems of Kerala, but conversions in the last five centuries or so have been mainly from lower-caste Hindus frustrated by caste traditions. The first Persian Christians to immigrate into Kerala were 472 families escaping the persecutions by Shapur II in 339; they arrived in Cranganore in 345, under a merchant called Thomas of Cana, and were granted land on the opposite bank of the Periyar river, where they were allowed to create their own bazaar and village around a church. Other groups fleeing Islamic intolerance in the 8th and 9th centuries settled elsewhere along the coast, notably at Quilon, and inland at Kottayam, but Christianity spread more by conversion than by immigration, and by the time of Vasco da Gama's arrival at Cochin in 1502, the number of Syrian Christians in Kerala was estimated at 200,000. The liturgy was Syrian and the doctrine Nestorian and, until the Portuguese stopped the practice, bishops were appointed from Iraq and Iran. The split from Rome occurred in 484, when the Persian Christians declared their refusal to accept the decisions of the Council of Chalcedon in 451. The Catholikos of the Nestorian Church resided at Seleucia-Ctesiphon on the Tigris, and turbulent proselytising activities resulted in the establishment of churches in Kurdistan, the Persian Gulf area, southern Arabia, Socotra off the coast of Yemen, and on the coastline of the Red Sea, culminating in a wave of conversions in Turkestan and South India. Nestorius taught in the 5th century that the Incarnate Christ comprised two *separate* persons, one human and the other divine, as opposed to the orthodox teaching which recognised the Blessed Virgin Mary as *Theotokos*, that is *Deipara* in Latin, or 'God-Bearer'. Nestorius declared this term used of the Virgin by the Greek Fathers to be incompatible with the full humanity of Christ, and proposed instead the term *Christotokos*, or 'Christ-bearer.'

Of course, over the centuries, the Christian churches felt the impact of indianisation, whether in heterodox teachings or in such sculptural features as the use of Peter and Paul images for guardian figures at the doorway of the Syrian church in Chengannur, or the decision to plan a monumental gateway with a balcony or hall for musicians above it as practised in a number of Hindu temples. When Vasco da Gama entered a Kali temple in the belief that he was entering a Christian church, the point of intentional similarity is clear.

The Portuguese, with their militant Roman Catholic orthodoxy, quickly made foes of the Muslims with whom natives of the Iberian Peninsula had been at loggerheads for centuries, and with the Jews whom the Inquisition had named adversaries even unto death, but they realised that they would have to coexist with the Hindu majority, and they began reacting tolerantly to the Syrian Christians, who by then had fallen off in numbers and zeal. When St Francis Xavier arrived in Kerala in 1542, he found an aged Nestorian bishop 'very obedient to the customs of the Holy Mother the Church of Rome', which may have been no more accurate than calling the late Patriarch Pimen 'very obedient to the customs of Russian Orthodoxy' after surviving two decades of unswerving loyalty to the Kremlin's moods and stating 'the social evils so typical for the life of many people today just cannot occur within our social structure'.

The first church on this site must have been, as usual with the founding Christians, of wood. There Vasco da Gama was buried in 1524, though removed to Lisbon's Jerónimo Monastery in 1538. It was dedicated to St Bartholomew. St Francis Xavier came here in 1543, and it is likely that the stone church was completed about three years later, when its first extant inscription is dated.

Portuguese Cochin must have looked very like Old Goa, with churches and convents, palaces, colleges, and mansions. But when the Dutch landed in 1663 they transformed St Francis' into a Dutch Reformed Church, and demolished a great deal of the Portuguese colonial town, including all the convents and the other churches, permitting the Catholics to create a new church in 1665 on the nearby island of Vypeen. The British took Cochin in 1795 but allowed the Dutch to keep the church until the Dutch handed it over of their own accord in 1804, and it remained in the Church of England until 1947, when it passed to the Church of South India. Portuguese gravestones are found on the northern wall and Dutch on the southern wall, confronting each other even in death.

I was asked to remove my shoes as in any Hindu temple, and a polite lady showed me an Old Malayalam grant of land for the church site. A tablet in the north wall is dedicated 'To the memory of Rev. Alfred Forbes Sealey, M.A. of Caius College Cambridge, late Director of Public Instructions in the Cochin State and Principal of Ernakulam College'; I found a brass tablet to John Hutchinson Aspinwall (1834-1884). Above the altar the Creed is written out for those with a short memory and the first of the Ten Commandments appears as 'Thou shalt have none of their Gods but me.' Light, simple, massive and as full of memories as a barrel is full of beer, St Francis drowses in the gratifying sun like Sir John Falstaff after a gutfull of sack.

The Cathedral of Santa Cruz was blown up by the British in retaliation for resistance, and its restoration completed in 1904.

The charm of Mattancheri, south of Fort Cochin, lies in its unassuming single-storey buildings, block-like street-planning, and its quiet eccentricity, with an opulent palace, an exotic synagogue, and a workaday market for coir and spices from which pungent aromas spread their perennial excitement. Pirates killed for these spices, and governments fought wars for control of their trade routes. Nowadays, you can buy a spice-belt made up of a dozen airtight pockets, each with a different spice: turmeric and tarragon, cardamom and ginger, pepper and oregano.

The Mattancheri Palace was built by the Portuguese as a gift for Raja Virakerala Varma (1537-61) of Cochin in 1555; until then the rulers inhabited relatively small and easily erected wooden mansions in the manner of the early Japanese emperors, who were constantly at war. This example at Cochin was quickly followed by other stone buildings throughout Kerala, from Calicut to Quilon, wherever wealthy rulers or noblemen felt vulnerable, or sought to found a dynasty that needed protection by thick walls and a durable sloping roof. Because the Dutch

*Cochin. Street scene*

139

*Cochin. Mattancheri Palace*

renovated the Cochin Palace throughout, it came to be known errone-ously as 'the Dutch Palace'. However, its plan of four buildings with a central courtyard fell into the category of artistocratic Keralan domestic buildings, though of course on a more majestic scale. In the centre is the Palayannur Bhagwati temple, and to the south another temple area devoted to Lord Shiva and Lord Krishna.

The first gallery on the upper floor of the palace displays vivid por-traits of the Cochin Rajas from 1864, though the dynasty began in the late 15th century with Unni Rama Koil I (*d*. 1503). Here are Rama Varma (1864-88), Kerala Varma (1888-94), Rama Varma (1914-32, the instigator of industrial and economic development in Kerala), and finally Rama Varma (1948-64). This Coronation Hall contains a fine 18th-century palanquin, but next door begins the series of murals in the Royal Chamber and three other apartments which constitute the glory of Cochin pictorial art.

The Royal Chamber is covered with 48 murals, all but five devoted to scenes from the *Ramayana*, the balance depicting scenes from the *Krishna Lila*, such as Krishna playing the lute in panel 9. The Ramayana scenes begin with the *putrakameshtiyaga* or 'sacrifice for the birth of a son' and end with Sita's release from captivity. R.V. Poduval has dated these paintings to the second half of the 16th century, but H. Sarkar prefers the second half of the 17th century, when the building took its present shape. The *Krishna Lila* paintings are later, and the ground-floor pictures with a Europeanizing tendency may be of the 19th century. The crowded murals in tempera (not strictly frescoes, therefore) leave not a single space untouched; the *horror vacui* is theological as well as artistic, for just as the Christian God is everywhere, so are the Hindu divinities, filling up every niche in creation. Perspective is not an issue here: there is a range of receding planes, each cardboard-thick so that an individual two or three rows back might be concealed by one of two limbs of others, but remain in the same dimensions, gentle, half-smiling, with a faraway look in the eyes that might conceal deep meditation or a sudden thought. Gods and mortals are shown full face. Above the window, panel 8 shows Ganapati, remover of all obstacles. Next to the portrait gallery, a portrait of Lord Vishnu remains unfinished. The magnificent panel 13 is dominated by Lakshmi on her white lotus as universal mother, the consort of Lord Vishnu as Roman Catholic Mater Misericordiae. Narada, who warned of the coming incarnation of Vishnu, is shown as a white wandering messenger, with the vina or lute, which he reputedly invented: the Indian Orpheus. Ten avatars or manifestations of Vishnu are painted on the lowest row. Panel 20 is an image of green Vishnu as Lord of Tripunithura Temple with the Naga king at the back. The next galleries show palanquins, with the costumes of the last Cochin Raja, Rama Varma. Palms greet the azure sky in the palace grounds, as you look out of the windows.

Two rooms on the ground floor, the women's bedchambers, have murals retelling the story of Kalidasa's *Kumarasambhava* and puranic stories.

### Jewish Kerala

Jewish settlers first reached Kerala through Cranganore, or Shingley as they called it, at a time conjectured in the 1st century A.D. by a number of authorities, including local Jewish tradition. This Jewish home called Anjuvannam near Cranganore was reinforced by successive waves of immigration, to the extent that between the fifth and fifteenth centuries Cranganore could be considered a self-administered Jewish principality. Marco Polo notes Jews in Quilon and 15th-century travellers record Jews in Calicut. In 1524 a massacre of Jews by local Muslims led to the virtual abandonment of Cranganore by Jewish survivors and their appeal to the Hindu raja of Cochin for refuge, based on the grant of copper plates about 1000 A.D. by the Hindu king Bhaskara Ravivarma I (962-1020). The Hindus welcomed the Jews and in the 1560s a Jewish town and synagogue were established in Mattancheri, Cochin. The Portuguese in Malabar persecuted the Jews wherever they could find them:

we have a letter from Afonso de Albuquerque asking the King of Portugal whether he could be permitted to exterminate Jews from Portugal and Spain 'one by one, as he found them'. Cochin's Jewtown was crushed bloodily by the Portuguese, against whom the Jews fought on the side of their traditional allies the Lords of Cochin and their subsequent allies the Dutch, who arrived in Cochin in the 1660s. The 132 years of rule by the Protestant Dutch allowed Jews to recover their prosperity, and in 1686 Moses Pereira de Paiva, a former Portuguese Jew living in Amsterdam, listed 4 synagogues and 128 Jewish families in Cochin and 6 synagogues elsewhere in Malabar. The British also tolerated Jews in Cochin, and their numbers declined again only after 1947, when they decided to make a new life in their Holy Land.

While in Cochin, their main activities were the import and export of such commodities as pepper, coral, timber, rice, cotton goods, and they followed the professions of jeweller, bookbinder, contractor, estate-agent, and architect, the most distinguished figure being the merchant family of David Rahabi, who arrived from Aleppo in 1646. His son Ezechiel played a vital diplomatic role in the Netherlands East India Company, dealing with Indian Christians, Hindus, Parsis and Muslims,

*Cochin. Synagogue (1568)*

142

*Cochin. Coir matting being loaded*

and merchants in Denmark, Portugal, the Netherlands, England and France.

Cochin Synagogue may have been built in 1568, but the Portuguese attack of 1662 meant that it had to be heavily restored in 1664; the clock tower dates from 1760 and the Cantonese tiling from 1762.

Jackie Cohen is an elder of the White Jews' Synagogue at the end of a cul-de-sac in Jewtown, Cochin, which serves twenty-five persons in seven families. Visiting hours are 10-12 and 3-5 except on Saturdays and other Jewish holidays. 'Oy,' he grimaced, 'fifteen more years and there'll be no more community here. Everyone goes to Israel, they die off, the youngsters don't want to know.' He sold a reproduction copper plate to a Bermuda-shorted American paying in dollars ('Keep the change and good luck!') and told me that the Black Jews' Synagogue in Cochin was abandoned fifteen years ago, mebbe twenny, who knows? His hands spread in perplexity about the ineluctable gnawing of time at his vitals. The windows looked out as from a drawing-room, and the spinning gold-crowned Ark of the Law gleamed expensively below its plush red triangular cloak. Nineteenth-century silver and glass could have come from an Amsterdam synagogue. Apart from the very fact of its survival, the greatest wonder of the Cochin synagogue is the shining

143

tiled floor, all the colours of blue and white beneath the wooden ceiling with its sloping roof. In the courtyard I found a slab from the Kochangadi synagogue (1344), the oldest in Cochin, about 2 km away, now in ruins.

## Back to Ernakulam

After exploring dingy spice shops and little coir factories in shade made black by contrast with white dusty sunshine, I headed back on the ferry towards Ernakulam. What could be left of the Jewish community there? On Jews' Street I found no sign of them, but in Market Road a familiar enough building made me stop short in amazement: surely the nursery called Cochin Blossoms had been laid out in front of an old synagogue? Yes, this was the original Kadavumbagam Synagogue, and though disused it has not yet been knocked down, but remains protected by Joseph Elias, 'Distributor for Sutton Seeds (Calcutta), tropical aquarium fishes and tanks, we do undertake landscape designing and garden arrangements'. With alacrity he took me through to the dustladen synagogue. 'Nobody uses it now,' he told me, 'we have only four families in Ernakulam. The main exodus to Israel occurred in 1948, then in 1957. Nobody wants to stay here now.' 'And you, Mr Elias?' 'I'll go too, one day when I'm too old to work at my flowers. Our colony is at Nevatim, near Beersheba. They'll always take me in, but in the meantime I like it here, sure.'

Paico Bookshop on Broadway, parallel with Market Road, is not very obvious: look for the sign on the upper storey; the shop prides itself on a splendid stock of Keralan history and art, and general Indian books too. The Friday Mosque in Ernakulam and the Shiva Temple are not particularly worth a second glance, but you should not miss the Parishath Thampuran Museum in the Durbar Hall, where relics of the former royal family and Mughal paintings vie with sculptures on Durbar Hall Road not far from the Kerala State Handicrafts Emporium. Another museum worth a special detour is the Hill Palace Museum 13 km away at Tripunithura (also closed on Mondays), because this was the seat of the former royal family, where cavalry accoutrements, coaches and palanquins are displayed in a worthy setting.

Organised boat tours of Cochin harbour representing very good value leave at 9 a.m. from Sea Lord Jetty, calling at Willingdon, Mattancheri Palace, the White Jews' Synagogue, St Francis' Church and Bolghatty: a packed morning if you are pressed for time. This will leave your afternoon free for wandering around Ernakulam, and in the evening you may choose a Kathakali performance. There is usually a choice of three venues, starting at 6.30 or 7 and lasting about an hour and a half, including explanations in English. The most charming theatre is that beside the Cochin Cultural Centre on Durbar Hall Road; and you might visit Art Kerala, near Chittor Road and Church Landing Road junction. I chose the See India Foundation on Kalathil Parambil, organised on his roof by P.K. Devan, who introduces the programme in English and has practised the art of Kathakali all his life, like his father before him, who danced till he was 97. If you cannot see an all-night drama in your journeys through Kerala, Mr Devan's brief introduction on a dark roof in Ernakulam provides a whiff of the magic that is Kathakali.

Kathakali consists of three elements: the sung narrative, led by the director or Ponnani with a large gong and assisted by a Sankiti with cymbals; the drum accompaniment led by the Chendakkaran with a cylindrical drum and assisted by the Maddalam with a barrel-shaped drum; and the danced mime, dancers echoing the narrative without speaking or singing but emphasising each point with bells resounding on their stamping feet. Masks are no longer worn, being replaced by intricate symbolic makeup, but the enormous headdress is retained in modern Kathakali, which is headquartered at the Kathakali Kalamandalam, founded in 1930 by the poet Mahakavi Vallathol at Cheruthuruthi, north of Trichur on the road to Shoranur. There they also teach the ancient temple art of Kudiyattam, literally 'acting together', which introduced the clown to Keralan temple drama, and Mohiniattam, or 'Dance of the Temptress', comparable with Bharata Natyam on the Coromandel coast.

Kathakali itself may have its roots in the dance drama called Krishnattam (still performed in Guruvayur temple), and the similar Ramanattam, of the 17th-18th centuries, but its whole ethos is pervaded by a commingling of Aryan influences from the north with rituals long consecrated in the south: that hybridisation which has given us a united India today. Kathakali texts comprising songs and narrative were written by rulers, who also took part in performances as dancers, illustrating the close relationship between religion and state. Tampuran of Kottayam (1665-1743) wrote, acted and danced in four such plays; Balarama Varma of Travancore (1724-98) wrote six; and the great patron of Kathakali Utram Tirunal (Maharaja of Travancore from 1847 to 1860) wrote another. The discipline is as arduous as that of Russian ballet, for boys recruited at the age of ten must refine their mind and body every day for seven years before they are allowed the smallest stage part. He trains every limb and every facial muscle, especially his eyes, neck and hands. The movements of the face convey the nine *rasas* or dramatic emotions: tranquillity, fear, loathing, desire, wonder, courage, pathos, anger and ridicule. The mudras or hand gestures may total only ninety-five in the abstract, but according to their significance in the drama they produce almost five hundred meanings. Whereas in the Japanese Kabuki theatre, specialised professional *onnagata* (male impersonators of women) have 'refined feminine beauty to the extent that it exceeds

*Ernakulam. P.K. Devan's Kathakali Dance Company*

146

the beauty of real women in many ways,' to quote Yasuiji Toita and Chiyaki Yoshida, the woman-impersonator in Kathakali may be called up to act a woman one day, then a hero or god the next.

Kathakali is very much an 'art dance'; the ordinary Malayali folk took no part in performance, partly because of the endurance and time required to train as a dancer, but also because caste regulations forbade most Malayalis to enter their own temples until the present century. True folk dances performed at popular festivals such as Onam are never taught in academies, so they tend to change with the generations.

Wherever you are in Kerala, ask round for an Ottan Thullal performance, which may take place at any time of year. It is a one-man show, in colloquial Malayalam, with accompaniment by two or three musicians of whom one sings. The text will be a partly-improvised ballad, like the mediaeval ballads of Spain or Provence, in which a familiar text (in Kerala often a Rama or Krishna story) is embroidered with local or topical backchat calculated to raise a laugh at the expense of politicians, local bigwigs or bureaucrats. A performance may take place at two in the afternoon or six in the evening and last about two hours, the venue being a market-place, perhaps, or a temple platform. First the singer invokes Ganesha and Saraswati, joined first by the drummer and then by the dancer's lightning-quick steps to draw the audience's attention to his spotlight. The dancer will then sing an opening verse of the ballad, enacting it with mudras and body movements and facial expressions, varying his tempi and occasionally stopping, to allow the instrumentalists into focus. Ottan Thullal was devised by Kunjan Nambiar in the mid-18th century, and has developed from his rather aristocratic style into a nudgingly jocular populist style not above crudity. You can recognise an Ottan Thullal dancer by the green make-up covering part of his face, the knee-length skirt, bells above his calves, and a naga-king headdress.

### A Ferry to Varapuzha

King prawns at the Mandarin Hotel just east of Ernakulam Town rail station, followed by fresh fruit, prepared me for a leisurely afternoon along the backwaters north of Cochin to the idyllic village of Varapuzha. Though Kerala is only half the size of Scotland, its population of 18 million Malayalis comprises 4% of India's total, in only 1% of its area. Most of the schoolchildren and farmers seemed to be dodging on and off our ferryboat, the *Water Lily*, as it swung from shore to shore, crashing on crates, banana boxes, and hurling off bicycles and gunny sacks. The passengers divide themselves into men and boys fore, with the captain scribbling importantly at his lurching desk, and women and girls aft, their eyes flashing with dazzling curiosity; not a word of English or any other language but Malayalam is spoken: it is as if a hundred metres out of international Cochin the countryside swallows all traces of foreignness: the swaying palms utter only Malayalam, that constant fluvial murmur that sounds like a perpetual iteration of sounds like 'pamayatarapinam kalayatinappural'. The tone is feminine, gentle, like a ballet-dancer on her points, but the speed is unnervingly supernatural, like a soughing zephyr which one cannot hope to understand but might easily blow one away.

In his poetry, Vallathol N. Menon made the Malayalam language 'sing and dance', observed Hridayakumari, 'flow as a grand river of the plains, walk in splendour like a queen, and be gracious as a goddess.' The gentleness, the liquid vowels, above all the bubbling rapidity of Malayalam gush and flow from Vallathol's voice. Of course we cannot reproduce this cataract of sweet vowels, coconut water to English bitters, but here is a slight flavour from his poem in praise of Krishna *Ambadiyil chenna Akrooran* ('Akroora goes to Ambadi'):

> *His cloud-dark hair decked with peacock feathers*
> *Trails down, its knot undone,*
> *And on his brow, with glittering pearls,*
> *His* tilak *gleams with beads of sweat.*
> *The saffron silk swirls down*
> *From his shoulders, grimed with dirt;*
> *His body, stained with grass and mud,*
> *Shines like an uncut jewel on all facets.*

The *Water Lily* chugged past Tata Oil Mills, stopping every few minutes to embark a wizened crone with a durable brown shopping bag or to disembark two schoolboys conversing with the rapidity of machine-guns. Chinese-style fishing nets at thirty degrees mimicked palms and their branches splayed like delicate green fingers into a radiant turquoise sky. These waterways are thoroughfares as in Venice or Amsterdam: lads doze or fish in rough rowboats, susurrous waters enchant our ears as they flow past, divided like fleeing foam assassins. Ramshackle canoes with patched sails glide across our bows while their brown owners sit entranced, anaesthetised by the downturned bowl of sky centred over their dark heads. Chinese-style nets hover like ghostly parallelograms all along the palm-fringed shorelines. My notions of island and mainland merge as we putter from one bank to the next. Millions of cocopalms breathe life and wealth into these continuing miles; they teach grace and beauty to girls with eyes of burnt sienna and lustrous black hair entwined with red and white flowers.

In conversation with a clerk in a private firm, Mr Johnson of Madathi Parambil House, Pizhala, I learned of his Sunday jaunts into the countryside, and of his passion for such Malayalam writers as the novelist M.T. Vasudevan Nayar, the poet O.N.V. Kurup, and the short-story

*Waterways between Ernakulam and Varapuzha*

writer K.N. Pillai. Is Kerala communist at the heart, as it has so often voted in recent years? 'We have a way of communism that is very strange, peculiar to Kerala. We are not beggars, but we want to live with dignity. The big politicians in the north in their a/c offices have too much corruption. Capital like in United States is not our way: communism like in Russia is not our way. What to do? No prime minister will be all in all in this country, even first-class, one is shifting house and another is coming up but the people are staying the same. Poverty is there, difficulties are there, unemployment is there.'

I asked if he became homesick for those wondrous expanses of sea, canals and coconut groves. 'Once I take family for holiday in Bombay - what for? I see dirty houses, dirty offices, everyone is sleeping down in street. Straightaway we come and never go off back even if supposing we get chance.' We floated beyond the Coconut Pest Control office, which seemed deserted, between patchwork-sail boats being paddled by sinewy men, with not a spare ounce of fat on their straining bodies. A pair of hooligan crows holed a sack with voraciously-sharp beaks and began to tear at the contents, as at a canvas corpse. A few minutes after leaving Cheranellur we berthed at Varapuzha, where men were taking a bath in the river at the end of the day's labours, and women pounded the family washing.

Until the last boat left back towards Cochin, I strolled in Varapuzha, swallowed down cool drinks, selected bananas, suffered the ritual humiliation of any tall fat Westerner giggled at by groups of schoolgirls, and peered into private homes and gardens, whitewashed with dashes and splashes of startling colours – pastel blue, dark red, and electioneering slogans for K.V. Thomas and his rivals. A riot of jungle threatened to engulf the village: you leave a lawn alone for a week and you find pampas. Why visit Varapuzha? Because it is at the end of the ferry link: I should gladly have walked on if my time at Cochin had been longer, but the remorseless enemy time had forced me back. Tomorrow I was set for legendary Cranganore.


## Cranganore

We have already found the Jews at Kodungallur, as the town is called now, or Muziris as it was known to the adventuring Greeks, though we need not date their arrival as optimistically early as the 6th century B.C. Greeks and Romans both called at Muziris, and the Periyar river is equated with Ptolemy's 'Pseudostomos' for Alexandrian ships would have been carried here by monsoon winds from July to September. Christians came following Muslim repression in Iran in the 8th century, and Black Jews are known at Cranganore in the 12th century, though their traditions claim immigrations from Babylon and Yemen long before our era, inherently unlikely given their colour, which seems to prove to everyone but themselves that they originate from low-caste Malayali Hindus who rejected the faith of their birth for the more egalitarian system imputed to Jehovah.

Cranganore itself is a mute witness to its own historical significance, for little has been done in the way of excavation, and its Portuguese fort called Kothapuram remains derelict. Muslims too are said to have landed in Kerala first at Cranganore, but the mosque attributed to a certain Malik ibn Dinar as early as the seventh century seems later, and its outer walls rise from a tiered basement that you would expect on any Brahmanical temple. Islam took root in the 8th-10th centuries on the coast of Kerala and you might well expect Cranganore's two-storey mosque to date from that epoch. In any event, Cranganore – like Surat in Gujarat – has an air of dilapidated glory that tugs at one's memory like a kite in the wind: once seen, never obliterated.

Cranganore appears to be escaping from the mainland into its watery nemesis: the Arabian Sea to the west, to the north and south the mouths of the rivers Chetvai and Azhikode and to the east inviting backwaters. The annual Talapoli festival at the Bhagavati temple lasts for four days at the turn of December to January.

150

## Trichur

Trichur lies at the crossroads for Palghat and Tamil Nadu to the east, Calicut to the north, and Cochin to the south. You can stay in the old Residency, now a Government Guest House on Palace Road, with airy rooms always associated with a more opulent past. This is handy if you have been attending an all-night Kathakali performance at the Kalamandalam 30 km to the north. Special night-long performances are held on 26 January, 15 August, 18 September and 8 November, beginning at 8.30. The school is closed every weekend and all April and May. Visitors without an appointment may watch classes in progress from 4.30 to 6.30 a.m., from 8.30 to noon, and from 3.30 to 5.30 p.m. Non-Hindus will not be allowed to enter Trichur's wonderful Kerala-style Vadakkunatha Kshetram, dedicated to Lord Shiva, but as usual any Keralan temple is worth travelling to for its external features alone. 'Trichur' is a name deriving from the phrase 'Tiru Shiva Perur', meaning 'Lord Shiva Town' and the centrally-located temple proclaims its allegiance discreetly, with low red-tiled roofs and an almost Japanese tact in the subtle low walls in such extraordinary contradistinction to the towering gopurams of Tamil Nadu. Within, the largest shrine is the northernmost, dedicated to Lord Shiva, circular at the perimeter, with a square sanctuary; in the centre is the Shankara Narayana Shrine, also circular, with dazzling 18th-century murals on the passage including scenes from the *Mahabharata* and a reclining Lord Vishnu on Ananta, his serpent-protector and mount. The southernmost shrine is the Rama, the heroic incarnation of Vishnu in the *Ramayana* whose exploits course through an Indian's imagination like blood through his veins: he is a Henry V, Romeo, and resourceful adventurer combined, a Robin Hood capable of austerity and self-abasement, a Francis of Assisi for his attachment to the monkey god Hanuman, but the personification of marital fidelity. Western literature has no-one like him: neither Ulysses nor Roland, more than the *Kalevala's* Ilmarinen, more than Aeneas, more than Zhivago. The Rama shrine at Trichur is square, with a square mandapam to the west. Kerala's most important shrine to Lord Rama can be found 30 km away: the Tiruvilamala Shrine at Triprayar (with fine sculpture and woodcarving), not far from the Kutalmanikyam shrine at Irinjalakuda dedicated to Rama's brother Bharata.

Trichur's major festival is Puram, celebrated in April-May on the great open square in front of the Vadakkunatha Temple, with a procession of caparisoned elephants six abreast, their Brahmins bearing tall silk parasols, peacock feathers and fly-whisks. At night fireworks irradiate the black sky like a premonition of general resurrection.

Puram is a truly authentic folk-festival of Kerala, as is the week-long harvest festival called Onam in the month of Chingom, between August and September.

The Great Elephant March announced by Kerala's Department of Tourism for mid-January includes a spectacle of 101 elephants at Trichur, but has been denounced by Prathikarana Sangham, 16 Vanchi Lodge, Trichur, as a crude dollar-earning device without any roots in native beliefs or culture. 'Kerala was rich in natural resources', mourned a spokesman for the movement, but 'gradually the resources shrank, so the state is now short of electricity, water, grains and vegetables; our agriculture is stunted. Industrial growth is stagnant. Only the tertiary sector of education, business and health is increasing. All our resources have been drained out, and replaced by modern consumer articles. In short, Kerala is a colony of multinationals and transnationals. More than three million youth are unemployed. The state tries to hide the real state of the people by staging Great Elephant Marches. It is a betrayal of the people and people's culture.' Such an outburst I find quite understandable; indeed, only the most vigorous compaigning protected Venice from the indignity of staging Expo 2000, just such a trumpery invasion. But elephant marches keep the tourist economy flourishing and provide unemployment for hundreds, if only for a few days: moreover, no-one can deny that elephants form an integral part of Keralan life. And there is every opportunity to inspect authentic Keralan arts and culture at the Kerala Sahitya Academy and the Kerala Sangita Nataka Academy in Trichur. Pelicans clack at the Zoo (closed on Mondays) which has lion-tailed macaques and a good snake park, but I cannot say a great deal for the Aquarium. Near the Zoo the Art Museum (closed on Mondays) has a fine collection of folk jewellery, bronze sculpture, Kathakali figures, and traditional lamps.

The mooching wardens of the place are not caretakers, for they take no care of anything at all; they are not guardians, for guardianship involves paying attention to whatever they are to guard. They might be messengers, though they seldom appear if a message is to be carried. They are not guides, for they have no knowledge of the objects they brood among, or if they have they do not impart it to schoolchildren or casual visitors. They will tell you with glee that there are no postcards or guidebooks for they were, if they ever existed, so popular that they quickly sold out years ago. They are not doorkeepers, for they are seldom to be seen by a door, unless it captures the sunlight, in which case they will draw up a chair, and close their eyes in gratification. They spend their time gossiping with their own kind, drinking tea, and looking perplexed if asked the way to the adjoining room, or to the exit. Their god is the God of Closing Time, who is to be propitiated by ensuring that all heathens are herded out of his shrine well before his bell sounds, or his ceremonial gong. Why employ such people? What function have they ever performed that cannot be done by others? They cannot attend to plumbing in the toilets (the job of the lowest menial specially emp-

*Trichur. Art Museum. Guardian sculpture*

loyed for the purpose), they are not armed to prevent robberies, they cannot show visitors the greatest treasures for they candidly do not know which they might be, and they do not clean, dust, polish or make inventories, all tasks to be undertaken by others, invisible or non-existent. Each has the distinct impression that in some way he contributes to the well-being of society, the proof being in his weekly wage. His job is clear: it is to be employed, so that at least one family man is provided for in a country which could never afford to pay actual unemployment benefit. We must thus never derogate from his dignity by questioning the worth of what he does, for the fact that he does nothing at all makes him no less of a human being.

## Guruvayur

Thirty km from Trichur is the 'Dwarka of the South': Guruvayur. The fact that Guruvayur is a Hindu pilgrim centre will not put off the connoisseur of India, for of course the pilgrims themselves form an endless kaleidoscope of human behaviour: you can just sit on your haunches and watch them. Lord Krishna is known here as Guru Vayurappa, and his temple became important in the 16th century, according to Innes' *Malabar Gazetteer*. I have not seen it, and it is not open to non-Hindus, but I understand that the temple is square in shape, with a square central two-storey shrine, gold-plated flag-staff 33 metres high and a 7-metre

*Guruvayur. Sri Krishna Temple. Sanctum*

154

high lamp-pillar. Postcards on sale locally compensate for what you miss, such as the nearby Parthasarathy Temple, dedicated to Lord Krishna as Arjuna's charioteer, and Lord Shiva's shrine at Mamiyur, 500 m away. We have already seen the value to the lower-caste Hindus of the satyagraha at Vaikom, but the later Guruvayur satyagraha proved equally significant in the struggle for the emancipation of the untouchables. The Zamorin opposed unrestricted entry to the temple of Sri Krishna, but the Kerala Provincial Congress started satyagraha in 1931 and exerted such pressure that in a local referendum held later 70% of voters agreed temple entry for harijans. Guruvayur festivals occur in February-March (ten days, with an elephant race and processions), April-May (Vishukani), August-September (Ashtami Rohini) and November-December (Ekadasi, with the temple music festival called Chembai Sangita Mela). Vishukani is the rice-sowing season, when firecrackers explode to frighten evil spirits from the fields. Immediately they wake, villagers must look first at their *vishukani*, a vessel stuffed symbolically with coins, jewels, fruit, rice-grains and any other precious commodities set before a lamp to ensure a good harvest and a prosperous season. Reasonably-priced accommodation can be found at the Elite Tourist Home and Tourist Bungalow (both in East Nadu) and Sri Valsam Guest House.

### Calicut

Calicut has its own airport, but I took the 10.30 Mangala Express out of Shoranur Junction (the English shot snipe hereabouts in the season), stopping at Pattambi, Kuttippuram, Tirur, struggling into Parpanangadi at 11.40 and Calicut an hour later, the Lakshadwip Sea having accompanied us in limpid blue waves along the whole ineffably beautiful route. Some boards proclaim the town Kozhikode, but as so few tourists come here nobody really cares what you call the town, lethargic as its cows under the fierce midday sun. It is hard to envisage, as auto-rickshaws parp about their lawful business, and women in red and gleaming golden saris steer their unswerving way, loaded with shopping, that Calicut once competed with Cochin and Trivandrum. The ruling Zamorin could, according to the *Roteiro de Vasco da Gama* (1498), 'muster 100,000 men for war, with the contingents he receives' and Duarte Barbosa in 1516 described the city of Calicut as 'very large' and the Zamorin 'became greater and more powerful than all the other (Kings)'. The light cotton textiles we know as 'calico' derive their name from Calicut, which was favoured by seafarers for its natural harbour. Calicut arose in the 13th century, after which its cottons and spices found their way to Venice and Basra. Pedro de Covilham arrived in Calicut around 1486, but it was his compatriot Vasco da Gama, arriving here in 1498, who began the long period of suspicion and trade, mistrust and temporary alliances, which marked Indo-Portuguese relations. The Chinese and Arabs found in Calicut an easy-going free port where they could berth to replenish provisions and all-important water supplies. The Chinese even established their own fort (*Chinakotta*) near the larger fortified palace (*Koyilkotta*) which gave its name to both Calicut on the Malabar Coast and possibly also in another context to Bengal's Calcutta. The Zamorin early supported the Arab traders, whose concessions gradually led to a virtual monopoly, and a long-term relationship with the Middle East and Arab states in Africa. Each successive Zamorin tried to expand his sphere of influence, first to Tirunavai and Talappilli, then south towards Cochin and north to Nileswaram. The Zamorin was not a despot as understood by Karl Wittfogel in his *Oriental Despotism* (1981), but an autocrat with a council of ministers who would remind him of his obligations and duties while invoking customary law. An inner circle of four chief ministers and an outer circle of lesser ministers surrounded the Zamorin, who appointed a *Naduvazhi* for each of his districts of *nadus* and called upon these district governors for men in times of conflict. In 1516 Duarte Barbosa observed 'many clerks in his palace. They are all in one room, separate and distant from the ruler, sitting on benches, where they record all the royal revenue, his alms, the wages he provides, and petitions presented to him. Seven or eight always stand before the king with pen at the ready and blank paper ready to record his commands'. The death penalty was incurred for murder, dacoity or other robbery offences, and treason.

Early Zamorins made a great contribution to Keralan culture, in particular by means of the Revati Pattathanam, a week-long literary assembly of poets and scholars held in Calicut's Tali temple. Unfortunately, of all this past glory, little survives: words are vanished into air, clerkly deliberations into dust. The local Muslim population, the *mapilla* (*anglice* Moplahs) have an interesting quarter with their own mosques, and will reminisce about their rejection of Portuguese Vasco in 1498, their conquest of the shortlived Portuguese colony three years later, and their gradual if reluctant acceptance of different overlords and intruders. The Portuguese were finally allowed to set up a factory in 1513, the British in 1616, the French in 1722 and the Danes in 1766, when the Zamorin set his own palace on fire to avoid falling into the hands of Haidar Ali. The East India Company quietly seized the place in 1792, and both Anglican and Roman Catholic churches silently report stages of these conquests for the hearts and minds of men, not to speak of their ginger, pepper, and cardamom. Some might think that the port of Beypur about 11 km to the south has more appeal, especially for Tipu Sultan's fort and the 11th-century Temple of Shiva, but if you can sniff antique tragedy at Carthage or Troy, you will not be disappointed in the pungent smell of it through Calicut's dung-strewn streets. You can stay near the bus station at Nelima Lodge, or at Beach Hotel on Beach Road.


## Mahé, Tellicherry, Cannanore

These three stations on the Shoranur-Mangalore line hide totally different histories. Mahé is a corruption of Mayazhi, the Malayalam name conjoining *mai*, black, and *azhi*, river-mouth, which the French neatly switched to honour the Governor of Pondicherry, Mahé de Labourdonnais, for the little enclave belonged to France until 1954, and chose to keep its identity as part of the Union Territory of Pondicherry thereafter. Even now the town has a ramshackle French feel about it, as though characters from Graham Greene, Somerset Maugham, and Joseph Conrad might bump into Humphrey Bogart round the next street corner. On elevated ground, Mahé watches the river flow seamlessly into the sea, though few craft disturb its calm. A mission house built by Swiss missionaries seems an intrusion, but then the Hand of God might be held rightly ubiquitous by those pressing claims against Islam and Hinduism.

Tellicherry is Mahé's British competitor, only 7 km away, with a factory founded as early as 1683 by the British East India Company from its base in Gujarat at Surat, thus colonising the spice coast of Malabar. The Cherikal Raja allowed them a square fort here in 1708, protecting their interests in coffee and tea from the Western Ghats and Mysore plateau, and cardamom, ginger and pepper from coastal Kerala. The bazaar is of endless interest, as usual, with textiles and spices predominating, and you can see the ruined defensive walls, the opulent golden beach, and the characteristic Moplah houses. Mangy dogs skulked through sunken lanes. A Belgian and his wife and young daughter had rented rooms near the beach: they stayed at Kovalam before, but found too many rowdy foreigners disturbing, and prefer idyllic Tellicherry. The lady crooned 'What shall we do with a drunken sailor?' to her little girl, who spurted round a sandcastle with whoops of joy. 'We're on our way to the Laccadive Islands', Dirk assured me, 'but we haven't got there yet.

I squeezed between standing passengers out of the bus from Tellicherry, and squinted into the brilliant afternoon of Cannanore, where I had booked into the Government Guest House on the beach. Once the capital of the Kolathiris, Kannanur is etymologically 'the town of Krishna', but plenty of Moplahs still live here, and it was not unknown for women to rule the port and hinterland. The Portuguese built their Fort Sant' Angelo in 1505 to command the harbour and defend their factory, though a contemporary Italian declares the 'zenzari pochi e non cusi boni come quelli di Colcut' (*Archivio Storico Italiano*): 'the ginger is neither as abundant nor as good as in Calicut'. The 16th-century Portuguese church and factory can be found near the sea, and the royal palace round the bay south of the fort.

'Come,' commanded a voice, and a Muslim called Ibrahim ushered me into a shady tented hovel where a boy of about ten was pouring sickly sweet milky tea from his greatest possible height down to near his feet, from one sticky glass into another. I tried to pay of course, as always, but Ibrahim crinkled up his face wrinkled by sixty fierce Keralan summers and offered a one-rupee note to the lad for two teas and change. Ibrahim had been a fisherman, and still goes out occasionally at night, but mostly he watches the breakers quilting the coral reef, and struts bowlegged but a free man among the citizens of the town where he was born. The stress of life we find so hard to come to terms with in Western Europe is a concept he would never try to grasp: instead he makes do with the little Allah has seen fit to give him. And that, Allah knows, is enough. He looked pityingly at me, a man harassed by the need to know, to travel, to explore and investigate, to take notes and take photos, to ponder and evaluate. If all you ever need or love is in Cannanore, why subject yourself to the physical strain of travel, the expense of lodgings, the mental strain of learning new languages, interpreting and asking questions? We talked low for half an hour, a haunted modern Faust, and a complacent quirky Sancho Panza who would not accept the challenge to accompany Quijote if asked.

The rail link to Mangalore wanders northward again, and the road inland eastward to Mysore via Nilambur's great teak plantation, or via Sultan's Battery. Near the Battery are the prehistoric cave paintings of Edakkal Caves (8 km) and Tipu Sultan's fort of Panamarram where the local ruler was besieged by the British in 1805. Low to my left sat the fat red sun, like a lion's bloodshot eye close-up, bleary to all appearances yet sudden to pounce. Its deep crimson rays ringed a splaying banyan beside the road then died. The old lion had fallen asleep.

# III: GOA THE GOLDEN

Reminiscing about days in Goa, the epithet 'golden' is evoked by those many hours of brilliant sunshine, excellent beaches, and the Chapel of the Blessed Sacrament in the Cathedral, Old Goa. White is the colour of the houses, Panaji's Our Lady of the Immaculate Conception, dhotis worn by the many Hindus, and foamy breakers on the shoreline. Upland forests roam green and lush towards the border with Karnataka; the sky and Arabian sea glitter with untroubled blue; red is for the bougainvillea that spreads wherever it catches hold, from Lake Mayem to the fort of Tiracol.

A colony of the Portuguese for 451 years until 1961, Goa formed a Union territory with distant Damão and Diu until 1987, when Goa became the twenty-fifth state in the Union of India. Its capital was known to the Portuguese as Panjim, and nowadays as Panaji, a marvellous mixture of traditional and new buildings on the left bank of the Mandovi. You must see Old Goa in your mind's eye humming with three hundred thousand people with a vast additional vagrant or transient population of traders and sailors, mainly from Portugal, but also from China, the Arab World surrounding India and the rest of Europe. It was greater than contemporary Lisbon. In the early 17th century Portugal's population rarely rose above 1½ million, yet an average 2,700 emigrated each year to share in the fabled wealth of the Indies, including journeys onward to Macao or Indonesia's Spice Islands. This outflux ultimately ruined Portuguese agriculture, and impoverished the towns, so that Portugal's over-extended colonial adventure ended in tears and poverty, from a golden age which was never truly golden except to a tiny minority of merchants and administrators, churchmen and aristocrats.

With the Arabian Sea to the west, the Western Ghats on the east, Maharashtra's coastline to the north, and Karnataka's coastline to the south, Goan territory spreads about 105 km north to south and only about 600 km west to east, but within these small dimensions Goa boasts several important rivers from the Tiracol in the north to the Galgibaga in the south: the most important are the Mandovi and Zuari, which meet at Cabo, west of Panaji, making the capital almost a cape city. To the east the foothills of the Western Ghats provide spectacular views and appropriate sites for natural sanctuaries: Bondla and Molem off the road to Belgaum and Cotigão in the deep south off the highway

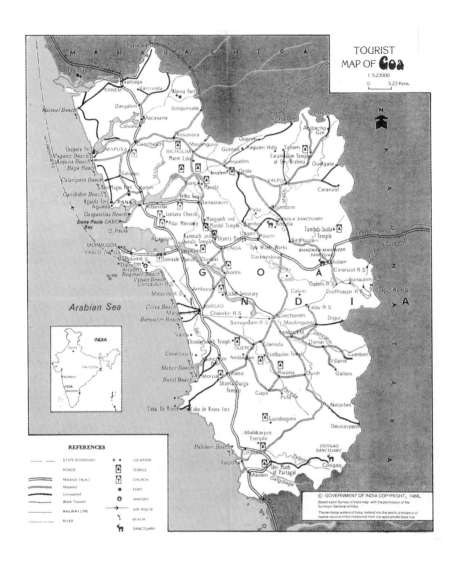

TOURIST
MAP OF **Goa**

1:5,23000

0        5.23 Kms.

Arabian Sea

REFERENCES

STATE BOUNDARY

ROADS

　Metalled (N.H.)

　Metalled

　Unmetalled

　Black Topped

RAILWAY LINE

RIVER

⊛ ●   LOCATION

△    TEMPLE

✠    CHURCH

■    FORT

○    AIRPORT

→    AIR ROUTE

⚓    BEACH

🐾    SANCTUARY

© GOVERNMENT OF INDIA COPYRIGHT, 1988.

Based upon Survey of India map with the permission of the
Surveyor General of India.

The territorial waters of India extend into the sea to a distance of
twelve nautical miles measured from the appropriate base line

160

to Mangalore. Cottages can be hired at Molem, which is a good centre (via Colem railway station) for Dudhsagar Waterfalls, accessible either by train (Dudhsagar station) or on foot through magnificent scenery.

The beaches may look inviting, and they are, but there is no substitute for involving oneself in the social, religious, historical and artistic life of the people, which is best done using the ubiquitous public and private buses, river cruises, and taxis, motorcycle taxis and auto-rickshaws. River ferries take passengers across the Zuari from Dona Paula to Mormugao, across the Mandovi from Panaji to Malim (Betim) for Mapusa and the north, and across fourteen other unbridged rivers. The rail link between Bangalore in Karnataka and Miraj in Maharashtra has a feeder line from Londa Junction to Margao for Panaji and Vasco da Gama for Dabolim.

Dabolim International Airport (30 km from Panaji) is used for charter flights throughout the world, and internally for Indian Airlines connections to Bangalore, Bombay, Cochin, Delhi and Trivandrum, and Vayudoot connections to Pune and Hyderabad.

### Arriving by Sea

Daily sailings from Panaji to Bombay (except Wednesday) and Bombay to Panaji (except Tuesdays) were interrupted during the disturbances in Sri Lanka. Your hotel or travel agent can confirm whether these Shipping Corporation of India connections are running when you need them. Richard Burton took three days to reach Goa from Bombay in 1846, but nowadays a level twenty-four hours is the norm, give or take an hour for tidal conditions. The schedule is interrupted in monsoon, from July to September, but I recommend the sea trip because that is, after all, how the Portuguese first saw Goa, sailing down the Mandovi into their self-designated 'promised land'. You have spent the night restless or asleep in your bunk, awoken perhaps at Ratnagiri port by the engines shutting down or restarting, the mingled shouts of warning or greeting in Marathi, Konkani, Gujarati, Hindi, Tamil, and those puzzling noises emitted at intervals by all ships no matter how majestic or humble. I couldn't sleep, of course, amid the sensual excitement of the early hours, and opened my cabin door to absorb the sights, smells and sounds. A Goanese in Western shirt and trousers was gazing up at the stars.

'Menezes,' he bowed slightly, displaying teeth as evenly white as freshly-hewn Carrara marble, and handed me his card. Under a lamp I read, 'G.A. Menezes, Johnson Aerated Waters, Guddi, St. Jose de Areal, Salcete, Goa.' He seemed a little startled when I asked him for a few Konkani proverbs, but I pointed out that I had recently written the introduction to a new edition of Jayakar's *Omani Proverbs* and suggested that if you wanted to discover the underlying preoccupations of a nation, its proverbs might reveal more than its propaganda. 'Prothom bhugt, magir mught', suggested Senhor Menezes, or 'you can't think until you've eaten', more elegantly expressed in the Latin 'primum vivere, deinde philosophare'. 'Fula voroun vavlli vikta' means 'selling string beneath the flowers', or placing the best goods on top and the inferior below. My favourite, with the first lights of Goan territory winking offshore, was 'Zhanktam zhanktam ganvkar zalo', which I guessed meant 'Softly softly catchee monkey', but actually means 'By shouting he won the village rights'; that is, by persistence he attained his desire, or 'softly softly catchee monkey'...

Shining brass-edged portholes allowed me to glimpse my first views of Goan shores at breakfast. There is Fort Chapora above the mouth of the river Chapora, then cliffs above a line of beaches beginning at Vagator and ending at Sinquerim below Fort Aguada, before the boat rounds Aguada headland into Aguada Bay opposite Miramar Beach. Here Fort Aguada Beach Hotel seems to raise a standard of peace against that Portuguese military installation, and we have arrived in modern Goa, dedicated in great part to the cult of leisure. Even the Goanese on the boat are probably coming back for a holiday from jobs in Bombay or the Gulf States such as Kuwait, Bahrain or Oman. The favourite Goan word for their attitude is *sucegad*, a Konkani adaptation of the Portuguese *sossegado*, calm or tranquil, a frame of mind dictated partly by the tropical climate and partly by an instinctive yet philosophical acceptance not so far distant from the Spanish *mañana*, Italian *domani*, and Arab *bukra, insh' Allah* syndrome. Why do anything quickly when there's all tomorrow not touched yet? Such intuition finds formal expression in Buddhist serenity and the supreme stillness of many Hindu gurus, some justly enough pilloried in Peter Brent's absorbing *Godmen of India* (1972).

*Sucego* is not a feeling that one can experience in the urban pandemonium of Panjim, Mapusa or Margao, much less in Vasco da Gama. It is suspended animation, breath-held bliss that reminds you of Italian *dolce far niente* without the stigma of laziness; in *sucego* one is always on the point of bursting into activity, but not quite yet...

You can breathe in the atmosphere of *sucego* at villages like Chandor, Curtorim and Raia in southern Goa. My own favourite *sucegado* village is Loutulim, north of Raia, on the road from Margao to Ponda, in Salcete taluka. The village centres on a baroque-style parish church asymmetrical with its tower to the right and the rest arcing towards a little high crucifix above two solar quadrants flanking a tiny rose-window. The shady graveyard opposite has nothing melancholy about it, but rests somnolent in long sunlit hours. The mansion of the Miranda family is reached through gates leading to a formal garden. The great house was built shortly after 1700, with a façade of classical rectangular windows, individual upper-floor balconies, and the red tiles so typical of

162

Goan homes. As I write this it is still a family home, so only the family can invite you in, and they are often away. A living is made more easily in Bombay these days. The Old Goa families dispersed when the city became unhealthy, and spread throughout the Old Conquests to lands they were to farm in semi-feudal splendour, patronising craftsmen and keeping up a colonial princeliness we recognise in Tuscany as well as in Sintra or Estoril.

## Early Goa

Amusingly arrogant Eurocentricity sees Goa through Portuguese-coloured spectacles, as existing in a spatio-temporal vacuum before Afonso de Albuquerque drove out the army of Ismail Adil Shah, Sultan of Bijapur, in 1510. This is no more reasonable than the dating of Calcutta or Madras to Georgian and Victorian times, much as those cities changed in the 19th century.

No, 'Gomanta' appears as early as the *Mahabharata*, which in its first recension dates from the 9th century B.C., and it is the Kouba of the ancient Greeks. The Mauryas ruled Goa in the 3rd century B.C., followed by the Andhras or Satavahanas of Kolhapur (a city on the route north to Pune) in the early years A.D., the Bhojas of Chandor in the 4th century, King Anirjitavarman of Kumbarjuva in the 6th century, the Chalukyas of Badami (580-750), then by the Silaharas (feudal owners under the Rashtrakutas) and by the Kadambas (feudal owners under the Western Chalukyas of Kalyani).

The Kadamba dynasty had been founded by a Brahmin from Karnataka called Mayuravarman about 420 A.D., to judge from a later inscription in the Belgaum region, but they did not attempt to overthrow Chalukyan overlordship of the Konkan, the area of Western India incorporating Goa. The Kadamba king ruling as Shastadeva I seized Goa – then Gove or Gopakkattana – from the Rashtrakutas in 973: it is this date which serves conventionally as the basis for Goan chronology when Goan identity and independence are discussed. Shastadeva actually ruled Goa from Chandrapura, now the village of Chandor about 10 km east of Margao, just inside Salcete taluka, to the west of the border with Quepem taluka. In this Sindabur of the Arab geographers, a Kadamba-period fortress (11th-14th centuries) enclosing a temple to Shiva has been excavated. We know that Shastadeva maintained a fleet for defence and trade and the whole region became a 'Hindu lake', with the spread of predominantly Chola power to Java, Bali (where Hinduism remains paramount to this day), the Champas of Indochina, the Khmer in Cambodia and the Sailendra of Malaysia. The Cholas also governed Sumatra and Sri Lanka by naval supremacy: it is a valuable corrective to Eurohistoriography to stress and remember the power of the Cholas in South India from the 9th century to the 12th.

163

Jayakeshi I, Shastadeva's son, realised the value of establishing a capital closer to the harbours on the Zuari (*zuar* means 'island' in Konkani) and Mandovi (*mand* means 'toll'), and chose Goa Velha on the Zuari, not to be confused with Old Goa, east of Panaji and opposite Divar Island (also spelt 'Diwadi'). Jayakeshi II (ruling 1125-47) made a significant dynastic alliance when marrying a daughter of Vikramaditya VI (1076-1126), a Chalukya of Kalyani, for this extended his domains into Konkan once more. The last Chalukya, Somesvara IV (1184-1198), was defeated by the Yadava dynasty, and found refuge with Jayakeshi III at Goa Velha, as Govapuri was later known. Jayakeshi's son Tribhuvanamalla decided strategically to follow the ascending Yadava star, but around 1310 the Muslim armies of Malik Kafur descended from the north, taking Warangal in Telugu lands, then Dvarasamudra of the Hoysalas, and Ma'bar of the Pandya dynasty. Malik Kafur seized 'six hundred and twelve elephants, ninety-six thousand *maunds* of gold (a flexible measure, by some peoples understood to denote two lbs. and by others up to 160!), several boxes of jewels and pearls, and twenty thousand horses', and by 1326 considerable parts of the Deccan and South India became tributary to the Delhi sultanate.

Regrettably, all the palaces, temples and public and private buildings of Kadamba Chandor and Govapuri have perished, and if you want to immerse yourself in the atmosphere of 13th-century Hindu Kadamba life, you'll have to journey east into Sanguem taluka for two Shaivite temples: one near Surla (taking the Sancordem turning north just short of Darbandora on the Belgaum highway), and a less spectacular example at Curdi, just beyond the end of the road south from Sanguem town. The Sri Mahadeva temple at Tambdi (Surla) corresponds to other Western Chalukyan and Yadava temples, with its raised plinth, main hall, vestibule and sanctuary below a sikhara (spire) carved with bas-reliefs of an elephant conquering a horse, Shiva and Parvati, Vishnu, Brahma. One can only conclude that the temple was left alone by the vengeful Muhammad bin Tughlaq because of its isolation from avenues of power.

Not much remains from the Vijayanagar period either, from the early 14th century to 1469. Some scholars suggest that the Hindu adaptation of Buddhist rock-cut laterite caves at Arvalem (Bicholim taluka) must be of Vijayanagar date. The original excavation dates between the 3rd and 6th centuries, but each of the six caves was incongruously endowed with a proud Shiva lingam. The same happened to the Buddhist hermitage at Rivona (beyond Sri Damodar Temple, Zambaulim, Sanguem taluka) with a Vijayanagar image of Hanuman the monkey-god. Quite recently a new and exciting series of four free-standing sanctuaries has been identified at Khandepar; as at Rivona, these may have been inhabited by Buddhist hermits, for river water is easily obtainable close by, we are far from busy towns, and clues abound such as pegs for hanging lamps and robes, and niches for cult objects. They are currently considered Kadamba monuments of the 11th century: we know because the Sanskrit scholar Hemachandra mentions such monks conversing with King Jayakeshi I.

The Bahmani dynasty of the Deccan arose out of an insurrection against Muhammad bin Tughlaq in 1345, and 'Ala ud-Din Bahman Shah was crowned two years later, bringing Goa under his Muslim sway before his death in 1358. Within twenty years the Bahmani Sultan Mujahid had been killed and Goa had passed under the sovereignty of the Hindu Vijayanagar rulers, who appointed Madhava Raya their regent in Goa. It was Madhava, keen to reassert Vedic learning in an area ardently proselytised by the Bahmani Muslims, who settled Hindu scholars in three places, one of them the Old Goa which was later to be overrun by the Portuguese. The Brahmapuri here on the Mandovi is now known to have been chosen for its antiquity as a revered site of a previous Brahmapuri established under King Tribhuvanamalla and destroyed by Bahmani zealots.

The struggle for Central India between Hindu Vijayanagar (ruled from Hampi) and Islamic Bahmani Deccan (ruled from Gulbarga until 1425, then from Bidar) made a constant battlefield of Goan territory, where the emphasis on administrative headquarters gradually moved from the Zuari river and its hinterland to the northern Mandovi shores. There Madhava Raya's Brahmapuri was demolished, to be replaced by a new Muslim town called Ela, and Gopakkapattana (Goa Velha) suffered the same fate.

Yusuf Adil Shah, Sultan of Bijapur, created a fabulous palace in Ela, but it has been almost totally lost: the only survivor is a basalt doorway presumably rescued from a Hindu shrine from before the 1470s. This palace is recorded to have been used in 1560 as the Palace of the Inquisition (for which see Anant Kakba Priolkar's *The Goa Inquisition*, Bombay, 1961); as the most distinguished building in the city of Ela it was used by the Governors of Goa until 1695, and Yusuf created a two-storey summer palace at the village of Panjhe (now Panaji, the Portuguese 'Panjim', and known from a Kadamba inscription of 1107 as 'Pahajani Kali') which was defended against the invading Portuguese of 1510, and later became, with changes and restoration, the present Secretariat, just west of the Tourist Hotel and east of the Steamer Jetty.

This is where we tie up, the Bombay steamer and the tumultuous, running, shouting hordes that emerge from all sides with crates and packages, live chickens and shopping bags, cardboard boxes and battered suitcases with flight labels of Gulf Air and Biman, Air India and Vayudoot. Like the fearful, excited Portuguese mariners of Afonso de

165

Albuquerque (who first captured the summer palace of Adil Shah in Panaji), we are ready to explore Goa.

## Old Goa

The story of Portuguese Goa begins with the conflict of two men, Dom Francisco de Almeida and Afonso de Albuquerque. Almeida was founding Viceroy of Portuguese India, at Cochin, assuming office in 1505, and Albuquerque his successor was named Governor in 1509, some months before Almeida's murder by assassins at Saldanha Bay. Almeida's view was that Portugal should command the seas, confining their land possessions to factories defended by mighty fortifications against all possibility of capture.

Albuquerque's vision – more grandiose and worthy of *Os Lusíadas*, the epic poem by Luis Camões consciously based on Virgil's *Aeneid* – contradicted that of the pragmatic Almeida and corresponded with that imperial fantasy embodied in the British Raj. Whereas Almeida emphasised the value of factory-fortress bases in Quilon, Cochin and Cannanore, Albuquerque insisted that Portuguese overseas possessions should not be within the gift of native Hindu and Muslim rulers, with their whims, demands for tribute, and changes of fortune with repeated conquest and reconquest. Portugal should have permanent overseas lands, not governed from peripheral Cochin, but from the more strategically central Goa. Moreover, while Portugal could work with Hindu allies, they feared growing Islamic power in the subcontinent, and Albuquerque felt the ambitious statesman's need to subdue his nearest rival, the Sultan of Bijapur, whose Golden Goa was the jewel in the crown. Almeida had believed that in the long term Portuguese lands would be attacked and ravaged by local enemies, and of course each proved right in his way. Portuguese India survived threats and attacks across four and a half centuries, as Albuquerque had argued, but eventually succumbed as Almeida had surmised.

On 25 November 1510 the city of Old Goa was attacked by the Portuguese in 28 ships carrying 1700 Portuguese, with Hindu allies in the service of a Hindu-born sea-captain called Timoja and the Raja of Gersoppa, Timoja's father-in-law. Yusuf Adil Shah had left Goa with 4000 Turks and Persians under Rasul Khan, of whom half were reported killed in the onslaught, with the loss of forty Portuguese killed and 150 wounded. The victorious Albuquerque, merciless in war and religion, ordered that all Muslim civilians should be murdered, and their homes and mosques razed to the ground, which is why Old Goa today seems an entirely Christian city. By faith, perhaps, but by works? 'Utter desolation', mourned Richard Burton.

I hear the shrieks of slaughtered children; the blood of innocent women stains the bougainvillea. As you wander around Old Goa today, remember the swamps in which mosquitoes bred, and the lack of hygiene which caused the spread of cholera from 1543 until the city was abandoned at the end of the 18th century in favour of Panaji. Among the churches of white Bassein limestone red-tiled houses, mostly of two storeys, provided accommodation for a colonial people doubtless yearning for the sparkling mountain air of Tras Os Montes or Beira Alta.

Until the 1630s you would have sailed to Old Goa from Panaji, but then the Viceroy, the Conde de Linhares, constructed with slave labour the causeway nearly 3 km long which still connects Panaji to Ribandar, with salt flats to the south. 'Ribandar' means 'Harbour of the Kings', and was settled by the Vijayanagar rulers, and still possesses charmingly polychrome or whitewashed houses which could be transported to Sintra or Estoril without loss of face. Porches and verandahs with beautifully-carved pillars add a subtle Indian feel, and yes, the reds and yellows do feel a little too tropical for the coastline beyond Lisbon, then the bus jolts into a main square so monumental that you might think of Pisa's cathedral and leaning tower, perhaps, or an Andalusian town in siesta.

This is Old Goa, virtually deserted nowadays. From the bus I headed for the roundabout, then wandered left down to the Mandovi ferry for Divar Island, to reconstruct in my mind the Portuguese advent and invasion. At the jetty I turned to face old Goa, while cold-drinks vendors serenely surveyed my quivering body. I had succumbed once more to mental malaria: shaking with excitement on being at a historic crossroads, as I had felt at Persepolis and Cuzco, Peking and Bukhara. As on the field of Agincourt or the bombing of Dresden, I felt stirred in the invisible crucible of events that changed the world; here is the abandoned shipyard, an arsenal now silent (closed as recently as 1871), shadows of the customs house, the faintest scent of the bazaar now gone forever, hinted incense of the Dominican church razed in 1841 to provide stone for new barracks. Vanished are the goldsmiths, bankers, merchants and craftsmen, with any trace that they ever lived: Roman Ostia has more to show than the 'most handsome street of Goa', called Straight Street, a Rua Direita.

Passing through the Viceroy's Arch of laterite with a riverine façade of green granite and the arms of Vasco da Gama, I nodded to the statue of the great man commissioned in 1597 by his grandson the Viceroy Francisco da Gama. The arch was rebuilt in 1954.

On the left I found the only surviving fragment of Adil Shah's former palace, set unobtrusively like a legless beggar beside the way to the Church of St Cayetan. It must date from the time of Sabaji, the last Hindu ruler before the Muslim conquest of 1471. Basalt pillars on a platform are surmounted by a lintel, unmistakably Hindu yet left here for some reason when the rest of the palace was removed in 1820 to

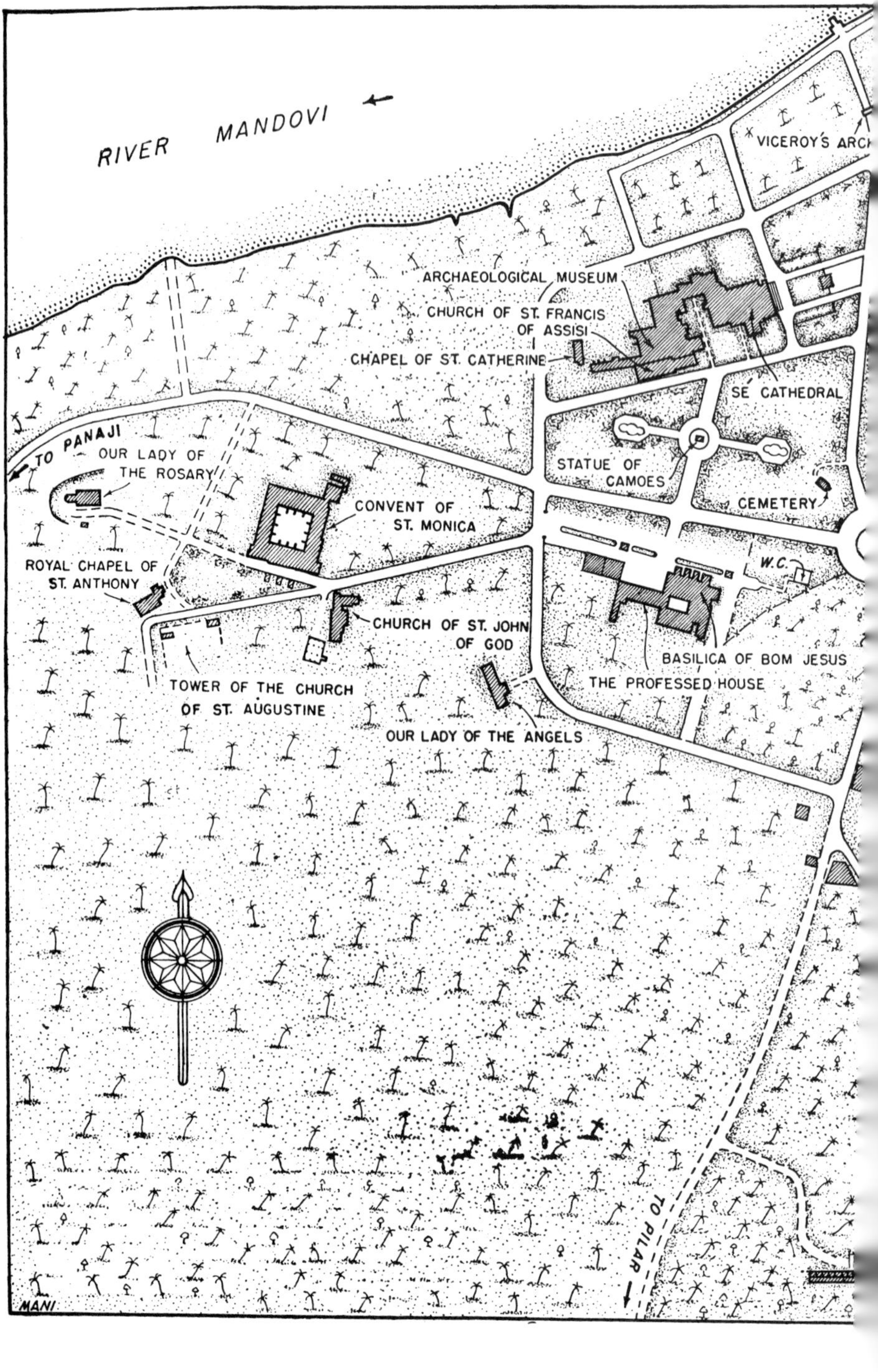

RIVER MANDOVI

VICEROY'S ARCH

ARCHAEOLOGICAL MUSEUM
CHURCH OF ST. FRANCIS OF ASSISI
CHAPEL OF ST. CATHERINE

SE CATHEDRAL

TO PANAJI
OUR LADY OF THE ROSARY

STATUE OF CAMOES

CEMETERY

CONVENT OF ST. MONICA

ROYAL CHAPEL OF ST. ANTHONY

W.C.

CHURCH OF ST. JOHN OF GOD

BASILICA OF BOM JESUS

THE PROFESSED HOUSE

TOWER OF THE CHURCH OF ST. AUGUSTINE

OUR LADY OF THE ANGELS

TO PILAR

MANI

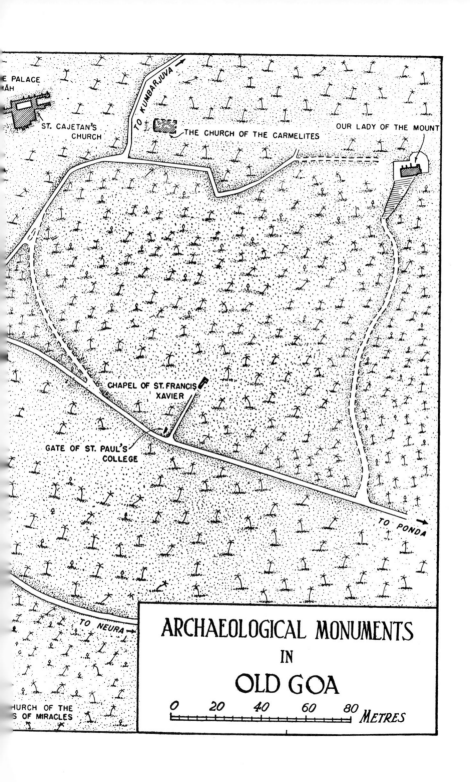

E PALACE
ÁH

ST. CAJETAN'S
CHURCH

TO KUMBARJUVA

THE CHURCH OF THE CARMELITES

OUR LADY OF THE MOUNT

CHAPEL OF ST. FRANCIS
XAVIER

GATE OF ST. PAUL'S
COLLEGE

TO PONDA

TO NEURA

HURCH OF THE
S OF MIRACLES

ARCHAEOLOGICAL MONUMENTS
IN
OLD GOA

0    20    40    60    80
METRES

provide building stone for Panaji.

St Cayetan's, formerly dedicated to Our Lady of Divine Providence, was built by friars of the Theatine Order sent from Italy by Pope Urban III to convert the 'heathens' of Golconda. They were understandably refused permission to proselytise by the Muslims ruling there, and took some consolation in recreating in 1656 for Old Goa a replica in miniature of San Pietro in Vaticano, at least from the inside, in some respects: its classic Corinthian portico with pilasters, and its high attic storey and graceful dome. Several times restored, it is now again badly in need of another coat of whitewash, and it would help if flapping pigeons could be induced outside. Its associated monastery, restored in the 18th century and more recently, serves as a theological college.

The Theatines or Clerks Regular of the Divine Providence came from an order founded in 1524 by two members of the Roman Oratory of Divine Love; Giampietro Caraffa, later Bishop of Chieti or Theate and Pope Paul IV (1555-9), and the Vicentine Gaetano Thiene (1480-1547), canonized in 1671 as St Cayetan. Bitter opponents of Martin Luther, they were equally opposed to corruption within the Roman Catholic Church, and forswore ownership of property, begging, and all forms of luxury. Their austerity may have been the main cause for their failure to reach wider sympathy in the populace at large. Certainly there seems to be little popular appeal in these scenes from the life of St Cayetan painted by minor painters of the Italian Baroque and shipped out east towards an uncomprehending populace.

Fungal growth appears in the monsoon season at St Cayetan's and elsewhere, when nothing ever really has time to dry (this factor can affect underpants in the same startling way, mottling green and black), and nobody can ever spend the time and energy to paint every building white afresh each year, so a kind of desperate rearguard action is fought to keep up appearances, then for a decade the struggle nought availeth so it is given up.

Behind St Cayetan's the road to Our Lady of the Mount (1510) leads past the Carmelite Church façade, all remaining of the church of 1621: the Carmelites left Goa in disgrace in 1707 for refusing to swear allegiance to the King. From Our Lady of the Mount take the southern path and at the main road to Ponda turn back into Old Goa for the gate of St Paul's College (1542) and the Doric Chapel of St Francis Xavier (c. 1544 in its original form, but in this version 1884). We are now back in the monumental complex of three zones: (a) the Cathedral, Church of St Francis of Assisi and Archaeological Museum; (b) the Basilica of Bom Jesus and the Professed House; and (c) the climb to Our Lady of the Rosary. Most of Old Goa is open from dawn till dusk, so you should make sure you see the Archaeological Museum and Portrait Gallery between 9 and 5: it is closed on Fridays. Housed in the huge monastery of the St Francis Church, its cloistered courtyard is well worth a quiet wander to lure your imagination back to the 17th century, when the former church of the Holy Ghost was demolished to make way for the present grandiose edifice.

In the museum, small scrapers and arrowheads prove Mesolithic habitation in the territory of Goa, and evidence of food-gathering emerges from the Late Stone Age. Hindu sculpture from the 7th century can be seen, with 12th-century hero stones from Quepem and an undated sati stone, but the best Hindu image is a mediaeval standing Vishnu from Savoi-Verem, north of Ponda. An extraordinary cultural mixture is provided by 16th-century inscriptions in Arabic, a 17th-century Hindu hero stone, and a lifesize John the Baptist in wood near a bishop's tombstone of 1786. Governors and Viceroys felt the need to immortalise themselves in oils, and we have lifesized portraits of Pedro de Alem Castro (1662) dressed more like a swashbuckling soldier than a gifted administrator, and Fernando Martins Mascarenhas (1690). The Portuguese determination to convert and dominate is exemplified by an array of small religious figures: St Anthony, St Augustine, near the tombstone of Dom Diogo de Noronha (d. 156), the first Captain of Damão. It was the age of extravagant intolerance, boundless convictions.

Those swaggering, ruthless Governors are all here, from 1547, when Dom João de Castro began the practice of limning the magnificent, to 1961. Dom Henrique de Menezes (1526) threatens and blusters, his hands reaching for weapons at the first sign of insurgence, but outside the windows matted, dense foliage proclaims that the jungle will take over after the most arrogant and longlived man has perished. Coins, notes and stamps of Portuguese India provide a collector's feast in showcases, but I continue to watch these black-eyed viceroys in case one 'scapes his rectangular frame and dodges away, sword unsheathed. Surely this heart is blameless: the friar-governor Dom Frei Aleixo de Menezes (1608-9)? No. The Inquisition that strikes terror into everyone who sees Verdi's *Don Carlo* dominated Goa too: priests and friars denounced, tried, punished, tortured, and condemned to death much as in a military court-martial.

On the one hand, a charmingly naive St Francis of Assisi adores a tiny crucified Christ in a 'primitive' landscape; on the other, a painting shows 'The Execution of Five Franciscans', each haloed and enchained, being beheaded by a scimitar wielded by the Emperor himself 'in the city of Marrocha in the Empire of Miromolim'. These muskets, swords and cannonballs were not for show, they were used and used again. Almeida warned us that this would happen: insurrection, insubordination, night attack, betrayal. Then the portraits end with Salazar and a photograph of the last Governor-General of Portuguese India, with the resonant names of Manoel Antonio Vassalo D'Silva. With unseeing eyes, two

Bombay socialites, giggling out of a sense of superiority to the rest of India, passed the solemn culmination of Portuguese domination and wandered down the stairs, the man teasing, his ticklish slender bride in an orange blouse pouting coquettishly in a manner she will lose in shall we say three years? Four?

Inscriptions in the courtyard below run the gamut from Marathi to Persian and Arabic, mainly of the 16th century. Images of Brahmanical deities include a Mahisha Mardisi of the 10th century and a Vetala of the 12th.

The Franciscan Church dates from 1661, for the first Church of the Holy Spirit (1521) had become unsafe by then, and only the original ornate Manueline west doorway survives. The monastery next door, built on the site of a demolished mosque in 1517 and restored in 1762-5, served as headquarters of the Franciscans in the East, and their church demonstrates the most astounding antithesis to the saint's teachings that money could buy. Indian Baroque rivals its Roman antecedents in scrolled pilasters, intricate gilding, sumptuous decoration, and paintings on wood displaying in pure Baroque ecstasy the high points from the life of the saint who would have abhorred this church, from its excessive size and grandeur to the excrescences of its idolatry of the founder of the order, surrounded as he is by wealth and visual splendour. Sacheverell Sitwell has educated our taste for Southern Baroque, so that I can appreciate now Sant' Ivo alla Sapienza as one of the perfect Roman churches, on a par with Bernini's stupendous creations, but one has to remain peculiarly resistant to the search for authenticity in sense and sensibility to avoid a suggestion that Francis would have shuddered deeply at the churches erected in his name and to his great glory. The rib-vaulted nave has no aisles, and the eye is led immediately to the steps up to the altar. 'Poverty, humility, obedience', announce the saint's vows amid the riotous glitter. Hollywood comes to Assisi, Old Goa.

Behind the Church of St Francis of Assisi rises the great Cathedral dedicated to St Catherine, patroness of the day when the Portuguese seized Goa. The largest Christian church in Asia, it was begun in 1562, but not completed until 1652. A Dominican church, it measures 180 feet by 250, with a façade 115 feet high. Again, the magnificence of the building seems to be a statement more political than architectural: 'we have taken ninety years to create this temple to our God because, as we are here until the end of time, speed of execution has no importance'. King Dom Sebastião (1557-78) is credited on the façade, in a Latin inscription to symbolise the universality of the Catholic Church, with the desire to build this Cathedral from the Royal Treasury, with his archbishops as administrators to see that the works were carried out. Designed by Júlio Simão and Ambrósio Argueiro, it was originally endowed with symmetrical twin towers, but one was damaged by lightning in 1776, and removed for safety. If you stand in front of the façade or east door (it backs on the ensemble including St Francis with its west door) you can envisage in front of you the Terreiro do Sabaio, or Square of Yusuf Adil Shah, with its Senate House (used until 1835), the Tobacco Store, and Palace of the Inquisition, all now wafted into oblivion. The secular life of the Terreiro having vanished, we turn round expecting to see the cathedral a mirage too, but there it remains, as solid as Vignola's Chiesa del Gesù on which it must have been modelled. The exterior is in Tuscan Ionic; the interior barrel-vaulted nave is interrupted on each side by tall white Corinthian pillars leading first to long-vista aisles, and then to a sequence of chapels. At the octagonal baptismal font St Francis Xavier is said to have baptised large numbers of converts in 1542. Old Goa was by then Christian by majority, as he relates in one of his letters (*Epistolae*, I, 124): 'After four months and more out of Mozambique, we reached Goa, a city entirely of Christians, *cosa para ver*' – an extraordinary thing. He found the Bishop, the Franciscan Recollect Fray Juan de Albuquerque like himself a Spaniard, a frail old man clearly suffering from heat, humidity and tropical fatigue, who embraced the missionary and 'bade him use his Papal briefs in any way that the goodness of his heart might direct'. So Francis Xavier went

*Old Goa. Cathedral*

173

to tend the sick and dying in the royal hospital, where he found Chinese, Malays, Sinhalese and Africans. Many so-called Christians were ill-instructed in the faith, so the future saint took up a bell like any other town crier and wandered through the streets and squares calling men, women and children to attend his instructions in the faith. As the *Monumenta Xavieriana* tells us, 'he explained each point so simply, that his audience could easily understand and this system was adopted elsewhere in India, so that everyone took to singing the Ten Commandments in the streets, fishermen in their boats, and labourers in the fields.' Truly the 16th century is the most ingenious age of hagiography: we have lost the faculty of innocent awe, learning sceptical irony with our adolescent humour.

How can we accept at their face value these chapels to Our Lady of the Virtues, St Sebastian of the arrowed martyrdom, the Chapel of the Blessed Sacrament, chapels and altars to our Lady of the Virtuous Life, Our Lady of Sorrows, Our Lady of the Three Necessities, Our Lady of Hope, before coming to the High Altar? No poetry after Auschwitz, asserted Adorno, and it seems that simple acceptance of theological virtues will be to the same extent tainted by our monstrous knowledge of man's ability to maim and murder man, whether the pointing finger of command belongs to Stalin or Pol Pot. The gilded carved altar writhes and coils as if half-alive: such too are the serpentine columns of the Basilica of the Infant Jesus across the main road.

The cathedral represents the formal, ecclesiastical grandeur of Old Goa; Bom Jesus is the ardent, familiar heart of the religious capital of the Portuguese East, endowed by Dom Jerónimo Mascarenhas, to whom a cenotaph is erected in the middle of the nave. The church was begun in the 1590s and consecrated in 1605. Its roof is modern, but the rest of the place is as homely as Lourdes or Knock, for we are dealing not so much with the church as monument but as place of pilgrimage, a dimension evading me wherever I turn. I see the sticks and stones, but cannot feel the spiritual zest of the bone-hungry, skeleton-hunters drooling over the shrivelled and disintegrating remains of St Francis Xavier, who were last allowed an uninterrupted sight of the saintly corpse in 1974, since when it has been visible through a hole in the coffin well above eye level in its own chapel on the south side of the transept. Lights gleam as if in a fairground and the sugary sentimentality of cupids and angels surrounding the opulent reliquary consorts well with the pedestrian Italian-style series of paintings showing events from the Jesuit saint's adventurous life, including kissing an ulcerous wound in Venice, or receiving the papal benediction on departure for Lisbon and the Indies.

He died at the early age of 46 at Chang Chun Shan Island off the coast of China, having evangelised Malacca in Malaysia, the Moluccas of

*Old Goa. Basilica of the Infant Jesus*

*Old Goa. Basilica of the Infant Jesus. Sarcophagus of St Francis Xavier*

176

Indonesia, Sri Lanka, and Japan. In his time he was lauded by the Jesuits for converting the good round number of 700,000 heathens, but it is clear that many of these so-called mass conversions were for the sake of propaganda ('more is better') than for any long-term spiritual benefit. Indeed, in Goa alone the Inquisition tried 16,172 cases between 1561 and 1774, testifying to a restive, antagonistic population all too difficult to coerce even in his own headquarters. He persecuted the Nestorians and loathed the Muslims, but one has to admire the single-minded tenacity of a man horribly susceptible to seasickness. Pope Pius X called him 'Patron of Foreign Missions', and he is regularly named 'Apostle of the Indies', but I like to think of him as 'Father Confessor to those suffering from mal-de-mer.' Somebody must be on our side. St Francis's sinuous figure in wood, hands hanging limply inward as he gazes in rapt adoration at Christ crucified in his left hand, looks pale from his last voyage, all his breakfast gifted to the briny below.

The great tomb, by contrast, seems to offer in death all the gilt and glory he despised in life, and was the gift of Grand Duke Cosimo III of Tuscany, commissioned in 1688 from the Florentine Giambattista Foggini (1652-1725) and finished ten years later, a riotous triple-tiered golden cake of sarcophagi, gleaming in marble and jasper, gloated over by alabaster putti. The remains of the saint himself have been lodged in a silver casket behind a silver statue of the saint made in 1633. Pilgrims seem to be convinced that a small bribe put into an offertory box will persuade St Francis Xavier to intercede on their behalf and I saw Hindu ladies distinguished by the *tikal* on their forehead as thoroughly impressed as Christian women following on in the rush. The saint's body needed to be protected, because one pilgrim bit off a toe and kept it in her mouth, refusing to release it to the church authorities, and took it back to Portugal. Part of an arm was sent to Rome at the request of the Church of Gesù, and part of a hand to Japan in 1619. Another toe which reportedly fell off spontaneously is conserved in the sombre but atmospheric sacristy, but I couldn't persuade the sacristan to show it to me. I passed up the stairs into an art gallery where devotional paintings of no great merit are hung, a visit worthwhile for the view down on to the tomb.

The monastery next door, finished in 1585 and only partly rebuilt after a fire in the 17th century and reconstructed in 1783, was the so-called 'Professed House' or oriental headquarters of the Jesuits, and still serves as quarters for a few Jesuit fathers.

Nearby eight barefoot urchins were playing soccer with the intensity of a Cameroon squad overcoming Argentina, and I found meals bubbling at the Hotel Datta Prasad, an open-air shanty completely off the tourist trail a couple of hundred metres away. For less than one American dollar I feasted off fish, rice, green vegetables, two bananas, soda water and hot sweet tea, while mosquitoes worried away at exposed sectors of my body. I nervously covered one bare foot with another, conscious of what happens to unguarded toes in Old Goa, but no lady pilgrim from Lisbon ventured to disturb my relative serenity. 'Gawawal!' squealed the westward boys, while the eastward team howled derisive dissent. My pale skin was turning the colour of boiled lobster, so I moved under the shade of a rough rush roof, as a pi-dog gazed in longing at that bubbling cauldron under the desultory eye of a plump Goan lady. The perspiring lady won.

The way to Our Lady of the Rosary winds upwards, as at Calvary, to a headland known as Holy Mount. On the left a barred gate leads to the Church of St John of God, a white building against a cloudless blue sky dated 1691-1721, with a convent founded by the Order of the Hospital-

*Old Goa. Church of St John of God, from the ruins of St Augustine*

lers of St John of God in 1685, rebuilt in 1951-61 after being abandoned in 1835, when many other buildings in Old Goa were left derelict. The label nowadays reads 'Franciscan Hospitaller Sisters Home for the Aged', but the church – with its west front of pediment and bulky white towers – lay closed to all clamour, and I proceeded uphill beside the fortress-like Convent of St Monica, built in 1607-27 for cloistered nuns as a retreat against the rugged sadness of the world outside. Now called the Institute Mater Dei, it is a theological centre founded in 1964. I did not dare summon its denizens with a modest request to look around, for I feared to disturb them at their orisons. The exterior is roundly masculine, sturdy, with Corinthian and Tuscan styles vying for ascendancy.

Above St Monica soars the ruined tower of St Augustine, too grand for its own good, for its vault crashed down in 1842, smashing the statue of St Augustine, and the façade and main tower fell in 1931, leaving overgrown the silent floors of this vast church and convent. They were raised first in 1512, then in 1597, and 1607, but even Golden Goa could not afford endless repairs to accident-prone churches, and nowadays the unluckiest chuch in Goa remains prone, disconsolate as a solid puddle. Once an imitation of a Gothic church, it now seems destined for a movie rôle in Gothic novels. The Royal Chapel of St Anthony (1543) was charmingly restored by the Portuguese in 1961 and serves as a distinctive reminder of 16th-century times, when the Augustinians raised it, and requested the statue of the saint, Portugal's patron, to be granted the rank of army captain and receive the emoluments thus due. To obtain his wages, the statue was solemnly (?) carried to the Treasury to receive the payment which one hopes was dedicated to 'good works'. The Royal Chapel has a doorway in a semicircular apse in front of the main façade, an intriguing feature.

We emerge on to a promontory overlooking the Mandovi, where 'Deste alto assistiu Afonso de Albuquerque em 25.xi.1510 a Reconquista de Goa', as a pillar still simply records. From this height Albuquerque directed the Reconquest of Goa, 1510. The Church built in 1544-9 to celebrate this victory, in this lofty place, was dedicated to Our Lady of the Rosary, and – with Bom Jesus – survives as the only other truly cruciform church in Old Goa. Earlier churches, like St Francis, have all been reconstructed, so Our Lady of the Rosary is now the oldest extant church in Old Goa, in Manueline style, with a main doorway through the lower floor of a triple storey tower. This west front, sturdy as a castle gate or barbican, has two small engaged cylindrical towers flanking the arched opening, and larger engaged cylindrical towers at the back of the square tower, in which bells are visible from ground level. The effect resembles that of a stairway and allows access to the upper part of the church, giving a busily secular effect, with the maritime twisted rope-moulding so typical of Manueline buildings to lash the building together like some spiritual vessel.

Another fascinating feature, within, is the Gujarati-style lower panel and columns of the tomb of Dona Catirina, wife of the Viceroy Garcia de Sa, near the main altar. Their nuptials were celebrated by St Francis Xavier himself, a fact which undoubtedly played a part in the decision to place her monument in such a crucial position, on the mount of victory, in the church built to honour a vow made by Albuquerque before his death. On this Holy Hill we look westward down to the Mandovi and Divar Island, towards the city of Panjim which would assume the mantle of administrative headquarters with the gradual dereliction of Old Goa, by a Royal Decree of 1843.

*Old Goa. Church of Our Lady of the Rosary*

The three-metre statue of a poet in the garden north of Bom Jesus dates from as recently as 1960: it represents Luís Vaz de Camões (1524-1580), author of the great epic poem *Os Lusíadas* (1572), which sets out to accomplish no less than the narrative of Portugal and her exploits abroad over a century and a quarter which saw their empire extend from Japan to Brazil based on command of the oceans. The Portuguese prowess was due partly to the speed with which they disposed of the Islamic threat at home (by 1267), compared with the frustrations of the Spaniards until their Reconquest was completed with the capture of Granada in 1492.

Camões viewed the Portuguese enterprise as a patriotic poet, taking very seriously his country's claims as a civilising and Christianising power. His own father, a ship's captain, was wrecked off Goa then – surviving rescue on a plank – succumbed on dry land. Luís frequented the great University of Coimbra, as I did four hundred years later, and Lisbon court circles, where he began to write poems and plays. After an unfortunate love affair he left Lisbon in 1547 for Ceuta, where he lost eye; returning to Lisbon he was involved in a brawl but pardoned after nine months in jail on condition that he set sail for India, in May 1553. He returned seventeen years later, poor and frustrated, the manuscript of his magnum opus nearly ready to print.

The hero of his poem is Vasco da Gama, the great explorer who had died – significantly to the poet – in the year of Luís's birth; the analogy is with Virgil's *Aeneid*; for the followers of Aeneas to Rome, read the followers of Lusus, mythical settler of Portugal. But of course there is much more than plain tales of da Gama to the florid, passionate *Lusíadas*. Camões moves us with the poignant fate of Inês de Castro, excites us with the chivalric narrative of the Twelve to England, and stirs us on the Island of Love. His prophecies make eloquent reading, and his elevated style combines the best of classical and romantic diction. Not only a faithful factual record, the epic is a personal testimony to a life spent abroad in the service – not always suitably rewarded – of his country. Sir Richard Burton's English version of the *Lusiads*, which you might expect a masterpiece judging by the master's scholarship and brilliance, failed entirely to win the English over: he was so faithful to the text and the style of his sixteenth-century Portuguese author that he totally ignored the modern reader's requirements, and it fell from the press stone dead. The way to read Camões is to use the text edited by Frank Pierce (Oxford University Press, 1973) with the prose translation by W.C. Atkinson (Penguin, 1952).

Here is an extract, as Jupiter reassures Venus about the future of her beloved Portuguese, with my prose translation from Canto II:

*Goa vereis aos Mouros ser tomada,*
*A qual vira despois a ser senhora*
*De todo o Oriente, e sublimada*
*Cos triunfos da gente vencedora.*
*Ali, soberba, altiva e exalçada,*
*Ao Gentio que os ídolos adora*
*Duro freio porá, e a toda a terra*
*Que cuidar de fazer aos vossos guerra.*

*You will see Goa seized from the Muslims, and then become mistress of*
*all the Orient, raised high by the conquerors' victories. At that great*
*height, exalted, proud, they will keep at bay all those who worship idols*
*- all those who dare to wage war against your champions.*

Much later in *Os Lusíadas*, Vasco da Gama and his mariners are guided to the Island of Love, where a nymph foresees the 'future' of the Portuguese overseas, though of course Camões is retelling in summary what was already known to his contemporaries. This passage from Canto X implies a knowledge that Albuquerque took Goa briefly in 1509, then definitively in 1510.

*Que gloriosas palmas tecer vejo,*
*Com que Vitória a fronte lhe coroa,*
*Quando, sem sombra vã de medo ou pejo,*
*Toma a ilha ilustríssima de Goa,*
*Despois, obedecendo ao duro ensejo,*
*A deixa, e ocasião espera boa*
*Com que a torne a tomar, que esforço e arte*
*Vencerão a fortuna e o próprio Marte.*

*I see Victory, weaving palm-leaf garlands to crown the hero's brow*
*when, without fear of apprehension, he takes the most illustrious*
*island-city-Goa. Then, obeying fate's decree, he abandons it, and takes*
*the next chance to seize it back, for military skill and power can over-*
*come even Dame Fortune and the God of War.*

**Panaji** (its official name)
The declaration of Panjim's status came as a formality, because the Viceroys had already departed Old Goa in 1759, setting up new quarters in the former palace of the Adil Shah dynasty on the southern shore of the Mandovi. Nowadays the Government Secretariat, the restored palace, adapted and transformed, possesses that musty and faded aroma of yellowing dog-eared files with paper moistly warm like the tongue of a resting mongrel. Flies buzz; beneath and around us the dreaded slog of silent bookworms and beetles, woodlice and cockroaches, reduces solidity to dust.

The 17th-century Mamai Kamat House facing the Secretariat still houses the descendants of the original extended family, who possess a few shops and landholdings and live in ten family groups within the great complex.

Panaji's population is around 40,000 – a tiny number for an Indian state capital – and the atmosphere seems correspondingly intimate, when you compare it with Madras's 3½ million. Goans complain endlessly about the desecration of beaches and villages, but Panaji City has resisted many encroachments such as vast supermarkets or overblown hotel complexes, to its credit and benefit. Panjim glows with flower-decked open balconies, bright cafes, welcoming bars (there is no prohibition in Goa), and women dressed in bright European dresses (if Christian) or glowing saris (if Hindu). Glimpses to a *razangann* or inner courtyard will show you another world, nostalgic for a Portugal most will never have visited. The leafy suburb of Fontainhas contrasts abruptly with the noisy bazaars of Madras or Madurai: we are definitely halfway to Europe in atmosphere. Here one sees few of the southern Indian ankle-length lungis; rather more of the Maharashtran dhotis, but preponderantly the Goan prefers open-necked shirt and trousers, with dusty shoes, and occasionally a briefcase announces the businessman, clerk or entrepreneur: the Goan is likely to succeed as a man of the world.

I stayed in Fontainhas at the Panjim Inn, at E-212 31 January Road, an 18th-century mansion with fourteen charming old-fashioned rooms, some with antique furniture such as the *almirah* or cupboard-wardrobe and four-poster beds, and many with verandahs. Amid houses of the nobility, and corner shops, the Panjim Inn has always belonged to the Heredia family who welcome you now to a home they once inhabited themselves. The Tibetan waiter, his face still shocked by the Chinese invasion of his country, brought me on to my balcony one pot coffee, one bouble omlett, two toas butter, and one jam ounce, as the bill explained. I offered him a seat but 'waiters do not sit down in India, sir'.

I heard a scuffling on the corrugated iron awning protecting the balcony from rain and sun. 'What is the noise?' I enquired of the Tibetan, wondering about rats or the occasional robust mongoose. The low-lidded Buddhist folded his arms in compassion. 'Heavy birds', he replied.

Like thousands of Tibetans he has settled in India as a refugee, and his knowledge of English enables him to take a wide variety of jobs in service industries.

Past a video shop I found opposite the Don Bosco School the offices of *Gulab*, a family magazine in both Konkani and English, and was welcomed by Bonaventure Peter Fernandes, the self-styled 'James Hadley Chase' of Goa, who writes his Konkani novels as Bonaventure D'Pietro. We talked about the future of Goan mansions: the Silva house at Margao, the Loyola Furtado mansion at Chinchinim, and the SBI

*Panaji. Panjim Inn, Fontainhas. Breakfast verandah*

building in Panjim. The Vasco da Gama Club, once owned by a Portuguese count, is being pulled down, as is the Macías Gomes house, a distinguished building that was allowed to crumble. The rising demand for living-space comes not from Goans themselves, but from immigrants who have turned the city of Vasco – now the main port – into an overcrowded slum, creating intolerable new demands for water and electricity which cannot be adequately met, and local unemployment, with a consequent rise in drug abuse and crime. Panjim, Margao and Mapusa are also crowded with Indians from other states, and only the villages of the interior seem relatively unaffected by that frenzy for change, speed, and money which demoralise the cities.

I was invited by a member of the ubiquitous Menezes family ('Aleluia Menezes & Sons, Hardware, Paint, Tools' reminded me of names in a Gabriel García Márquez novel) to take feni with him at Joseph's Bar. Normally averse to any form of alcohol, I took a gingerly sip of the drink distilled from palm toddy: it is an acquired taste, and I did not acquire it, but connoisseurs recommend cashew feni, distilled from the red cashew apple forming above the nut. Nothing is wasted in India.

On the waterfront G.X. Verlecar, Joalharia, the jeweller's, might give the impression that Portuguese is spoken, but in fact the younger generation, possibly partly for patriotic reasons, chooses not to learn Portuguese, and the signs can be quite misleading, as on a film set. At Pinto's Hairdresser close by I found an expert barber charging a pittance for a thorough haircut and shampoo. A dog pissed hurriedly near the door.

At the Rio Restaurant of the shabby Imperial Hotel, near the Old Bus Stand, I dined off prawn biryani before taking the *Santa Monica* river launch, garishly lit, for an evening cruise of folksong and dances down towards the Arabian Sea, and curving round into the Zuari, lights winking in confederacy from the shore. The tourists on the launch were mainly holidaymakers from Bombay, showing off and giggling, clicking snaps as the twilight shaded into dark, their flash bulbs irradiating the deck like miniature flares. One folk dance told the story of two beautiful girls wishing to cross the Mandovi, but the ferryman refuses because the river is in spate; they offer him their jewels, then their rings, and finally agree to dance especially for him... After forty minutes the tipsy Bombayites tired of harvest dances and traditional songs: they started baying for Hindi pops and the Italian pop *María*, requests granted despite the fact that the Goan tenor did not know the Italian words. Liquor induced the seated public to stand, sway and stomp in solo exhibitions of sensual display unimaginable in Maharashtra. 'Come', said a husky voice in my ear: a transvestite emerging after dark, the long nail on his little finger carmine. I eluded his grip.

Next morning I roamed out from Panjim Inn to the rising Church of the Immaculate Conception (1541) where, on the hill overlooking Church Square, tall twin towers reach up to the sky as a historic landmark for ships. The magnificent balustraded staircase invites you to climb it for the view, like the Spanish Steps in Rome, and so of course you do. An Australian backpacker with her money pouch strapped tight looked like a marsupial, curved forward to prevent her backload from pulling her to the ground.

'I have no faith in God,' she grumbled to me disconsolately, 'so why dye visit all these churches?' 'What you might have,' I suggested, 'is a touching faith in the power of history to heal your absence of faith or hope. You cannot feel the mystifying circularity of oriental life because you were brought up in the mystifying linearity of occidental life, but in a continent far removed from your origins.'

'It's all a mystery to me,' agreed the backpacker, wiping her perspiring brow as the women attending early morning mass shuffled into their accustomed positions. 'I wouldn't have come here pertickly, but me mate Charlene's stuck at the hostel sick as a sow and can't get out, so I'm doing the Immaculate Conception on my own.' 'Good luck', I waved from the altar of Our Lady of Fatima. The church, originally a small chapel, was renovated in 1619, and stands north of the 18th-century Friday Mosque renovated in 1935. Farther along Dr Dada Vaidya Road, on the opposite side at the T-junction leading to Dr Shirgaonkar Road, I found the Mahalakshmi Temple, emphasising the faith some Goans have always kept with India's oldest organised religion.

Richard Burton's *Goa and the Blue Mountains* (1851) reveals the young traveller at the outset of a career that would take him to Arabia, Utah, and the source of the Nile. He stayed in Panjim nearly a month, during which time he visited a convent to consult some sources for the book he was writing, and chanced to glimpse a beautiful nun who seemed melancholy. He thereupon conceived the romantic plot of carrying her off from durance vile to freedom under the British flag, where she could live happily ever after.

He visited the convent regularly now, to spy out the land, 'studying' folios of St Augustine and offering 'medicine' bottles filled with cognac to the prioress and sub-prioress whom he memorably described as 'more like Gujarat apes than mortal women'. From this point the adventure swings out of the Byronic into the realm of Sindbad the Sailor. The young sister appeared modest and moist-eyed with alarm at first, but eventually she accepted a bouquet with a billet-doux inside containing full instructions on how to elude her Roman Catholic captors. Burton prepared a fast lateen-rigged vessel known as a *patimar*, procured false keys to garden gate and cloisters and with two confederates, also disguised, decamped with... the sub-prioress! They had taken the wrong turning and entered the wrong room. With a shriek, the fat negress sounded the alarm, but the three men had by then disappeared into the tropical night, leaving the fair damosel to her unknown fate. When reading Burton and his fabulous sorties into Panjim's velvety operatic night, like Mozart's Don Giovanni or Rossini's Almaviva, my mind's eye turns to the young, pale nun and I see her as the young Virgin Mary in the London National Gallery paintings by Dante Gabriel Rossetti, *Ecce Ancilla Domini* (1849-53), where Mary cowers in uncomprehending fear before the angel of the Annunciation; and the serene *Girlhood of Mary Virgin* (1848-51), both as it happens contemporary with Burton's exploit.

Wandering east to Ourem Creek, I passed a temple to Hanuman, near which little black pigs grazed with that single-minded absorption we have learned to expect from the more pampered Empress of Blandings. I arrived at a small office or home, where a charming lady was brushing the courtyard with a twig broom. Over the door ran the legend 'Om Shanti, Rajayoga, Brahmakumaris Centre' – of course I went in. The lady in the turquoise sari herself entered the door and greeted me. 'Do you teach raja yoga here?' I enquired.

'Why of course,' she answered, beckoning me to a small bench.

'What are the hours?'

'Hours we have eight to eleven mornings, five to seven thirty evenings, can begin any day, most welcome.'

'What is the charge?'

'Charge we don't have. Only voluntary contributions we accept from regular students.'

Santosh then proceeded to tell me about the association, Prajapita Brahmakumaris Ishwariya Vishwa Vidyalaya, with its headquarters at Pandav Bhavan on Mount Abu. The sect was founded in 1937, but its first centre opened in 1953, and there are now 1,800 centres in India and overseas, including three centres and three subcentres in Goa. The sect preaches continence, purity of thought, words and deeds, and purity of diet, taking only food congenial to spiritual advancement, as prepared by a continent person practising yoga. In addition, one should take a daily lesson of God's knowledge and pay attention to divine virtues such as introversion, contentment, tolerance, humility, righteousness, detachment and sobriety. One should remember Shiva or God or Allah (the yogi may call Divinity by any name he chooses) constantly, at work or at play as well as while secluded. The Brahma Kumaris sect requires no mantra, no *japa* or incantation, no breath-control, no rosary. What this type of yoga calls for is a steadily-acquired knowledge of God the Father who is Shiva, plus a keen aspiration to be united with Him through the practice of purity.

It is strange how the asceticism of Brahma Kumaris yoga contrasts

with the freedom from carnal restraints practised at Bhagwan Shri Raj-
neesh's Osho Commune in Pune, where the majority of worshippers are
Europeans. Just as Buddhism split from Hinduism to prefer the Middle
Way, so I courteously expressed my inability to become enchanted by
vegetarian chastity towards union with a God in whom I cannot believe.
'I am looking into your eyes', murmured the lady, 'and you reflect
already the perfect serenity we teach. Why should you come here?' I felt
chastened: I seek the unsettling, the distant, the inchoate, the *Deserto
dei Tartari*, and should gladly have taken Dante's place through the
Inferno, through Purgatory, through Paradise, just for the insecurity and
danger of the adventure. A charming little white kitten scuffled with a
fallen leaf at the edge of the lane where thoughtless traffic roared along.

Glistening with coconut oil against heatstroke, I strolled parallel with
Ourem Creek and found the Archives of Goa, with a cannon outside
and within a Ganesh image from Verna in Salcete taluka. Dr P.P.
Shirodkar, the Director, spoke with me about the influence of the Nath
cult in Goa. The Nath or spiritual leader is considered in this cult the
only pure soul, while everyone else is human, and there are no castes.
Nathism arose in Bengal by the early 10th century and quickly spread
throughout India. The doctrine states that Shakti created the universe,
Shiva nurtures it, Time destroys it and Natha brings *mukti*, or liberation.
Though Shiva was their Adinath and their chief human guru one Mat-
syendranath, it was Goraknath who spread the cult, followed by nine
other spiritual leaders (avatars of Goraknath) and the child-saint pro-
digy in Maharashtra Dnyandev, whose 9000-stanza poem *Dnyaneshvari*
(1289) influenced every generation of Hindu philosophers, and even –
this ranks with St Matthew's obsessive emphasis on showing Old Testa-
ment auguries of the New – the extraordinary *Christapurana* of Fr
Thomas Stephens (1549-1619) written in the Marathi current in the
early 17th century. The Nathas took honey and opium, and allowed
themselves every kind of meat but beef and pork. Numerous Nath
teachers and saints have shrines throughout Goa today: Bhairava;
four-handed Ravalnath also called a Kshetrapal, a deity who protects
the locality from climatic disaster, witchcraft, and snakebites; and the
three-headed Dattatreya, combined Shiva, Brahma and Vishnu in one.

Dr Shirodkar is also the author of *Goa's Struggle for Freedom* (Delhi,
1988), and stands for the correction from a Eurocentric view of Goa to a
more indigenous frame of mind. The Historical Archives has the largest
collection of Portuguese-domination literature in Asia except for the
Lisbon Archives, and is regularly used by scholars from all over the
world, being especially rich in primary manuscript sources.

Out of the Archives, I wandered down Rua Ourem, crossing Pato
Bridge to the Department of Tourism, where I met A.M. Viegas, a
tourist official here for twenty-eight years – going back to the Por-

tuguese period. I asked him about reconstruction of the Mandovi bridge, which collapsed in 1986, killing four people; years later the bridge remains as it was and the crossing to North Goa has still to be made in a ferry that looks like a World War II landing craft. 'This will be done', consoled Mr Viegas. In June 1987 the new Goa state government announced that tourism would become a state industry, enabling all future hotels to receive a 25% subsidy, and land for hotels could be compulsorily acquired by the state. Protesters demanded public discussion before the master plan became law, but some were jailed and on release formed part of a new Vigilant Goans Army. 'The creation of tourist ghettoes' claimed Roland Martin of the VGA, 'had meant fishermen lost their jobs, homes had been destroyed and local people had become subservient.' A.M. Viegas admitted there had been conflict and corruption, but according to a UNDP report there is still plenty of scope for expanding tourism in Goa. In the capital area there can be no development of a zone extending from Campal to Miramar, the Fontainhas district, and the whole of Old Goa. Tourism is the logical service industry to counteract low employment, without the pollution that heavy industry brings. New beaches will be opened, with adequate parking, changing-rooms and restaurants, and nothing will be allowed to disturb beaches within 200 metres of the sea. Harmala Beach, for instance, lies only 200 metres back, so rumours of development there are unfounded.

The Church in Goa has joined the VGA in condemning the industry of tourism, because of the danger it perceives 'to the moral fabric'; nudism, drugs, free sex, easily available alcohol have been among the cited dangers. Moreover, while citizens of Bardez receive water supplies for about one hour a day, the Taj Hotel in Candolim receives water twenty-four hours a day, and benefits from a 50% government water subsidy according to the VGA.

Genial, tolerant and well-informed, Mr Viegas appreciates the difficulties of Goans who feel hard done by the advent of five-star tourism, but feels sure that a compromise can be reached. Twenty thousand foreign tourists must be found beds, food and water each season, and the popularity of Goa is unlikely to decrease, as the flood of hippies decreases to a trickle, and charter tours of the middle classes from Europe constantly increase.

In Hotel Mandovi I browsed in the ground-floor bookshop, selecting a reprint of R.S. Whiteway's *The Rise of Portuguese Powers in India 1497-1550* and Khushwant Singh's novel *Delhi*. Over a vegetable curry I skimmed the day's Panjim *Herald*, with news of the recapture (by tranquilliser darts) of a national park lioness, the death by burning alive of three children in Maharashtra, birthday greetings to Mrs Maria Farreo of Chinchinim, the winning tickets (a Honda scooter top prize) in the raffle organised by St Mary's Convent High School in Mapusa, and an ad by Dr A. Bagalkot running 'Golden Opportunity! Don't be Disappointed!! Before or After Marriage!!! For the Real Charm of Healthy and Happy Married Life, to regain lost vigour vitality & strength and all secret diseases of both men and women.' The headlines were devoted to a fire destroying 73 km of telephone cables at Bambolim.

One-act play contests were announced at Bicholim (in Marathi), Assolna (in Konkani), and at the Kala Akademi in Panjim. If you feel like a stroll along the banks of the Mandovi, from Campal to Miramar, you will find the Arts Academy (Kala Akademi) on Bandodkar Marg just north of Dr Bragança Pereira Road, the latter named for the eminent ethnographer who served as President of the Permanent Commission of Archaeology. The Academy runs its own Goa Symphony Orchestra playing Western music and classical-style music by Goan composers, and organises performances of folksongs, dances, and drama. The Konkani-language *mando* is predominantly a love song, though it may reflect social comment, as in 'Expensive Days', a song performed by the Mohan Orchestra of Vasco da Gama:

> *Disandis hi mhargai choddot veta;*
> *Ixttamno, amcher vhodd odruxtt ieta.*
> *Aslolo bankantlea duddvancher jieta:*
> *Naslolo pejecho nis pieta.*

> *(Every day the prices rise;*
> *Friends, we're in for a quick demise.*
> *The haves can live like bankers and kings:*
> *The have-nots survive on free water springs.)*

You might be lucky enough to see the martial dance called *ghode modni*, the Christian *jagor* folk-drama, Portuguese-style folkdances such as the *corradinho*, the central Goan *mell* dance, and the Hindu *dhalo* dance, or their *fugdi*.

Gujaratis brought to Goa their male percussive stick-dance the *tonyamel*, and the female harvest-dance called *gof*. If you travel among the villages, you may see towards evening a story-teller in the traditional vein, telling *kahanis*, often in the form of a fable, and these may occasionally be seen in carnivals, especially the national three-day secular carnival announcing long Lent.

During my visit an Uttar Pradesh festival packed out the Kala Akademi, but the greatest concentration of activities there runs from November to December, with drama festivals in Marathi and Konkani, the annual art exhibition, and concerts including Christmas carols and sacred music.

Before a Kala Akademi concert, take an hour in the Santa Inez quarter for the parish church and the Museum of Goa, situated in the Ashir-wad Building (9-1 and 2-5.30; closed on weekends and public holidays).

## South Goa

The night bus from Mysore I designate the greatest rumpus thumpus uninterruptus parping ear-shattering experience of South India lived up to all I had heard about it and, rather than continue north to Panaji, I summoned up a shriek - above the general uproar - to ask the bus driver to slow down at Margao's stop for Benaulim, where I intended to rent a room, or failing that a mattress, in the beach resort. An auto-rickshaw bore me into the Arabian Seashore dawn at 5.45, and I knocked quietly, then with a little more conviction, at the door of L'Amour Beach Resort. Nobody came. At 6.20 the first Goan emerged from an upstairs room. 'All room full', he stated with unmistakeable finality. 'May I sit in a chair?' He silently gesticulated to a rickety chair in the kitchen, and began to stir last night's nameless victuals in a pot on the stove. Ten minutes later another two cooks arrived to spoil the broth. Bemused with fatigue, I stumbled out to Johncy Bar and Restaurant where a deck-chair stirred and silently agreed to my suggestion for omelette, coffee, toast, butter and jam. Watching a moving circus of flapping crows, sad but ever-hopeful pi-dogs with damaged ears and egos, and the first of the morning's circling seagulls, I sat alone in my sagging

*Benaulim. Beach restaurant, with pi-dogs*

wicker chair painted blue and white and surveyed the marquee. Its sand floor looked as though a metal-detector had produced a trove, then vanished taking it away. Pull-tops and lager tins, flattened cans and squeezed soft-drinks littered the soft sand: then an urchin with a rake pulled up the débris as the early sun hauled its bald pate over the blue horizon. Outrigger boats perched on the beach expectantly like resting members of a tug-o'-war team.

## Margao

I strolled back to Margao through the palm-groves, as trim men in short-sleeved shirts and western trousers gradually swelled the stream of pedestrians joining the world of work. A woman sat by the road, breast-feeding her baby with the assurance of a Sienese madonna. In Margao I found a tour company operating a whole-day tour of South Goa, and spent the time before departure visiting this town, much changed since Liberation.

Today it is over-crowded, its once-renowned cleanliness and tidiness just a memory. Jorge A. Barreto, the pioneer of modern Margao, would shudder at the litter in the street, and the grimy condition of commercial buildings. The Town Hall and Municipal Gardens still seem relatively well-tended, but the modern architecture of Margao looks tawdry beside that of the colonial era, such as the 1564 Church of the Holy Spirit, rebuilt in 1675, and the aristocratic town houses on the central square. The da Silva House known as Seven Shoulders dates from 1790, when the original da Silva served as secretary to the Viceroy. Look for its classical façade on to the street below a high-pitched roof and ambitious peaks. The interior has been affectionately maintained by the present da Silva family, who still use some rooms and the private chapel. The furniture is of the exuberant Eurasian Baroque, the original Portuguese aesthetic spiralling into fantastic cornices and curlicues, rich chandeliers and heavy-looking cabinets, tables and wardrobes betokening wealth and security.

And do not imagine that 'village life' outside such towns as Margao must have been any simpler or less grand. No: the wealthy Goans chose to create mansions in their local environment, where they would be grandees in a large feudal economy.

The Portuguese took Tiswadi taluka including Panjim and Velha Goa in 1510, and by 1543 had added Bardez and Salcete talukas to their sovereignty. So as the capital of Salcete Margao early became Christianized, and allied itself with the new conquerors to everyone's benefit.

Salcete is Goa's richest agricultural district, producing coconut, rice and cashews commercially, and enough fruit and vegetables for domestic consumption and often for sale, preponderantly papaya, bananas, mango, and the Malayalam *chakka*, Portuguese *jaca*, in English jack-

*Margao. Municipal Library*

fruit, confused by the excellent Rumphius and even Linnaeus with the plantain *Musa sapientum* though the botanical name of the jack-tree is *Artocarpus integrifolia*.

It was only in the 18th century that Ponda and Sanguem talukas, Quepem and Canacona, Pernem, Bicholim and Satari fell under Portuguese rule, Pernem being the last to be ceded – in 1778 – by its ruler in gratitude for their help against northern rivals in Maharashtra. Zealotry had died down by now, explaining why the north and east of Goa were never effectively Christianized.

Margao could hardly be taken for Faro in the Algarve, or an inland town near watery Aveiro, but the gracefully-arched two-storey white and red building housing the municipal library possesses its own charm, as does the monumental cross facing the west front of the church of the Holy Spirit, on broad Church Square. And if you have the chance to see other churches in this area, look for those in Curtorim (9 km from Margao) and Verna (on the way to the Zuari), where the bliss of Goan *sucego* will overpower you by stealth.

## Colva to Cabo
Santos hailed me as 'mister' for the South Goa tour, and the tumultuous bus, its loudspeaker blaring Hindi popular songs in a seamless band,

193

*Colva. Beach*

sped along the 7 km to Colva Beach. 'It's excruciating, isn't it?' commiserated the man in the next seat, a charming Goan with a wife and daughter.

'Which part of Goa do you come from?' I enquired.

'Actually, Wood Green,' he replied, 'but my hardware shop is in Primrose Hill: Chalcot Road, I don't know if you know that area.' Dominic D'Silva had emigrated so many years back that his daughter speaks English as her first language, but they wanted to come back and see the old country and, in January, I can well appreciate his preference. Past coconut groves, the silver sands at Colva spread invitingly. 'Ten minutes', commanded Santos. Entrepreneurs spread their fresh coconuts for hacking: 'take milk, take meat', they beckoned. I swallowed the natural goodness while watching two brightly-dressed girls by a pool cleaning freshly-caught shellfish. A rowboat leant luxuriously to starboard, lazy as a vacant sunbed.

North from Colva you cruise through Cansaulim's roads narrow enough for only one bus-width among groves of cashews ripening from February to May. Past Dabolim Airport, for international as well as domestic flights since 1983, we came to Vasco da Gama, which has overtaken Panaji as a port. Political parties appealing to a partly illiterate electorate identify themselves by symbols more than by sophisti-

*Marmagao. Manganese and iron ore ready for export*

cated political platforms. In India one votes for film stars, dynasties, or personalities known in society. 'Vote for Boat' urged one hoarding: 'Vote for Wheel' countermanded the next. 'Vote and elect Elephant'. 'Vote Lion.' 'Vote for Cycle, G.L.P.' Long after elections, thousands of posters remain pasted up because nobody bothers to pull them down.

Vasco's Church of St Andrew dates from the 16th century, but the modern city teems with industrial and commercial concerns of the late 20th century on the edge of Marmagao or Mormugao and its deep-water anchorage, its special handling and loading equipment for ores making it seem like any northern European port, except for the heat and humidity. The capital was in the process of being moved from Golden Goa in 1703, when one Viceroy even headquartered at Marmagao, but the idea was abandoned a few years later, and industry rather than administration claims Marmagao and Vasco nowadays. Marmagao, with its broad avenues and neat bungalows, was designed by a town-planner called Maravilhas, literally 'Marvels'. There is a ferry from Marmagao to Dona Paula if you want to reach Panaji quickly, and this has the advantage of giving you the chance to see iron-ore barges on their way to dump their cargo beside the harbour. Manganese and other ores have replaced the more romantic cargoes of diamonds (the trade fell off in the 1720s) and the transshipment of Moluccan spices.

The old fort of Marmagao, which protected civilians during the emergency of 1683, when a Mughal army threatened Goa, has long ago vanished, but one can visualise the fortifications here from the surviving example commanding the northern shore of the Mandovi at Fort Aguada. Other fortresses commanding susceptible headlands – from south to north – include Cabo de Rama south of Betul Beach, Fort Aguada, Fort of the Wise Men (Reis Magos), Chapora, and Tiracol.

The regular daily tour then enters the Seminary, church and school of the All-India Mission of the Society of the Missionaries of St Francis Xavier, founded in 1887 by Fr Bento Martins.

Anyone thinking that the mission apostolate of the Christian Church has crumbled away will be interested to see the expansive grounds of the Pilar Seminary, with its magnificent view over the Zuari estuary and Marmagao harbour. Today the Society has a Bishop (of Port Blair, Andaman and Nicobar), 133 priests, 24 brothers and 112 students, not to mention over 70 pre-novices and 21 novices, and operates 33 houses in eight states and three union territories. Dispensaries offer free medical aid to the poor, who also benefit from rice-banks, co-operative societies and model farms. After a pre-novitiate period, seminarists experience one year as novices, three years of graduation in Nagpur, a year of work in the missions or schools, and finally four years of theology, after which they are ordained as priests. They run their own print-

*Pilar Seminary. From the top of the printing works*

ing press, and have opened a museum (8-1 and 3-6) with a model village house and objects from the zenith of the Kadamba kingdom (1005-1311).

Dona Paula Beach resort is a boating paradise, with speedboats and pedaloes for hire, named for a Viceroy's daughter who, legend relates, fell in love with a local fisherman whom she could not marry for good 'social' reasons yet, unconvinced, insisted on committing suicide by leaping off this headland. To the east of Dona Paula stands a pseudo-Portuguese holiday village called Cidade de Goa and designed by Charles Correa, who was also responsible for Panaji's new arts academy, and suggests that his beach village has the visual appeal of a Moroccan casbah. Within, rooms are conceived in three styles: Portuguese, colonial, and Gujarati. The South Goa tour doesn't take you to the Prainha Cottages, with showers, balconies and communal dining-room, so the area is deserted and for some tastes all the better for it, with the Pescador restaurant close by. Romantic, unspoilt (for the time being!) and quiet, these cottages may be more expensive than the average Goan hotel room, but those dedicated to beach life will find them enchanting.

Jutting out into the Arabian Sea is the 'cape' or Cabo atop which can be seen the latest in a long sequence of buildings; a local shrine gave way to a Christian chapel, then a Portuguese fort begun in 1540 which ended

*Dona Paula. Beach resort*

197

by protecting a nearby Franciscan monastery of 1594, expanded in 1610-2 and 1636, with its own Church of the Blessed Virgin Mary. The Portuguese military abandoned the fort, leaving sufficient ammunition in the monastery for the peaceable brothers to protect themselves with four bronze cannon.

The British entered Goa in 1797 and stayed until 1813, establishing at Cabo a new military hospital and barracks which the Portuguese destroyed in 1848, when the monastery was taken over by the Archbishop of Goa as his official residence. In 1866 the Governor-General took it over as his rural residence and the Raj Niwas we see today is the official residence of the Lieutenant-Governor of Goa, a fine mansion mainly of local laterite with elegant verandahs and superb sea views.

### Around Ponda

At the Tourist Hostel in Panjim we stopped for lunch: the kingfish tasted prime, with ample salad and cold beer. The all-day tour takes in Old Goa in the afternoon, then continues on the road to Ponda via Sri Mangesh and Sri Shantadurga.

The Mangesh temple near Mardol village, mostly of the 18th century but of 16th century foundation, is generally viewed as the most important Hindu temple in Goa. Mangesh is another name for Shiva, and his temple rises in the centre of a large compound. The great 'film-voice' singer Lata Mangeshkar is from this village. Drums beaten on the left of the entrance summon pilgrims, who rush as if to a bargain sale, choosing a plate of offerings for Lord Shiva from the vendors at the temple gate. A priest decked in white presents the offerings to a Shiva image covered in heavily ornate silver decorations, and worshippers implore intercession for their own private cases. 'Make this our journey safe'. 'Allow the unworthy woman thy bond-slave to bear a child.' The priest smears a red *tilak* on her brow with a wrinkled brown index finger and moves smoothly to the next supplicant. Enormous crystal chandeliers dominate the opulent ceiling. The deepstambha or lamp tower outside might be considered an upright tower of Pisa, with its graceful arched niches divided by seven ascending pilasters, the whole tapering into a dome topped by a kalasha, or ceremonial pot. Cashew and pineapples locally grown stood in piles and pyramids awaiting eager buyers from the towns. Seventeen lads played cricket to the exclusion of every other thought against the temple wall, without admonition.

We are in Ponda taluka, which has enjoyed freedom of Hindu worship since the liberal constitution of 1833, and equality of Hindus with Christians since the declaration of republic status in 1910. At the height of anti-Hindu repression, images from the Old Conquests were smuggled into Ponda taluka, and temples which had been allowed to deteriorate soon found new decoration and rehabilitation. Near Sri

*Shanta Durga Temple, near Ponda*

Mangesh are the temple to Lakshmi known as Mahalasa Narayani, the Amritsar-like temple to Ramnath, and the Sri Shanta Durga temple to Goa's special goddess of peace, symbolising reconciliation between Shaivites and Vaishnavites. Muslims now comprise only about 4% of Goa's population and are found mainly in Bicholim and Vasco. Forty-one per cent of the population is Catholic and the remainder form a Hindu majority dominating the interior.

Shanta Durga in the village of Kavalem was filled during my visit with a political rally, though over-resonant amplification made comprehension virtually impossible. The whole meeting took on the aspect of a quasi-religious ritual, in which the faithful participated. The tapering

199

lamp tower had been freshly whitewashed: I expected to see a flight of doves emerge from the round-arched niches. A temple was built here in the 16th century, far enough from the Portuguese Inquisition to be safe, but it has enjoyed many centuries of rebuilding, accretions and endowments, so that the present temple centred on the 16th-century image of Durga from Kavelesi (Salcete taluka), is essentially attributable to the Maratha sovereign Shahu and dates from 1738, when the Marathas attacked Goa and almost completed their conquest. 18th-century and 19th-century accretions often seem unsightly in western buildings, but the pious East places more emphasis on religious intent than artistic coherence, so such irregularities seem piquant rather than aggressive.

As at every other active temple, a row of women squats with offerings before them; the pilgrim acquires merit by buying a garland, bananas, or a neatly-composed plate of different foods, and offering it in the temple, usually through the mediation of a priest at the main shrine. Shanta Durga for instance has several side shrines, but the main press is to catch a glimpse of the central image.

The connection of Ponda taluka with Islam can be judged from the ruined Safa mosque, found off the road to Banastarim. Built by Ali Adil Shah in 1560 as a defiant demonstration of Bijapuri Islamic conquest, the mosque was ravaged by the angry Portuguese, but enough remains to welcome visitors on the occasion of Muslim festivals such as 'Id al-Adha and 'Id al-Fitr. Graceful yet austere, the little rectangular mosque provides a limpid counterbalance to the riot of baroque imagery on nearby Hindu temples, though its great rectangular water tank seems oddly ill-at-ease in this Muslim context, for an ablutions area would be expected on the eastern flank, so one might infer that it is a Hindu temple tank. However, the ornamentation and arches around the tank prove it to be contemporary with the mosque. Remains of columns show that the tilting roof would have been extended to protect Muslims at prayer during monsoon rains: the mosque would have been too small to accommodate all worshippers at major festivals, or even at Friday congregation. Within, a Western clock consorts oddly with a tall mihrab and modestly-proportioned minbar. The Safa mosque represents the nascent Bijapuri style, before its flowering in more grandiose Vijayanagar times, comparable with the decorous Najdi-style sandstone mosque in al-Qasim confronted with the enormous new Prophet's Mosque in al-Madinah al-Munawwarah.

Only one other important mosque in Goa should be seen (if one excludes the Friday Mosques in Sanguem and Panjim) and that is in an area with a large minority of Muslims even today: Bicholim. Here the Namazgah Mosque was created in the 17th century under no less a figure than Akbar, the future Mughal emperor, after a victory over the infidel Portuguese.

The conductor on the bus from Ponda lodged two fingers into his mouth, whistled, and yelled 'Rao re!' twice, mechanically, like a sweaty brown robot. The *carreira* or bus service employs as drivers failed airport pilots who take the crown of the road at a speed approaching that of Concorde, but with a much greater decibel count, bouncing up from rocks by the uneven roadside whenever they pull up with shrieking brakes as another bus swerves round a corner, splaying passengers from one side to the other while the conductor shoves through the ruck of heaving humanity, roughly twice the maximum load permitted.

## North Goa

The full-day North Goa Tour organised out of Panaji at 9 a.m. takes the ferry and bus to Mapusa, and generally encompasses the Arvalem waterfall, Sri Datta Mandir, Sri Vithal Mandir, Lake Mayem (lunch here or at Mapusa), Mapusa town, the beaches of Vagator, Anjuna and Calangute, and the area of Fort Aguada.

This omits the atmosphere of villages and mansions off the beaten track, including the small town of Pernem. As you travel north to Pernem, you are aware of approaching Maharashtra, with its wild and windy plateau, unkempt fields, raggedy urchins, and the sheer oppressiveness of distances. Goa is manageably small by Indian standards, but Maharashtra straggles north almost indistinguishable from the vastness of Karnataka. Pernem resists the encroaching, eroding far horizons of Maharashtra, but it compromises its Christianized Goan evolution by making room in its taluka for many Hindu temples. One is a complex of five temples 7 km away from the village at Parshem devoted mainly to Sri Bhagvati, but also to Sridev Ravalnath, Sri Sateri, Sridev Bhivangi Panchakshari and to Brahma. Another is a complex of five temples at Mandrem (20 km from Mapusa) dedicated to Sri Sapteshwar, Sri Bhagvati, Sri Narayan, Sridev Ravalnath, and Satpurush-Rampurush. In the village of Dhargal, 14 km from Mapusa, stands another Shanta Durga temple, with an image rescued from the iconoclastic Portuguese in Bardez, and protected here since then.

In Pernem itself, one of the major sights (never shown on an organised tour) is the Deshprabhu Museum, in the entrance courtyard of sixteen courts around which the landowning nobles (as Viscounts) made their grandiose home. The façade dates from the 19th century, but the museum reveals the life of many generations as the Deshprabhu family sought the best conditions for itself and its workers in an area Portuguese since 1778.

I hovered on the threshold of Panaji Tourist Hostel, avoiding the bookshop offering postcards at 2½ rupees each when anxious boys of eight or ten were offering them at 10 for 3 rupees, and the tour guide hollered 'Not Goa, Not Goa!' and we all – with a majority of Indian holidaymakers and about four foreigners – trooped on the free ferry *Goa Jivan* to cross the Mandovi amid jostling youths and serious businessmen with neat black briefcases or cardboard cartons tied up with string.

'Please allow me to introduce myself', said a quietly-spoken Gujarati. 'Hitendra M. Vyas of 7/B Sudershan Society 1, Near Naranpura Post Office, Ahmadabad.' 'You're on holiday, Mr Vyas?' He shook his head in affirmation. 'I don't understand this Konkani, Marathi they are speaking. I am speaking English, this way everyone understands first glance.' On the bus, the *only* language of communication was English; a northerner grumbled 'this is Hindi land, everyone should be speaking Hindi' but such wish-fulfilment is patently far from the truth, for the languages of Goa are basically Konkani, Marathi and English, with Hindi and Portuguese a long way behind. The film music tapes had soon been turned up so loud that I begged for relative quiet: I could make out nothing the guide was saying, and Mr Vyas had to yell in my ear to make himself heard. Eventually, a lateral thinker in the front seat agreed to sit in my place so I could be *behind* the loudspeaker, which was left all day at full volume.

The bus from Panaji ferry to Mapusa passes Alto Porvorim, the Holy Family High School, Motel La Joy, beautiful villas in wooded grounds,

*Panaji. Broken bridge across the Mandovi, from the northern bank*

Porvorim itself, and Monte de Guirim before flumfing breathlessly into the fumefilled hurly-burly of the bus-stand. Coconut palm trees mark Goa's verticals, and ricefields her horizontals. Bamboo groves, common enough in North Goa, have not marked Indian sensibilities as they have marked the Chinese or Japanese artistic tradition. Yoked oxen ploughed in the fields, cashew nuts were being harvested, and eldritch banyans splayed their enormous limbs by the roadside. We are climbing into the breeze-swept hills round Sankhali, the Portuguese Sanquelim, near the iron-ore mining region of Goa. The Sri Vithal Mandir is named for the tribal deity of the Ranes, a Rajput tribe compelled by politics to emigrate south in the 18th century. Their complex history in Portuguese Goa saw them on the side of the colonials then battling against them. Sri Vithal is an aspect of Lord Vishnu, like the Vithoba aspect (both hands on the waist) worshipped at the pilgrimage town of Pandharpur, east of the inland road from Goa to Bombay. And indeed Sri Vithal Mandir looks much more like a northern Indian temple than a typically Goan shrine, and though restoration has recently been carried out by descendants of the immigrant Ranes, some of the original columns have been left visible. You can ask to see the temple cart, if it is not on show. Next to the temple in Vithalwadi, Sanquelim, stands an old Ranes house on great stone columns with an impressive façade. The Chaitra-Purnima festival held in April is especially significant here, and the Datta Jayanti Festival every December at the Sri Datta Mandir, set in an areca-palm grove close to pipal and kadamba woods.

Datta was, with Soma and Durvasas, one of the three sons of the Brahman god Dattatreya, who incarnated aspects of Shiva, Brahma and most particularly Vishnu. Datta Mandir is visible above a low white wall, with a red-tiled roof protecting an open-air mandapam in front of the sanctuary to Trimurthi, the trinity of Brahma, Shiva and Vishnu. A handful of vendors in shorts squatted hopefully beside the entrance: one sold me Britannia Glucose D biscuits, made in Hungerford Street, Calcutta, and I munched Bengali biscuits beneath a Goan sky, as worshippers hastened to provide votive offerings within. A Hindu policeman with a whistle posted himself near the mandapam to stop anyone wearing shoes from soiling the shrine. Tamils have to buy melon slices in English from a lady at her fruit-stall: she understands no Tamil and they have no Konkani.

'Where are you from, Uncle?' piped up a little lad, who darted out of the way as a sacred cow lurched to gobble a melon rind at his feet. A Sanquelim woman at a fruit-stall sat on a machete handle, elegantly passing a fresh papaya along its blade, instead of chopping it macho-like from the shoulder. I thought of that story in Kipling's *Plain Tales from the Hills* in which a parody of an English Miss visualises India as 'divided equally between jungle, tigers, cobras, cholera and sepoys'. Like most of

India, Datta Mandir at Sanquelim will never see any of them: it basks instead in that Hindu rota of night and day which *in parvo* may stand for the wheel of destiny. We enter the temple as far as it is licit; we take part in the spiritual adventure as far as our understanding will permit; and we return, enhanced to a greater or lesser degree according to our sympathy. Mr Vyas from Ahmadabad smiled vaguely at me with that tolerance abundant in India as rice-grains, and we resumed our rackety, rickety busride to the waterfalls of Arvalem.

A cul-de-sac which might be at the farthest point of Shangri-La leads to a narrow path with a tenuous village preceding a Hindu temple. Arvalem waters are used to irrigate fields of rice (the staple food), coconuts, cashews, pineapples, jackfruit and areca nuts. The temple, shruggingly ascribed locally to the 13th century, is dedicated to Rudreshvara, a destructive aspect of Lord Shiva, but my guess would be that animists paid homage to their nature spirits as long ago as prehistory. Certainly, however, the temple as we see it now postdates the Portuguese, who destroyed one of its several predecessors without daring to put a Christian church in its place. Who here could have protected saints or sacraments? A priest descended to the foot of the waterfall with an offering from one of our group. Crows and gawping ravens, well accustomed to such fare, dived down to gulp the balls of rice before they could disintegrate. I bought four sweet little bananas tasting like solid hot sugar. A heavenly chorus of birds irradiated the dense foliage and blue sky. White foam scudded down the waterfall over shiny red rocks below, between dry, dusty boulders. Everything is red with fine dust from local opencast iron-ore mines. Weeks later I should still be combing red dust from my hair and finding dry red rivulets edging towards the hole after my bathwater had run away.

The road from Sanquelim to Mapusa passes through Bicholim; off the road, in a surprise of blue, lilts Lake Mayem in its cradle of red dust below an endless range of trees. Thirteen tourist cottages operated by the Government of Goa offer an idyll beyond all cities, all towns, all villages. A double room cost Rs 70 (off-season Rs 50) and a single only Rs 55 (off-season) and many will prefer this magnificent situation, with a perpetual breeze, high, green, and tranquil, to crowded beaches at Colva or Calangute. But the coupon-system at the Government Tourist Hotel leaves much to be desired: milling, not queueing, is the order of the day, and the racket is horrendous. I opted for chicken biryani with roti and a soft drink, lunching with a mining engineer from Bihar. The menu was provided only in English. A family from Orissa splashed by the lakeside, decorously as befits Hindus. Christians from Bombay were howling with glee in two pedaloes, swishing past each other as if in dodgems at a fairground.

The North Goa tour does not stop at Narve (5 km southwest of

Bicholim), so you could do this on your own, while staying at Mayem. Here is the fine Hindu temple devoted to Sri Saptakoteshvara of 1668, with a precious faceted lingam called Dharalingam brought from the original Narve village on Divar Island during the Portuguese persecutions. The name of the temple derives from Shiva, 'Lord of Seven Crores' or seventy million, being the number of demons destroyed by the virtuous Lord, iconographically shown either as the lingam – as here at Narve – or as Bhairava, 'the terrible destroyer', who haunts cemeteries and cremation mounds wearing sepents round his head and skulls as a necklace. Sri Saptakoteshvara is painted blue, with white columned-corners and white window-frames, and represents a type of temple very common within the so-called New Conquests. Its mandapam is arcaded and adjoins the sanctuary like a portico, with a water tank in front and a lamp-tower on a dais. The main temple is tripartite, with a raised central part, and two lower aisles. The shrine-dome rises on an octagonal drum.


## Mapusa

I cannot really recommend the crowded, smelly hustle-bustle of Mapusa, except as a centre for touring from the centrally-located Hotel Satyaheera just above the turmoiling bus station. A little Hanuman temple across the street woke me at six one morning with bells and prayers, and unremitting traffic reminded me that I was unlikely to go back to sleep. On Fridays that is no problem, because the colourful market, especially rich in decorated earthenware pottery such as the cockereliform *gurguletta*, enlivens 'Mapsa' as the town is pronounced (Mapuça in Portuguese) beyond expectation. But on any other day you just sit on the Satyaheera porch and watch the ancient buses polluting the atmosphere with clouds of grey poison. You can get a bus to Chapora every half-hour, and to Panaji ferry at virtually any time of day.

## Tiracol to Anjuna

Probably the best beaches in Goa are these least visited: near Tiracol in the northernmost corner. No tours go there, and the single-nave church within Tiracol fortress is a quaint and charming survival: the rest of the fort is now the Terekhol Fort Tourist Rest House, with twin-bedded rooms or dormitory accommodation, run by the Goa Tourism Development Corporation. The Portuguese fort protected both estuary and harbour, for little danger lay from landward, and the dry moat is artificial, the whole looking quite impregnable.

The next river south of the Tiracol is the Chapora, the Portuguese version of Shapur, named by the Adil Shah dynasty who built the great fort that dominates Vagator or Chapora Beach. A manual sugarcane

*Vagator Beach*

press forced sweet liquid into a row of glasses, with a spot of lime juice and a trace of ginger added like quicksilver, by the hands of a concert pianist or a conjuror. Goa has only about 70 km of beaches so – with six five-star hotels each occupying 2.5 km of beach – it is hard to work out where the fishermen will land their catches if the nineteen new five-star hotels planned are actually ever built. Domestic Indian tourism to Goa increased from 120,000 in 1973 to 300,000 in 1978, and 496,000 in 1983 to 762,000 in 1988, the most popular season being October-January, except for the most popular month of all, which is May. Foreign tourism rose over the same period from 8,371 in 1973 to 23,000 in 1978, and 34,000 in 1983 to 93,000 in 1985, since when it levelled off, remaining below a critical point of 100,000 due partly to a reduction in the provision of new hotel rooms. Hippies or their successors in the lotus business stay in cottages in the village of Anjuna, but a new Vagator Beach Resort caters to the slightly wealthier.

Anjuna Beach has a sign at the bus stop 'Don't Dabble in Drugs', but the message comes too late. A number of local Goans derive part or most of their income from such dabbling, and foreigners easily succumb, even if they do not seek out drugs. A shy girl from Bengal asked me 'one question, please. If 'duplicate' is two and 'triplicate' is three, what is one? My friend she says 'oneplicate'. And what is 'complicate': four or more?' So far from answering her, I couldn't even replicate. English strikes Indians as unfairly strange, and yet they still struggle gamely on, when most English people have difficulty spelling 'separate' and 'accommodation'.

Anjuna has a flea market where backpackers and elusive hippies come out of their huts and cottages to buy and sell clothes, guitars, cassettes and paperback books.

Green men, willowy women in beige, ambitious blondes, bearded Allen Ginsberg lookalikes with gimlet stares capable of penetrating reinforced concrete, hashish addicts with foolish smiles, efficient Germans with liberated womenfolk, the kind of sunken-eyed expatriate whom you met once in Tangier at Paul Bowles's place, even more ambitious blondes, and perhaps a maroon-robed escapee from Osho Commune in Pune: Anjuna mixes Woodstock with Greenham Common, the Manson Commune with Club Med.

'See y'aroun'' drawls a skinny Californian in a Belair T-shirt and torn jeans shorts, carrying a six-pack of beer from an ice-cart. The bicycle is their tripmobile, and nocturnal are their habits. Nude bathing is prohibited, but what the hell? Everybody does it, and if there is no significant corruption of minors, and the drugs generally fall within the soft end of the spectrum, the authorities generally turn a blind eye and a deaf ear. Tacitly, it is agreed that festivities should be celebrated as far as possible from towns and villages where respectable Goan families might be outraged. Occasional raids add to the spice of Anjuna. There are few hotels in the area: the idea is that you try to rent a room, or a whole cottage if you can, for a period, but six-month and four-month leases to foreigners have become so common here and at Calangute/Baga that the building supply seldom satisfies the demand.

### Calangute and Aguada
South of the lovely Baga beach runs the paradisiac extent of Calangute beach, west of the village of Saligao. The Church of the Mother of God in Saligao, also known as the Rosary, has an unexpected Gothic Revival exterior of 1873, unlike the baroque façades you can find elsewhere in

Bardez such as at Apora, on the road to Vagator, or the 18th-century church at Candolim near Fort Aguada.

At Calangute the Backwalk Drama Society were presenting the Kathakali drama called *Kiratam, or the Divine Savage* twice nightly at 7 and 8.35, including a lecture-demonstration helping a novice audience to follow the 24 stylised gestures, 9 facial expressions and poses. I arrived at 6 one evening to see the artistes making up, and fitting their elaborate costumes. Lord Shiva was played by Karuna Karan, Lord Arjuna by Shiva Das, and Srimati Parvati by Anil Kumar. Flesh-tinted faces denote women, saints and priests; green faces identify heroes, kings and warriors; jagged patterns in red and white on green indicate the audacious man who might succumb to evil; jagged patterns in white on red and black reveal evil characters, sometimes with superhuman abilities. Yellow is made by grinding a block of sulphur, blue from the indigo plant, green from mixing blue with yellow, black from soot.

Calangute in the Sixties I recall being the sole preserve of hippies, drunken, drugged, and cavorting naked by moonlight. *O tempora, o mores!* Nowadays it is 'officially' the 'best beach in Goa', with rush umbrellas mounted decorously around tree trunks, Anthonian's Caterers Bar and Restaurant (showers Rs 2; toilet Rs 0.50), and the buzz of charter-planes from London and Frankfurt overhead.

'You want nice girl at Baina, Vasco, mister?'

'Why, aren't there any nice girls left at Calangute?' My shady informant curled his lip: 'all too good here, big police clean-up, no good. You come with me to Baina, facki-facki.' Dogs loafed in the shade, hoping for an evening breeze. Gasping hot crows sat back inertly, with their beaks open. A row of vendors negotiated with Danes for briefcases, backpacks, capacious suitcases of low quality. I gratefully drank down a sweet lassi, then swung on to our moving bus as it lurched to Fort Aguada.

Aguada has many aspects: the round 19th-century lighthouse (inactive since a modern lighthouse was installed) can be visited every afternoon from 4 to 5.30; the fort itself built by the Portuguese in 1609-12 to command the Mandovi approach to Old Goa is transformed into a jail; but for rich tourists the zone is home to the Fort Aguada Beach Resort (up to Rs 1000 for a double room) and the even more exclusive Aguada Hermitage (up to Rs 3250 for a double), both operated by the Taj Group.

Fort Aguada rears above the crashing breakers, the most massive and seemingly invulnerable of all Goan fortresses. Constructed in 1612, the fort was reputed to have around eighty cannon to protect it on all sides, with at its highest point the Church of St Lawrence (1630). In the 17th century Fort Aguada was transformed into an island castle by means of a moat dug on the only landward aspect. Fresh water emerged from a

*Mapusa. Friday market, with earthenware jars*

well now not to be seen because it lies within the confines of the jail. Some outer bastions have crumbled into the Arabian Sea, but others have been destroyed, with a view across to Cabo Fort. If an enemy breached these first lines of defence, Reis Magos (on the north) and Gaspar Dias forts would have provided another stiff test. Reis Magos (1551) covers a Hindu temple; it cannot be visited because it too is now a jail, but the Church of the Wise Men (1555) can be seen, and is evocative for anyone who has made the pilgrimage to Assisi, for it became a missionary outpost of the Franciscan Order, and was the first church built in Bardez taluka.

## Out of Goa

As no de luxe hotel exists in Mapusa, anyone staying there will have to choose between the Tourist Hotel and the Hotel Satyaheera, both on the main square beside the bus station. The Government Tourist Hostel seems always to be booked out, so the Satyaheera is your only hope, and that too often has few vacancies. The restaurant is very slow ('Kindly spare us just 25 minutes to prepare your food') and the bathroom window has open slats through which mosquitoes rush in a manic bid to taste your blood before the rest; I closed the bathroom door but it didn't fit, and the battalions of mosquitoes triumphantly swished through to occupy the high ground, the low ground, and the area around the bed. I lit a green coil against them at each side of the bed, they coughed briefly, and then continued zooming practice, pausing only for sanguinary refreshment from my exposed flesh.

The early morning bus to Pune filled with diesel at 6.30 at a filling-station just above Mapusa on the Bombay road. A crow on the neon bulb against a sickle moon above the petrol-station glowered balefully in its parallel universe, hoping for stray pickings. Pope John Paul II had visited Goa from 5-7 February 1986, and his 'Call of the Lord to Unity' handbill 'courtesy Canara Bank' was peeling in the wind. Our bus bore the legend 'Mother Mary Bless Our Way'.

My excitement mounted, for I was on my way to Maharashtra and Bombay, the subject of my next book, *Western India*, which will also explore the variety of Karnataka, once called Mysore State, from the coastline near Mangalore and the hills of Coorg to the Hoysala temples at Belur and Halebid, the ruined Vijayanagar capital of Hampi, and the extraordinary northern Muslim cities of Bijapur, Gulbarga, and Bidar.

# Useful Information

## When to Come

The best months for South India are November to late February, but as it often rains in November and December, my suggestion would be start around the end of the first week in January, and stay as long as you can. Hill stations such as Ootacamund in the Nilgiris, or Periyar in the Cardamom Hills, will always be cool, and sometimes even cold in January.

Here are the maximum temperatures of some South Indian cities in degrees Centigrade.

|        | J  | F  | M  | A  | M  | J  | J  | A  | S  | O  | N  | D  |
|--------|----|----|----|----|----|----|----|----|----|----|----|----|
| Cochin | 30 | 30 | 31 | 31 | 30 | 29 | 28 | 28 | 29 | 29 | 30 | 30 |
| Madras | 28 | 30 | 33 | 38 | 40 | 39 | 36 | 35 | 34 | 33 | 30 | 28 |
| Panjim | 30 | 32 | 32 | 33 | 34 | 31 | 30 | 30 | 29 | 31 | 33 | 34 |

Panjim and the beaches of Goa enjoy their high season over Christmas and New Year, festival weekends, and school holidays peaking in May. It really is better to avoid the South during those periods, the torrid pre-monsoon heat of late April to mid-June, the monsoon downpours of June to August, and the post-monsoon humidity of September and October. Of course, these timings are subject to fluctuation: in Rajasthan the so-called 'rainy season' did not appear at all for several years until 1989. In Madras and Madurai the rainiest months are October and November. By contrast Goa's rainfall drops to zero in January and February and soars to a maximum 900 mm in July! In the far south, Trivandrum averages a low of 20 mm in January-February, and highs of 250 mm in May, 330 in June, 215 in July, and 270 in October.

## How to Come

International airlines fly direct to Bombay and Madras, without the need to connect, and it is worth paying a little extra if necessary to avoid the internal congestion, delays and even cancellations currently plaguing domestic air travel. Of the destinations currently covered in *South India*, airports can be found at Dabolim (Goa), Coimbatore, Cochin, Trivandrum, Madurai and Tiruchchirappalli (Trichy for short). I can't honestly recommend travelling anywhere by air in India, except if you have to cut short your journey for illness or lack of funds. Landscapes and the human dimension are sadly reduced from an aircraft, and one comes to India to experience the colour and the tumult, not to remove oneself from it by an aerial tube.

Rail travel is for the connoisseur of nostalgia, steam trains making their ponderous way across vast tracts of lush coastal palm groves (south from Ernakulam). Anyone who has enjoyed Paul Theroux's *The Great Railway Bazaar* (1980) or Heather Wood's contrasting *Third-Class Ticket* (1983) will need no second urging to try these slow, efficient, charming trains, whether meandering inland from Bombay to Goa via Pune and Belgaum, or chugging out of Madras west to Mysore or Salem, or south to Trichy and Cape Comorin. If you can't spare 4½ hours for the mountainward trip from Mettupalayam to Ooty, then at least the last 1½ hours from Coonoor should be enjoyed, preferably from the front compartment, first class.

But the serious traveller must use the buses, for they are not only faster, more frequent and thus more convenient; they also go to many more localities than the rail network covers. You can buy local city sightseeing tours and longer regional tours from a host of companies in Panaji, Ernakulam and Madras. These are very cheap and, because numerous, competitive. Public buses may be cheaper still, but they are less comfortable, more crowded, yet must be used for a number of destinations (like Guruvayur or Vellore) where organised tours seldom go. Air-conditioned buses are available on all long-distance routes, and again prove an astounding investment measured against what you would pay for a similar journey in Western Europe, America or Australasia.

You cannot currently hire a self-drive car in India, but many companies offer a chauffeur-driven car by the hour, day or week. This has virtually no advantages in cities or major towns, but can save time in visiting out-of-the-way sites in Tamil Nadu. In towns, wherever distances are – frequently – too great for a casual stroll, I fall back on the friendly auto-rickshaw man, agreeing on roughly half the initial asking price if his metre is 'not working'. Some small flat towns (Pondicherry, Mahabalipuram) offers tongas or cycle rickshaws, and virtually *anything* is better than exhausting yourself and risking dehydration by trying to walk everywhere. Again I stress: *always* settle on a price before starting. Enough English is spoken to define your destination and figures in rupees, no matter where you are in South India.

### Accommodation
I have stayed in South India at palaces and doss-houses, first-class hotels of the Western type, and pilgrim hotels intended for Hindu families.

There is little correlation between price and value, though anyone expecting luxury might stick unadventurously to the major chains, such as the Taj (Madras, Goa and Madurai), the Oberoi (Goa), the Welcomgroup (Goa and Madras) and the Spencer Group (Madras and Ootacamund). The Ashok hotels include Kovalam.

## Tamil Nadu

In *Mahabalipuram*, you have the choice of a select beach resort, such as those extending north from the town towards the Ideal Beach Resort, the most intimate and friendly, run by a charming man dispossessed by the Sri Lanka Government and given refuge by the Indian Government. If you can't find a room there, the next best alternatives are the large Silver Sands Beach Resort and the medium-size Golden Sun, which is heavily patronised by Russians. Alternatively, you can stay in the centre of Mahabalipuram, and if you want to spend extra time at the great monuments here, the Mamalla Bhavan, next to the Bus Station. One has to say, from personal experience, that this is the world's most popular conference centre for the Mosquito Aerobatic Hordes abounding at leisure in pouncing uproar round about midnight, which is how Mahabalipuram got its acronym, so it is worth investing in a room with a net or coil if you don't carry around your own mosquito net. If the seasons puzzle you at Mahabalipuram, the peak runs from mid-December to late January, with high season before and after it, off season from mid-April to late June, and low season from early July to late September.

In *Kanchipuram*, you have a choice of Raja's Lodge near the bus station or the Ashok Traveller's Lodge near the rail station.

*Pondicherry* has a good selection of hotels: I like most the Seaside Guest House at 10 Goubert Avenue. A pleasant Government Tourist Home is on Uppalam Road, near the rail station. Sri Aurobindo International Guest House on Gingee Salai is the most central hotel, for those keen to explore vestiges of French colonialism in this extraordinary city.

*Tanjore* (in Tamil, Thanjavur) was crowded during my stay: it clearly needs a couple of new top-class hotels. The best choice is the Hotel Tamil Nadu (fully booked as a rule) just two minutes' walk from the rail station. Near the bus station are Hotel Karthik and Sri Mahalakshmi Lodge, ideally sited for the Palace and Brihadeshvara Temple. The Ashok Travellers' Lodge is too far out of town: a stricture applicable to the equivalent hotel in *Trichy*. I preferred the central Hotel Anand at 1 Racquet Court Lane, and the equally convenient Hotel Arun, 24 State Bank Road, though friends suggest the more expensive Sangam on Collector's Office Road, and there is always the local Hotel Tamil Nadu, handy for the bus station.

*Madurai*'s Taj Group hotel is the Pandyan, on Alagarkoil Road, where you can also find the equally expensive Hotel Madurai Ashok, and the cheaper Hotel Tamil Nadu, not to be confused with the cheaper and more central Hotel Tamil Nadu on West Veli Street, vastly preferable because of its situation beside the bus station. Also close at hand is the Hotel Aarathy, just round the corner at 9 Perumalkoil West Mada Street.

Elsewhere in Tamil Nadu, the state-run Hotels of that name can be recommended, and are often booked several weeks ahead, as at *Rameshwaram*, the hill stations of *Ooty* and *Kodaikanal*, and the Cape Hotel at *Kaniya Kumari* (Cape Comorin). At Ooty, my preference is for the maharajah's summer palace called Fernhill Palace Hotel, though it is far out of town; the views from the back, over Ooty's slopes, are magical at dawn and dusk.

### Kerala
The Malabar Hotel, on Willingdon Island (for the airport) is the best hotel, but as inconvenient as the Bolgatty Palace Hotel (1744) on Bolgatty Island. *Ernakulam* town is the hub of the Cochin archipelago, whether you are using boats, buses or trains, and Gandhi Road has a range of excellent and reasonable hotels from the Abad Plaza (most expensive) to the Grand and Woodlands (mid-price). I like two hotels on Market Road: the Blue Diamond ideal for shops and Bijus Tourist Home, close to the main jetty for ferries to Willingdon, Fort Cochin, and Mattancheri, and the cheap, quick meals at the Indian Coffee House on Cannon Shed Road corner.

Staying in Fort Cochin itself has a special appeal: try the Seagull Hotel, with fine harbour views.

*Trichur* is a comfortable bus ride from Ernakulam on the way north to Calicut on the coast or Ooty in the Nilgiris or Periyar in the Cardamom Hills, but you can find accommodation there at the Elite International or the Tourist Bungalow. *Calicut* offers a Tourist Bungalow, the Maharani on Taluk Road or the Alakpuri Guest House on Jail Road. South of Cochin, Kerala becomes even more spectacular, with inland waterways connecting Alleppey with Quilon. In *Alleppey* I liked best the expensive and rather distant Alleppey Prince Hotel, and the much cheaper but clean and friendly St George's Lodging not far from the Hindu temple and the Dhanalakshmi Lodge. *Quilon* has the usual choice between a central location (Karthika or Iswarya) and a picturesque location outside the town, in this case the one-time British Residency, now a Tourist Bungalow. *Trivandrum*'s central hotels include the Pankaj and Onkar Lodge, both on Gandhi Road; the beach at Kovalam has a number of new hotels as it becomes increasingly popular, the best being Kovalam

Ashok Beach.

*Thekkady*, for the Periyar Wildlife Sanctuary, has the magical Aranya Niwas Hotel, which I cannot recommend too highly, for cuisine as well as comfort.

## Goa

*Goa* has too many hotels, having developed too quickly; most are anonymous, gimcrack buildings reminiscent of Spanish ribbon resorts on the Costas. If you are on a charter flight, your hotel will be chosen for you. As an individual traveller, you can select the oldest de luxe hotel in Panjim, the Mandovi, on Bandadkar Marg (with excellent bookshop); the economical Tourist Hostel (handy for tours, and the jetty for the North Goa ferry); but I opted for the atmospheric late 17th-century mansion still in the Heredia family, and known as the Panjim Inn, 31 January Road. Many low-price hotels can be found in the district near the Post Office. But of course most people stay at the beach resorts, and this is a matter of personal preference, from the crowded Colva Beach or the commercialised Calangute Beach, to the relatively unspoiled Benaulim in the south or Tiracol in the north. I stress that Goa is too beautiful in its hinterland, and too significantly historically and culturally, for you to waste a great deal of time on the beaches, so Panjim and to a lesser extent Mapusa (for North Goa) or Margao (for South Goa), make convenient headquarters.

## Customs and Currency

To pay for accommodation, unless you are a member of a prepaid group, you must pay in rupees obtained by changing currency or travellers' cheques within India. This is simplified by the fact that many of the bigger hotels will change money for you and give you the necessary receipt, enabling you to pay your bill and, even more significant, to change money back on leaving the country. Don't try to change money illegally: it is not worth the risk of getting caught and those who do either get caught by tricksters or find that, at best, they have made a few per cent over the authorised rate. Hotels display the daily rate of exchange in dollars, sterling, Deutschmarks and a few other leading currencies, and anyone who has tried to change money at an Indian bank will know what a boon and blessing the hotels' service will be. But not all hotels will change money, and few hotels will change more than a couple of hundred dollars' worth on any one day: you cannot insist. Keep your receipts in different places, so that in case of loss or theft you have at least one receipt to show.

It is prohibited to carry Indian currency into or out of India, so a mixture of cash (small quantities) and travellers' cheques (the bulk) in easily convertible currencies should be carried in a variety of places, such as a waist-belt or a neck-pouch. I have a hip-pocket sewn up at the back and opened inside; ladies carry a bag in front of them or sew an inside pocket inside a skirt or jeans. Backpackers should never put money in a backpack, where it is neither visible nor secure. Replenish your small change each morning from your hidden store, when you take your malaria pills.

The currency throughout India is the rupee, divided into one hundred paise. Coins are minted in denominations of 5, 10, 20, 25 and 50 paise and one and two rupees, and notes are printed in denominations of one rupee, 2, 5, 10, 20, 50, 100 and 500. Take care of the notes, for it is quite common for a shopkeeper or hotel or restaurant cashier to refuse a note if it is torn on one or more edges. Holes caused by staples on the interior of a note are normally not a problem. Tipping in small denominations oils the slow machinery of travel throughout India: few are exempt from this golden rule.

As a rule of thumb, one avoids giving money to beggars, but produces one- or two-rupee notes for services actually rendered, like a small boy showing you to the correct bus in a crowded bus station in Madurai, or a station porter finding you a sleeping berth in the train from Bangalore to Trivandrum when all hope seemed lost forever. The 18 hour-trip can seem a very long night indeed without one.

Small change, I emphasise here, is very hard to come by, and you should take every chance to change larger notes into smaller denominations. ALWAYS KEEP IN RESERVE YOUR AIRPORT DEPARTURE TAX, which in 1990 was Rs 300.

Customs searches entering and leaving India have in my experience always been conducted perfunctorily, simply, and scrupulously; you are treated neither like a leper nor a mafioso. As usual, you may bring in 200 cigarettes and spirits (up to 0.95 litres), but remember that many states in India have introduced Prohibition.

Goods to be declared in the red channel on arriving at an international airport in India include any weapons, dutiable goods, high-value articles, or foreign exchange worth in excess of the equivalent of US$1,000.00. You have to fill in a form declaration the description and value of your baggage contents. The Tourist Baggage Re-Export form should be produced with listed articles at the port of departure, including such items as expensive personal jewellery, cameras, binoculars, radios and tape recorders.

On departure, you may export goods to a maximum value of Rs. 20,000, *except that* gold articles may not exceed Rs. 2,000 in value, silver Rs. 200, and non-gold precious stones and jewellery may not exceed Rs. 15,000. You may not export ivory, animal skins, antiques, and gold items such as ingots, bullion or coins. Moreover, if you have spent more than ninety days in India, you need an income-tax clearance

216

certificate from the foreign section of the Income Tax office in Madras, Bombay, or your city of departure elsewhere.

## Passports and Visas
Every visitor to India must have a passport, with a visa for India and special permits for any restricted areas that you plan to visit. The whole of South India is unrestricted unless you include the Andaman and Nicobar Islands (at present a permit can be obtained on arrival in Port Blair, but check this with your local Government of India Tourist Office before departure) and the Union Territory of Lakshadweep, the archipelago known in English as the Laccadives. For the Laccadives, allow up to six weeks for a permit from the Ministry of Home Affairs in New Delhi; this permit is then validated by the Secretary to the Administrator of Lakshadweep on Willingdon Island in Cochin, Kerala. The eighteen- to twenty-hour journey operates from Cochin about once a week on *m.v. Bharatseema* (with some air-conditioned cabins) or *m.v. Amindivi*. Tickets can be obtained from travel agents in Cochin, including Jairam on Willingdon Island.

Allow two weeks for your general Indian visa, after obtaining the visa form and supplying (currently) three passport photographs with the appropriate fee: higher if an agent obtains it for you. In the U.S.A. the Embassy is at 2107 Massachusetts Avenue, N.W., Washington, D.C. 20008, and there is a Consul-General at 3 East 64th St., New York, N.Y. 10021. In Britain, send passport, visa, photos and fee to the High Commission for India, India House, Aldwych, London WC2. In France, the Indian Embassy is situated at 15 rue Alfred Dehodencq, 75016 Paris.

To be on the safe side, I take photocopies of the first three pages of my passport and my Indian visa, and keep them in a place distinct from the passport itself.

## Health
Travellers have always experienced trials and tribulations of the digestive system when visiting a new country, and this is as true of India as anywhere else. You take precautions, therefore, to minimise risks. Never drink the water or use it to clean your teeth: there is a wide range of reputable mineral waters which you can order in restaurants or, in light plastic bottles, carry with you. I am never without a 'sticky bag', with sun-cream and water bottle, as well as my clean bag with camera, spare film, books and maps. Together these will fit unobtrusively into a cheap, tough Indian shopping bag found in any bazaar which can quickly be replaced if damaged or lost. Some people use Sterotabs with ordinary water, but sterilizing tablets can never be 100% sure, whereas the min-

eral water is, in my experience, completely safe.

Avoid the temptation of 'going native' with food, and keep as far as possible to your normal diet. This has become much easier with the spread of international-style hotels in Madras, Goa, Ernakulam, and beach resorts like those at Mahabalipuram or Covelong, and hill stations such as Kodaikanal, as popular with foreigners as Ooty. Familiar ingredients may not be found everywhere, but South India is astonishingly fertile, rice is abundant everywhere, and various kinds of bread can be found. An omelette is a safe standby, and potatoes are sometimes available. Most Indian restaurants are well accustomed to the more sensitive Western palate and stomach, and often reduce the amount of chili or curry when serving foreigners. If in doubt, make your wishes clear to the waiter: 'no chili!' Buffets are even more helpfully divided into Western and Indian-style counters.

Toilets exist everywhere tourists are expected, such as major sights, palaces, forts and museums. You may have to use a squat-type toilet, and you will usually have to provide your own toilet-paper, but more lavatories are being adapted to Western use as tourism spreads geographically and upwards into the de luxe category. You do not have to stay in a given hotel, or eat in a given restaurant, to use the facilities.

Injections needed for India vary from time to time and must be checked well before departure with your local doctor to allow time for the full course prescribed. British Airways, 65-75 Regent St., London W1 can advise if you have no medical registration. It is safe to assume that you need protection against cholera, hepatitis, polio, tetanus and typhoid, as well as of course malaria. Current suggestions for precautions against malaria include Paludrine (two daily) and Nivaquine (two weekly) but your doctor is in the best position to advise. Dehydration, sunstroke and exposure are all dangers to those travelling in South India, so make sure your head is covered out of doors, and your neck and face should be protected with your usual lotions. I have found locally-prepared coconut oil very effective against sunburn: it is cheap and emanates a pleasant odour, but it *is* greasy. *Take everything with you*, because not all chemists carry all preparations, and you will normally not want to waste precious time gallivanting for all-night drugstores.

It is virtually impossible to prevent all stomach problems, because your system is not accustomed to the new conditions and it consequently rebels. Take as little alcohol as possible, eat in moderation, and be prepared with pills such as Streptotriad, unless you are sensitive to sulphonamide. After diarrhoea or vomiting, avoid eating anything at all for twenty-four hours, rest as much as possible, and keep drinking weak tea or mineral water to avoid dehydration. Imodium works well, but may take up to a day to work.

After taking a shower or bath, rub or spray anti-insect protection on exposed areas of your body. Mosquito coils, lit before you go to bed, generally last long enough to dampen the ardour of biters in the dark. Remember to shut windows or put up screens before you sleep.

A universal bath-plug is a great boon in all but five-star hotels, but *do* remember to take it away with you when you dry yourself. If you have no plug, saturated toilet-paper stuffed into the hole will retain water as long as you need it. I always take to India my own shampoo sachets, toothpaste and shaving kit, hand-towel and soap in a soapdish. Most hotels will provide a towel and soap if asked, but service is often so slow that – on arriving in a new hotel after midnight – you often do not want to wait for it.

In a hot, tropical and often humid climate, even small cuts can turn septic quickly, so keep antiseptic cream and a choice of three or four dressings to prevent minor accidents becoming major.

## Clothing

Take as little as possible, but remember that nights in hill stations such as Ooty or Yercaud can be cold and, if you intend to travel in buses or trains by night, an anorak can double as a pillow. For long daytime journeys I wear an airfilled cushion on my shoulders to take the weight off my head and reduce wear and tear on my neck muscles (and bruising) caused by bumping and jerking.

Indians dress modestly and are genuinely offended by the sight of immodest Western shorts or short skirts, so it is sensitive to wear long trousers or long skirts, and hardwearing jeans.

If you intend to visit Jain temples remember that leather sandals and belts must be removed before entering, so plastic belts have their uses. The same applies to leather handbags or purses.

Even the best hotels do not insist on formal wear, so you can be relaxed except at formal dinners with dignitaries who will themselves take enormous trouble.

Using hotel swimming-pools, men must use swimming trunks; women should cover up in what might be thought in the Occident 'old-fashioned ways'. You can buy excellent, very cheap sandals easily removed before entering shrines, temples or mosques. In Kerala you will not be allowed within Hindu temples; elsewhere you will not be allowed inside the inner shrine. Cotton socks protect your feet against hot stone; bare feet quickly burn, and distract you from the pleasures of the senses and the intellect.

Hotel laundries and dry-cleaning services are trustworthy and cheap, but be prepared for heavy surcharges for urgent work. Damage is not unknown, and I tend to use running water in hotel bathrooms for hand-washing clothes which will normally dry overnight. Sachets of *Travel*

219

*Wash* or a similar detergent are practical.

## Speaking the Languages

Readers familiar with my previous travel guides will recall my view that learning one or more of the local languages will repay the effort in proportion to the effort. Sadly, this does not apply to South India, where you stand a grave risk of offending somebody by trying to speak a regional language. It is assumed that, in avoiding English, you consider your acquaintance ignorant, uneducated, stupid, or from a lower class, and this is – as elsewhere in India – thought to be offensive. Furthermore, each South Indian language has a restricted territory, so that by learning the Tamil of Tamil Nadu you are lost on entering the Malayalam region of Kerala, or the Konkani district of Goa. Even in country areas, any crowd can summon up someone who can understand and speak English, while in the cities it is likely that people you meet will have studied in an English-medium school from a very early age. However, it does no harm in Tamil Nadu to say *Vanakkam* (Tamil for Good morning! or Good night!) or *Nandri* (Tamil for Thank you!).

Interestingly, French is virtually non-existent these days in the former French-controlled Union Territory of Pondicherry, and Portuguese has suffered similar eclipse in the former Portuguese-controlled territories of Goa, Daman and Diu. So it's English as usual.

For those tempted into the invitingly soft and effervescent world of Tamil (or another of the Dravidian tongues of South India), language cassettes and grammars are available from reputable language institutes. But avoid like bubonic plague such efforts as *Learn Tamil in 30 Days* by N. Jegtheesh (Balaji, Madras, 21st ed., 1988) commonly found in Indian bookshops, for their helpfulness is severely circumscribed, as the following sample conversation might convey.

*Foreigner.* Yonder I see an elephant standing! How did it come here?
*Guide.* It is not a true elephant. It is a monolithic sculpture.

Tamils do not actually think that foreigners are so stupid that they cannot be trusted to distinguish a real elephant from its sculptural simulacrum. I don't know how good Mr Jegtheesh's Tamil is, but his English finds room for such fruit as quava, melan, poma-granite and pumple.

## Holidays and Festivals

Hindu festivals are fixed in accordance with the Vikramaditya calendar based on lunar months which begin with the full moon, and intercalate a thirteenth month of the year every thirty months to ensure the months stay consonant with the seasons. Years of the Vikramaditya era are often cited on monuments or in books, and you need to remember that

220

these years are 57 or 58 years *ahead* of the Christian calendar. The Indian Government has officially sanctioned a third era (Shak) which is 77 or 78 years *behind* the Christian era.

You are never far in time or place from a festival in India: it is almost impossible to steer an itinerary around them. So make the best of them, delay your progress and let the genius of the moment flow into your life. Thus, for instance, in January 1990, in addition to the Book Fair and Tourist Trade Fair Madras celebrated Vaikunta-Ekadasi on the 7th, Aruthra Dharsan on the 10th, Pongal's four-day festival from the 13th to the 16th, Thiruvalluvar Day on the 15th and Republic Day on the 26th.

Pongal, 'upsurge', is the popular name for the agricultural festival Makara Sankaranthi and is celebrated on the first day of the Tamil month Thai, when the Sun enters the house of Capricorn in astrological terms, that is the 14 January in 1990. The 'upsurge' is that of the froth on rice boiled in milk by the housewife. If the froth rises first to the east, the popular belief is that the coming year will be prosperous. Some of the rice is then offered to Hindu sun god, Surya. On the first day of Pongal, old clothes and kitchen utensils are burnt; on the second new rice is cooked to symbolise the coming season; on the third, cattle are painted, garlanded and given sweet rice; the last day is a holiday, when Hindus visit friends and relatives.

Muslim festivals move gradually through the calendar, changing every year in relation to the Christian calendar, so you can check with your nearest mosque or reference library about the month of Ramadan (Id al-Fitr is celebrated at the end of it) and the dates of the Islamic New Year (1 Muharram) or the Id al-Adha. The Hindu Holi festival is in March. April 13 is a public holiday to celebrate the New Year. Good Friday is an Indian holiday, as is Christmas Day. August 15 is Independence Day. Dussehra (September-October) and Diwali, three to four weeks later, offer spectacles well worth seeing in any large town. In February, Madras hosts a flower and fruit show and a motor-sport meeting, in March the Aruvthumuvar Festival, in April the Tamil New Year's Day, another flower show and São Thomé Festival, in August Vinayaka Chaturthi, in September the Velankanni Festival, in October Navaratri and Ayudha Puja, in November Dipavali, and in December a music festival.

## Books and Maps

Two basic reference books will answer most of your questions about the history and monuments of South India. The first is the latest edition of K.A. Nilakanta Sastri's *A History of South India from Prehistoric Times to the Fall of Vijayanagar*, originally published by Oxford University Press in 1955, which sets the scene for a sympathetic understanding of

221

the land and peoples. The second is *The Penguin Guide to the Monuments of India* (2 vols., Penguin Books, 1989), of which volume 1 by George Michell covers Buddhist, Jain and Hindu sites, and volume 2 by Philip Davies deals with Islamic, Rajput and European works. A good map, such as the Nelles *India* or the 1:4,000,000 *Indian Subcontinent* from Bartholomew, is of course indispensable. Local maps vary in quality, and you often have to fall back on the Michell and Davies.

Indian books, produced on low-quality paper and priced accordingly, can often be of high quality. I am thinking of Nainar Subrahmanian's *History of Tamilnad* (2 vols.) published in Madurai but available from Higginbotham's in Madras or Ooty and A.S. Menon's *A Survey of Kerala History*. On Goa the best text is by J.M. Richards (*Goa*) and the best illustrations by Anthony Hutt (*Goa*), both obtainable from Books from India, 45 Museum Street, London WC1 near the British Museum, whose stock of language, literature, travel, maps and guides is perennially replenished from Indian and other suppliers.

A final word. South India is still so inadequately documented that most details of the places and sights you would wish to recall are unillustrated in the above books and guides. So take plenty of pens and paper, plus more films than you think you will need, for the crowded days ahead. Everything is memorable, from saris and yoked oxen to exuberant stone carvings and rice-paddies glittering in radiant sunshine. South India will astonish and delight the sensual voluptuary and the subtle connoisseur alike.

# Chronology

**B.C.**

| | |
|---|---|
| *c.* 1000 | Movement of the Aryans into the south of India, except the extreme south, ending about the 5th century B.C. |
| *c.* 486 | Death of Gautama Buddha |
| *c.* 468 | Death of Mahavira |
| 321 | Chandragupta founds the Mauryan dynasty, extending as far south as Mysore |
| 268-31 | Ashoka, reigning in the north, establishes friendly relations with the Cholas and Pandyas (Tamil Nadu), the Satyaputras (Karnataka) and the Keralaputras (Kerala) |

**A.D.**

| | |
|---|---|
| *c.* 50 B.C.-100 A.D. | Roman Empire trades with South India |
| *c.* 50 | Putative mission of St Thomas to South India |
| *c.* 575-600 | Simhavishnu founds Pallava dynasty followed by his son (monuments at his capital Kanchipuram, Mahabalipuram, and elsewhere). Dynasty ends in 897 |
| *c.* 590-620 | Kadungon founds the Pandya dynasty (monuments at his capital Madurai, none of which survives, Tiruchchirapalli, Namakkal and elsewhere). Dynasty ends in 920 |
| 700-728 | Rajasimha leads Pallava dynasty of Kanchipuram |
| *c.* 846 | Vijayalaya founds Chola dynasty (monuments at Tanjore, Chidambaram and elsewhere). Dynasty ends in 1173 |
| *c.* 907 | Parantaka I strengthens Chola rule |
| 985-1014 | Rajaraja I strengthens Chola dynasty grip |
| 1077 | Chola merchants visit China |
| *c.* 1130 | Chera dynasty (monuments at Trichur and elsewhere). Dynasty ends in early 14th century |
| 1288, 1293 | Marco Polo in South India |
| 1302-11 | Malik Kafur invades South India |
| 1326 | Deogiri (later Daulatabad) becomes the capital city of Ghiyas ad-Din Muhammad Shah II when he abandons Delhi |

| | |
|---|---|
| 1336 | Harihara I (with Bukka) of the Sangama dynasty sets up state which grows into the Kingdom of Vijayanagar (monuments at Kanchipuram, of the Tuluva dynasty, Vijayanagar, Vellore and elsewhere) |
| 1367 | Vijayanagar Empire captures Kadamba kingdom, including Goa. Most of South India forms part of a Vijayanagar Empire, by the 16th century |
| 1489 | Adil Shah dynasty in Bijapur captures Goa |
| 1498 | Vasco da Gama lands in Calicut |
| 1509-30 | Krishna Deva Raya is ruler of Vijayanagar |
| 1510 | Afonso de Albuquerque conquers Goa |
| 1542 | St Francis Xavier arrives in Goa |
| c. 1550 onwards | Nayaks (local rulers) dynasty established (monuments at Madurai, Kanchipuram, and elsewhere) |
| 1565 | Vijayanagar defeated by Muslims; Founding of Mysore |
| c. 1570 | Rajas of Travancore found dynasty (monuments at Vaikom, Trivandrum and elsewhere) |
| 1639 | Madras is ceded to British by the Rajah of Chandragiri |
| 1646 | Shivaji attacks Bijapur |
| 1665 | British take over Bombay from Portuguese |
| c. 1680 | Wadiyar dynasty of Mysore |
| 1686 | Fall of Bijapur |
| 1687 | Pondicherry founded by French |
| c. 1710 | Sethupathi dynasty founded (monuments at Rameshwaram and elsewhere) |
| 1745 | Jesuits expelled from Goa |
| 1764 | Goan 'New Conquests' |
| 1767 | First Mysore War |
| 1780 | Second Mysore War |
| 1790-2 | Third Mysore War |
| 1797 | British Army occupies Goa |
| 1798-9 | Fourth Mysore War, and the capture of Srirangapatnam from Tipu Sultan by the British |
| 1813 | British Army withdraws from Goa |
| 1843 | Panjim becomes capital of Goa |
| 1854 | Bombay's first cotton mill |
| 1881 | First railways built in Goa |
| 1886 | Madras becomes HQ of Theosophical Society |

| 1947 | Partition |
| 1948 | Death of Mahatma Gandhi |
| 1950 | India becomes a Republic within the British Commonwealth |
| 1961 | Goa incorporated into the Indian Union |
| 1989 | Congress Party loses general elections to Mr V.P. Singh |

# Index

227

rickshaws, 21-2
Ripon Buildings, Madras, 16
Rivona, 164
Robert, D., 63
Romans and India, 45, 48, 108, 110, 119
Rumbold, *Sir* W., 102
Rumphius, 193
Russell, *Sir* Henry *and* Jane Amelia, 6

Sabaji, 167
Safa Mosque, Goa, 200
St Andrew's Church, Vasco da Gama,
    195; Madras, 16
St Anthony's Chapel, Old Goa, 179
St Augustine's Church, Old Goa, 179
St Catherine's Cathedral, Old Goa, 172-4
St Cayetan's Church, Old Goa, 167-70
St Francis's Church, Cochin, 136-8; Old
    Goa, 170-1
St George's Cathedral, Madras, 16
St John's Church, Trichy, 67
St John of God's Church, Old Goa, 178-9
St Joseph's Church, Trivandrum, 117
St Joseph's College, Trichy, 67
St Lawrence's Church, Aguada, 208
St Mary's, Madras, 3-6
St Mary's Armenian Church, Madras, 16
St Mary's of the Angels, Madras, 16
St Monica's Convent, Old Goa, 179
St Peter's, Tanjore, 62
St Stephen's, Ooty, 99, 101
St Thomas' Cathedral, Madras, 9
St Thomas' Church, Ooty, 101-2
St Thomas' Mount, Madras, 9-10
Salcete, 192
Salem, 90-2, 110
Saligao, 207-8
Samson *family*, 101
sanctuaries. *See* wildlife
Sandilya, 88
Sanguem, 164, 193, 200
Sankaram, 8
Sanquelim, 203
Sta. Cruz Cathedral, Cochin, 136, 38
São Thomé, Madras, 9
Saptakoteshvara, Sri, Temple, Narve,
    205
Saraswati, 42, 51
Saraswati, *H.H.* Jayendra, 28
Sarkar, H., 141
Sastri, K.A.N., 45, 221-2
Satari, 193

Satavahana *dynasty*, 163
sati and sati stones, 8, 171
Satyagraha, 124-5, 155
Schwartz, F.C., 60-2, 67
sculpture, 34-9, 48, 58-60, 117, 171
sea travel, 161-2, 217
Sealey, A.F., 138
seasons, viii, 206, 313
Sebastião, *Rei Dom*, 172
See India Foundation, 145
Seelayampatti, 129
Selvaraj, 21
Semmantham, 92
Sen, Mrinal, 117
Senapati. *See* Subrahmanya
Senate House, Madras, 13
Serfoji II, 60, 62
Shahu, 200
Shakti, 188
Shankara (Shankacharya), 27-8, 108
Shanmugham, N., 72
Shanta Durga, *Sri*, Dhargal, 201;
    Kavalem, 199-200
Shapur II, 137
Shevaroy Hills, 91
Shipping Corporation of India, 161
Shirodkar, *Dr* P.P., 188
Shiva, 7, 9, 21-6, 32, 37-8, 40, 43-4, 48,
    50-2, 54-9, 66, 68, 72-3, 77, 79,
    86-8, 119, 124-5, 140, 144, 151,
    155-6, 163-4, 187-8, 198, 203-5
Shiva Siddhanta, 80
Shivaji, 42
shopping, 17-19, 31, 46, 66, 68, 75, 77,
    79-80, 93, 99, 113-7, 118
Shoranur, 155, 157
Shore Temple, Mamallapuram, 38
Silahara *dynasty*, 163
silk and sericulture, 18, 129
Silva *family*, 183, 192
Simão, Júlio, 172
Singh, Ram, 13
Sinquerim, 162
Skanda. *See* Subrahmanya
Smith, John, Ceylon planter, 100
Snake Garden, Guindy, 3, 14
Snake Temple, Nagarcoil, 89
snakes, 14, 89
snooker, 103-4
Solagampatti, 64
Somesvara IV, 164
Son et Lumière, Madurai, 82
Spencer Group hotels, 213
spices, 1, 77, 108, 111, 126, 139, 144,

# LIBYA PAST AND PRESENT

APULEIUS ON TRIAL AT SABRATHA
*Philip Ward*

THE LIBYAN CIVIL CODE
*I.M. Arif & M.O. Ansell*

LIBYAN MAMMALS
*Ernst Hufnagl*

THE LIBYAN REVOLUTION
*I.M. Arif & M.O. Ansell*

MOTORING TO NALUT
*Philip Ward*

SABRATHA
*Philip Ward*

TRIPOLI
*Philip Ward*

# ARABIA PAST AND PRESENT

# OLEANDER MODERN POETS

# OLEANDER LANGUAGE AND LITERATURE

THE ART & POETRY OF C.-F. RAMUZ
*David Bevan*

BIOGRAPHICAL MEMOIRS OF
EXTRAORDINARY PAINTERS
*William Beckford*

CELTIC: A COMPARATIVE STUDY
*D.B. Gregor*

FRENCH KEY WORDS
*Xavier-Yves Escande*

FRIULAN: LANGUAGE & LITERATURE
*D.B. Gregor*

GREGUERÍAS: Wit and Wisdom of
*R. Gómez de la Serna*

INDONESIAN TRADITIONAL POETRY
*Philip Ward*

A LIFETIME'S READING
*Philip Ward*

MARVELL'S ALLEGORICAL POETRY
*Bruce King*

ROMAGNOL: LANGUAGE & LITERATURE
*D.B. Gregor*

ROMONTSCH: LANGUAGE & LITERATURE
*D.B. Gregor*

# OLEANDER GAMES AND PASTIMES